THE POLITICS OF DEVIANCE

THE POLITICS OF DEVIANCE

Anne Hendershott

ENCOUNTER BOOKS
SAN FRANCISCO

First paperback edition published in 2004 by Encounter Books, an activity of Encounter for Culture and Education, Inc., a nonprofit tax exempt corporation.

Encounter Books website address: www.encounterbooks.com

Manufactured in the United States and printed on acid-free paper.

The paper used in this publication meets the minimum requirements of ANSI/NISO Z39.48-1992 (R 1997)(*Permanence of Paper*).

FIRST EDITION

Library of Congress Cataloging-in-Publication Data

Hendershott, Anne B.
    The politics of deviance / Anne Hendershott.
    p. cm.
    Includes bibliographical references and index.
    ISBN 1-59403-049-9 (alk. paper)
    Deviant behavior. I. Title.

HM811.H46 2002
302.5'42—dc21
2002017915

10 9 8 7 6 5 4 3 2 1

CONTENTS

INTRODUCTION

"Why would anyone want to teach a course on deviance?" This was the incredulous response from one of my colleagues a few years ago when I casually mentioned that we might want to consider offering a Sociology of Deviance course for our undergraduate sociology students. As chair of the department, I thought that a decade-long hiatus from offering the course was long enough. I believed that we ought to present an opportunity for our students to learn about a subject that until the 1960s had been considered the most important field of sociology. But the faculty resistance was strong, and there were no volunteers to teach the course. As one professor said, "No one wants to teach about a discipline that died a generation ago."

Unfortunately, my colleague was correct about the death of deviance—not as a fact, obviously, but as an academic discipline. More than twenty years ago, many sociologists began to abandon the study. Courses on deviance, long viewed as foundational to the discipline of sociology, were gradually deleted from the catalogues on many campuses. In the past, these had been among the most popular classes on campus because of the fascinating and occasionally racy subject matter: the violation of cultural norms. Students analyzed topics ranging from promiscuity and cheating on exams, to addiction, pedophilia, deviant subcultures, organized crime and serial murder, in an effort to understand how deviant behavior is defined and shaped by society—how groups draw boundaries around acceptable behavior and punish violators. Courses on deviance offered an opportunity to explore how the concepts of "normal" and "deviant" evolved over time, in different societies, and how notions of "conformity" and "deviance" can affect the way we live.

The discipline of sociology, in fact, emerged out of a sense that individualistic philosophies placed too little emphasis on the moral ties that link people in society. In one of the first sociology texts, Emile Durkheim wrote that deviance is an integral part of all societies because it affirms cultural norms and values.[1] All societies require moral definition; some behaviors and attitudes must be identified as more salutary than others. Durkheim saw that moral unity could be assured only if all members of a society were anchored to common assumptions about the world around them; without these assumptions, a society was bound to degenerate and decay. In this functionalist perspective, we are creatures with unlimited desires, which need to be held in check. The function of society is to constitute a "regulative force," setting limits on individual actions. At the same time, Durkheim believed that it is impossible for any society to be free of deviance—even a "society of saints" will have its sinners—and moreover, that deviance will always be present in every society at about the same rate. The challenge for the sociologist is to determine which behaviors are considered deviant and subject to sanctions by a given society during a given time.[2]

From Durkheim onward, sociologists regarded identifying and stigmatizing deviant behavior as an indispensable process, allowing us to live by shared standards. Durkheim was especially concerned with the controls that become internalized in individual consciousness as a result of what society defines as deviant. Convinced that society must be "present" within the individual, Durkheim was led to the study of religion as one of the forces that create within individuals a sense of obligation to adhere to society's demands. But his interest lay primarily not with individual devotion, but with communal religious activities, the rituals that bind communities together and give meaning to the lives of the devout. Functionalist disciples of Durkheim, including such contemporary sociologists as Talcott Parsons and Robert Merton, likewise believed that identifying deviant behavior was central to the process of generating and sustaining cultural values, clarifying moral boundaries and promoting social solidarity. For much of the twentieth century, defining deviance was considered a fundamental activity of any society.

Today, however, few sociologists teach about deviance and even fewer write about it. Edited collections of classic articles on deviance are republished every so often, but only, it seems, so that we can wonder over how backward we were to take such thinking seriously. The only recent in-depth analysis of a subject once considered basic to sociology is a book entitled *The Sociology of Deviance: An Obituary.* The author, Colin Sumner, describes it as "a post-mortem of a field of sociology which has ceased to exist." In fact, Sumner cleverly advises readers that his book "deals with a corpse rather than a corpus of knowledge." To him, the terrain of the sociology of deviance resembles the Somme battlefield in 1918: "It is barren, fruitless, full of empty trenches and craters, littered with unexploded mines and eerily silent. No one fights for hegemony over a dangerous graveyard."[3]

Indeed, for the majority of sociologists today, the only reason to study deviance is to dissect the long-dead discipline in order to understand why so many sociologists once deemed it important. Most current sociology textbooks are critical of the notion of defining deviance and even more critical of any sociologist who might suggest that the concept was ever useful in helping us understand social order. For today's postmodern sociologists, conceptions of deviance cannot exist in a society that has been so dramatically changed by shifts in values, politics and social relations. The commitment to egalitarianism, along with a growing reluctance to judge the behavior of others, has made discussions of deviance obsolete.

No wonder that most sociologists, in the face of this juggernaut, have been disinclined even to speak of the concept of deviance anymore. To do so would require a willingness to discuss behavior such as homosexuality, teenage promiscuity, adultery and addiction in relation to standards of "acceptable conduct." And defining by consensus what is acceptable is exactly what has disappeared over the last thirty years. In the aftermath of the radical egalitarianism of the 1960s, merely to label a behavior as deviant came to be viewed as rejecting the equality—perhaps the very humanity—of those engaging in it. Most social scientists became convinced that the sociology of deviance was more about the imposition of selective censure by the dominant elements of society—the "construction" of deviance—than it was about deviant behavior itself.

One of the influential voices of the 1960s, C. Wright Mills, says in *The Power Elite* that privileged groups participate in a "higher immorality" in their ability to marginalize as deviant those in society who become troublesome.[4] For Mills and his followers, society's elites use their wealth, prestige and power to sustain their privilege and ensure that their interests become national policy. According to this model, the concentration of wealth and power in the hands of an elite undermines the claims of American democracy and marginalizes those at the bottom of the social ladder, who are called "deviant" as a way of justifying their suppression.

Discussions of power during the 1960s centered on the ways in which agencies of social control shape people's identity, behavior and lifestyle.[5] Weakened by this approach, the study of deviance was further undermined by a growing number of interactionist sociologists who effectively argued that deviance and conformity had everything to do with the response of others, and nothing to do with any defect in the individual exhibiting what were called "deviant behaviors." Erving Goffman, for instance, argued that simply being labeled "deviant" could change a person's behavior. In his influential book *Asylums*, Goffman tried to demonstrate that mental patients only *appear* crazy because they are housed in mental institutions where their "craziness" is labeled and observed. By this theory, when an individual's action is tagged as deviant, that label will be incorporated into the person's self-image and social identity. Deviance is thus a self-fulfilling prophecy.[6] It is a short step from such a premise to seeing the tagged person as blameless and those doing the tagging as guilty.

Labeling theory

The overt deconstruction of the concept of deviance began with academics, but popular culture also has played an important role in destigmatizing deviant behaviors.[7] For instance, Ken Kesey's novel and award-winning film *One Flew over the Cuckoo's Nest* became widely viewed as a metaphor for the repressive social order that destroys individuals. Kesey's story of a courageous mental patient was taken by readers and moviegoers as a parable on the malign power of social institutions that force others to conform to norms established by the power elite, and stigmatize them—even kill them—when they protest.

Meanwhile, scholars like Howard Becker began to infuse sociological theory with the romantic view of the deviant as hero. An entire generation of sociology students was formed in large measure by Becker's *The Outsiders*, which promoted the belief that "social groups create deviance by making the rules whose infraction constitutes deviance—and by applying those rules to particular people and labeling them as outsiders."[8] Students were soon being taught that the degree to which an act will be treated as deviant is dependent upon who commits the act, and who feels harmed by it. And in some important ways—especially in the creation of drug policy—Becker was right about the social construction of deviance. Yet he neglected the influence of advocacy groups in defining unacceptable behavior, and focused only the "outsider" as the victim of unfair labeling. When rules began to be viewed as relative, applied more forcefully to some than to others, the poor and powerless were soon seen as victims of a growing inequality in the labeling and censuring of deviance.

Although figures such as C. Wright Mills and Howard Becker are cited by academics today less often than in past decades, they helped to pronounce the death sentence on deviance theory. The work of French social historian Michel Foucault and other postmodern theorists confirmed the growing belief that the sociology of deviance was not so much a legitimate field of study as a means by which the powerful exerted control over the powerless. In *Madness and Civilization*, Foucault wrote that the old model of deviance was merely oppressive "middle-class morality" dressed up in sociological language.[9] According to Foucault, things like madness, murder, incest, prostitution, homosexuality, illegal drug use and robbery were not "deviance"; they were "categories of censure" which were gradually created, developed or re-formed in the course of establishing and mapping out new systems and territories of domination.[10]

Given the vogue of such ideas, sociologists who continued to write and teach about deviant behavior found themselves blamed for supporting the ongoing quest of the powerful to marginalize those they found troublesome. Courses on deviance were gradually deleted from the curriculum. By the mid-1970s, the overt deconstruction of the concept of deviance was complete. Writing the "obituary," Colin Sumner says that the "death blow" was dealt to deviance when sociologist Alexander Liazos concluded that the subject not only was biased against the poor, but tended to ignore the way that the "corporate economy" was much more violent than so-called "criminals." Concern about "crime in the suites" began to take precedence over "crime in the streets." Liazos pointed out sourly that undergraduates at Yale (and elsewhere) jokingly referred to the popular introductory course on deviance as the study of "Nuts, Sluts and Perverts" because the typical subject matter included mental illness, prostitution and all forms of sexual deviance, rather than what Liazos regarded as "real" deviance—"covert, institutional deviance."[11] According to Liazos, the "daily violence of the capitalist economy, in condemning so many to poverty, ill health and exploitation, was ignored because their agencies were the ones with the most influence in defining deviance publicly as the province of nuts, sluts, and perverts."[12]

In defending the marginal or powerless, sociologists shifted the focus of deviance to those persons and groups in society with the power to propose definitions. Attention began to move from the criminal, the drug addict, the prostitute, the mentally ill and the homeless, to those who were seen to have branded them as deviant, or "caused" their deviance. Greedy landlords were viewed as the deviants who caused homelessness, while a punitive criminal justice system that targeted the poor and oppressed was viewed as the cause of crime. It was a stunning about-face. Sociologists assumed as a matter of course that a behavior is classified as deviant only when it offends those with enough political clout to pass a law against it.

Best-selling books like William Ryan's *Blaming the Victim* were lauded as providing "an impassioned, often brilliant exposé of middle class ideology which caused us to blame the powerless for their powerlessness."[13] No longer would the culture of the underclass be seen as contributing to the entrenched poverty of those who were part of it. No longer would out-of-wedlock births, drug abuse and the absence of a commitment to education or a work ethic be considered deviant. Instead, all this would be viewed as rational adaptations to an increasingly oppressive society. ← Deviance "general sense" dead

Criminals were redefined as victims of an unfair economy that effectively locked them out of legitimate opportunities. The homeless were redefined as victims of an unfair housing market. Drug abuse was transformed from a moral and legal issue into a medical one. Drug abusers were then redefined as victims either of their own genes, or of an oppressive society that forced them to take drugs in order to dull the pain of their rejection. And nobody was stamped as deviant—except, of course, those unfortunate traditionalists whom the new power elite in academia and in the media increasingly saw as maintaining an outworn and always suspect middle-class ideology about deviance.

It was not quite enough to let the study of deviance die a natural death. Instead, sociologists over the last thirty years have produced hundreds of articles and books attempting to drive a stake into its heart. Entire academic careers have been built on a clever criticism of Talcott Parsons' functionalist theory of deviance, for instance, or a hostile attack on the conservative thought of Emile Durkheim. Colin Sumner maintains that the concept of social deviance disappeared simply because it had run its course: "Fatally damaged by waves of successive criticism and undercut by its own logical contradictions, it ceased to be a living force. Its time had passed and it did not recover."[14] Books like Sumner's have served as a warning to those who might consider resurrecting the study that writing about deviance in anything but a dismissive manner is simply not allowed.

YET A FEW OF US, seeing "deviance" as a useful concept in helping us understand social order, believed that reports of its death were greatly exaggerated—particularly as we watched an escalation in behaviors that would have been declared deviant in the past. Could the dramatic increase in teenage pregnancy, teenage suicide or drug abuse by urban and suburban youth be said to have been caused by a "power elite"? Do we merely imagine that we are accosted by the aggressive, mentally ill or drug-addicted homeless in our cities? We can read about the increase in gang violence every day in our newspapers, and witness the continuing problem of neglected and abandoned children each evening on our local news. At one time, all of this would have been called deviant—and by characterizing it as such and studying it, we would be doing something about it. But there were no deviants left, only victims. Behavior that is socially and personally destructive was on the rise, even if we chose not to call it by its proper name.

In the early 1990s, a lone voice encouraged sociologists to consider these problematic behaviors once again. Addressing the 87th annual meeting of the American Sociological Association in 1992, Senator Daniel Patrick Moynihan did the unthinkable: he spoke of a worrisome increase in deviant behavior. In a speech entitled "Defining Deviancy Down," Moynihan, himself a sociologist, talked about an alarming trend in American social life, warning that for the previous twenty-five years, "society has chosen not to notice behavior that would be otherwise controlled, disapproved, or even punished." According to Moynihan, the social scientists who composed his audience had been complicit in this neglect: *Neglect not death*

> Over the past generation, the amount of deviant behavior in American society has increased beyond the levels the community can afford to recognize. Accordingly, we have been redefining deviancy so as to exempt much conduct previously stigmatized, and also quietly raising the normal level in categories where behavior is now abnormal by any earlier standard.[15]

The speech was received with subdued applause. Few of those present were willing to be disrespectful toward someone who was one of them in his academic origins, and who as a legislator had always been supportive of social science research. But there were many sociologists at the meeting who thought Daniel Patrick Moynihan was wrong about deviance—just as he had once been wrong, they believed, about poverty.

Many of the sociologists who heard Moynihan speak in 1992 had not forgotten his prior foray into the subject of deviant behavior. In

1965 he had issued a government report pointing to the "breakdown of the family" and a "culture of poverty" as contributors to the overwhelming and seemingly intractable malaise of the inner city. He even had the audacity to predict that a community where a large number of young men grow up in broken families dominated by women is bound to become chaotic. The absence of fathers, he wrote, would have devastating consequences. In the view of many sociologists, these remarks were just a form of "blaming the victim."

And Moynihan appeared to be doing the same once again. The senator may not have realized that very few sociologists were willing even to use the word "deviant" anymore, and that the handful who did had been disparaged for "blaming the victim." In private conversations throughout the weekend conference, people wondered whether Moynihan understood what he was saying by suggesting that we revisit the study of deviance, and worse, that we view it from the now unpopular functionalist perspective. Functionalism was at odds with the seemingly more egalitarian and nonjudgmental postmodern position, wherein no behavior, however reprehensible, could ever again be characterized as deviant. Any young sociologist who applied the term would risk being denied tenure. So most of the audience simply dismissed Moynihan's speech as the "nostalgic" musings of an old-fashioned sociologist who had lost his way during his years in politics.

Most of the attendees at that conference were reasonably confident that no outsiders would ever hear Senator Moynihan's heretical message. Unlike the 1960s and 1970s, when dozens of journalists would attend the pyrotechnic annual meetings of sociologists, the 1990s brought scant press coverage to these events. Journalists had long ago learned that aside from a few quarrels over terminology, little of substance would be discussed. In a later autobiography, in fact, Moynihan recalled that "at a press conference held just before the address, a sole reporter showed up from a local Pittsburgh radio station."[16]

The following winter, however, the text of Moynihan's speech was published in the *American Scholar*. While those who attended the annual meeting might have dismissed the senator as hopelessly behind the postmodern curve, people outside the rarefied academic environment paid a great deal of attention to what he had said. In fact, the response to Moynihan's call was overwhelming. Praise came from both ends of the political spectrum, from the *Washington Post*'s Mary McGrory as well as *National Review*'s William F. Buckley. William Galston, an assistant to President Clinton, publicly supported the senator's message, as did conservative William J. Bennett. A literature search of the popular press since 1993 reveals that more than five hundred articles have been written using Moynihan's phrase "defining deviancy down." The expression began to appear in major policy addresses. It was often used by New York's new mayor, Rudolph Giuliani, as he began his work to improve the quality of life in that city. New York's police commissioner, William Bratton, used the phrase to justify his department's new get-tough policies. So did *New York Times* columnist A. M. Rosenthal in describing the behavior of the police officers who, in the past, had not arrested brazen drug dealers on the streets.[17]

Given this overwhelming public sympathy with the senator's speech, some social scientists began to think they had erred in their polite reaction to it. The corpse of deviance, whose autopsy they thought had just been completed, seemed to be stirring. It was at this point that the gloves came off and a series of articles critical of Moynihan appeared in academic journals. One sociologist accused him of developing a "partisan campaign slogan which was meant to serve as a weapon to beat down the opposition in debates over social policy." Some worried that pet liberal programs and policies might begin to be questioned for having contributed to defining deviancy down. For one social scientist, the "seductive expression that masquerades as a self-evident, uncontestable truism, is actually a loaded phrase with severe limitations."[18] The major concern of these academics was that people might again begin making value judgments about certain behaviors. Worse yet, the long-dormant sociology of deviance might be revived and a door they thought was locked forever would be reopened.

As it worked out, these concerns were justified. Despite the resistance from academia, Moynihan's turn of phrase has become ingrained in our political vocabulary, and variations have even been coined. When the Monica Lewinsky scandal erupted, for instance, some social critics accused Bill Clinton of having "defined the presidency down."[19] Everyone knew what that meant—even if they were unwilling actually to use the word "deviant" when referring to the President.

In his clever alliteration, Moynihan had captured the essence of a disturbing trend in the United States: the decline of our quality of life through our unqualified acceptance of too many activities formerly considered unacceptable. Out-of-wedlock births, teenage pregnancy and promiscuity, drug abuse, welfare dependency and homelessness all seemed to be increasing, even in a climate of prosperity. Worse, these behaviors appeared to be morally condoned.

At the same time, there was a parallel but opposite development that the senator did not touch on in his speech—a movement of "defining deviancy up." Powerful advocacy groups were successfully stigmatizing behaviors that had formerly been regarded as "normal" and even benign. Some of these redefinitions have had consequences. On the one hand, the efforts of advocacy groups like Mothers Against Drunk Drivers to stigmatize drunk driving has achieved tremendous success and saved lives. On the other hand, the movement to brand cigarette smoking as deviant and restrict it accordingly has now reached into smokers' own homes.[20] Likewise, expanding definitions of sexual harassment and date rape have had destructive consequences for sometimes innocent individuals caught in the new, politically correct definitions of deviance.

THIS BOOK EXAMINES the politics of deviance. If in the past it was wealthy and powerful elites who labeled others as deviant, this prerogative has now been seized by influential interest or advocacy groups. Women's groups and gay rights organizations, for instance, now have the ability to silence speech by those with whom they disagree. Health care professionals and advocates have succeeded in medicalizing drug abuse and other behaviors once considered destructive. But the academic and media elite have the greatest power because they can shape discussion and dramatically influence public perceptions. These changes in the intellectual landscape prove that Durkheim was right in his prediction that the rate of deviance recognized by a society is constant, and that deviance will occur and be identified in every society, even in a "society of saints." But in ways that he and the earliest sociologists would have found startling, the targets of the new labeling system have changed: from those at the margins of society to those at the center.

Yet the picture is even more complex. Despite these political and intellectual crosscurrents, there are signs that the fact of deviance is being rediscovered by ordinary people who have suffered the real-world consequences of the academic elite's rejection of the concept. Those whose communities have been broken by failed welfare policies, or whose families have fallen apart as a result of teenage pregnancy or divorce, are now speaking out about the moral chaos that is destroying their neighborhoods, their schools and their families. The pendulum continues to swing; where it will stop is not clear.

For more than thirty years, the evolving politics of deviance has demanded that we adopt standards of conduct that come from human will and desire as mediated by advocacy groups, rather than those that derive from reason and common sense. Social theorist Philip Jenkins has proposed that the current social constructionist environment can be likened to a marketplace in which activists compete to win buyers for their products.[21] As marketers well know, success in convincing buyers that they really want to purchase a new product, especially when they are perfectly happy with the one they already have, can be achieved only through creative packaging of the product. The packaging of ideas involves a complex system of communication aimed at reaching people on an emotional level, convincing them that they want a redefinition of deviance even though they never realized that they needed it.

The following chapters explore this "culture war" between traditional and postmodern definitions of deviance. My central argument is that moral good or moral harm can come to a society according to how this conflict is resolved. I do not believe that all behaviors are created equal. And no conception of what is morally right exists without a corresponding idea of what is morally wrong. The distinction between these—that is, the boundaries of deviance—must not be established by politically powerful advocates through savvy marketing techniques. I will argue that we must reject the marketplace model, and instead draw from nature, reason and common sense to define what is deviant and reaffirm the moral ties that bind us together.

- wants everyone to have the same moral thoughts on deviant behavior.
- wants no diversity

ONE

MEDICALIZING THE DEVIANCE

OF DRUG ABUSE

While various advocacy groups have been gaining influence in redefining deviance, in many cases the real power to define and control deviant behavior has moved into the medical realm.[1] The discovery of subtle physiological correlates to explain human behavior and the creation of elaborate and expensive technologies has dramatically increased the influence of medical institutions in informing public perceptions and policy decisions.[2] When deviant behavior is reinterpreted in medical terms, its modification and social control take the form of medical intervention.

The medicalization of deviance is especially evident in the area of substance abuse and addiction. Rarely a week goes by without some form of media event highlighting the medical model of substance abuse. Television documentaries as well as newspaper and magazine articles on addiction are often enhanced with sincere testimony from Hollywood or sports celebrities who claim to have learned about and accepted the disease theory of addiction through their own treatment for drug and alcohol abuse. Lauded as heroes when they confess the hold that drugs and alcohol have had on them, they are embraced by the media and the public and quickly transformed from addicts into recovering role models for others to emulate. With every new drug-related arrest of superstar athletes like Dwight Gooden and Darryl Strawberry, or actors like Matthew Perry and Robert Downey Jr., we are again inundated with information on the biology of addiction—and given another list of medical reasons for the failure of these celebrity addicts to withstand the lure of chemicals or to fulfill the promise of recovery.

In the case of Darryl Strawberry, for instance, we have learned from countless magazine articles and televised interviews with the fallen baseball star and his supportive wife that his drug relapses, like the reoccurrence of his colon cancer, are beyond his control. Shortly after his most recent arrest for escaping from a court-ordered treatment program to begin a four-day cocaine binge, his wife, Charisse, stated that she continues to support her husband throughout his many relapses in his *illness*—just as she has done throughout his cancer treatment. She maintains her unconditional support despite Strawberry's most recent claims to have been kidnapped by men who *forced* him to take the drugs during the four days he was missing. Mrs. Strawberry knows there is a large audience for claims that her husband's drug addiction is a disease that cannot be *treated* in jail. "Darryl is not a bad person trying to do good," she says. "He is a sick person trying to get well." Now acknowledged as an expert on the "disease of addiction" because of her several years of experience in dealing with her husband's drug problems, Mrs. Strawberry was recently named president of the Tampa affiliate of the National Council on Alcoholism and Drug Dependence.[3]

Likewise, in another court appearance following yet another drug-related parole violation and arrest, actor Robert Downey Jr. appealed to a sympathetic judge, claiming that he continues to struggle with his *illness* of drug addiction and should certainly not be punished for behavior that is beyond his control. Downey has had enormous success in convincing the criminal justice system, the public and perhaps also himself that he is afflicted by an uncontrollable illness. At the Emmy Awards ceremony in 2001, Hollywood peers gave Downey a standing ovation and lauded him for his work toward recovery. In response, as he was receiving the Emmy for his acting in a popular television series, the charming and talented Downey flippantly thanked his "fellow parolees" for their support. Sadly, only a few weeks after this triumph, the thirty-six-year-old actor was arrested once more on drug charges.

Instead of holding the actor responsible for this latest relapse into substance abuse and addiction, the media offered to transfer any blame for Downey's problem to Hollywood itself. One *Boston Globe* critic claimed that most people believe that "Hollywood should have given him space after his release from prison, and that producer David Kelley did him no favors by featuring him on the television series, *Ally*

McBeal."[4] In a television interview, *TV Guide's* Mary Murphy charged that by putting so much pressure on the ill Downey, "Hollywood itself became the enabler."[5]

When Downey was briefly incarcerated, *Vanity Fair* published a flattering piece lauding him for his "courage" in surviving his time in prison, and criticizing the criminal justice system that would deny freedom to such a "great talent." The publicity surrounding this article brought enormous sympathy for the now "besieged" actor. *Vanity Fair* helped to move public opinion and eventually the criminal justice system to grant Downey's early release.

"Courageous" role models such as Strawberry and Downey maintain that addiction is a condition in which substance abusers are gripped by a disease they have acquired through no fault of their own. They are bolstered in their beliefs by a powerful portion of the scientific community, by the treatment professionals, and by a constant barrage of television documentaries, movies of the week and films like *Traffic*— all decrying the punitive ways in which we are currently handling our national drug problem.

In an interview with the *Los Angeles Times*, screenwriter Stephen Gaghan claimed to have written *Traffic*, a drama about the implications of heroin smuggling from Mexico to the United States, in order to show the danger of stigmatizing the addict for his drug abuse. He sadly noted that the script was an effort to save the life of his friend Robert Bingham, a longtime heroin abuser who died before the film was completed. Gaghan blamed the former head of the Office of National Drug Control Policy, William J. Bennett, for Bingham's death. "The reason Robert is dead is that he couldn't talk about his problem publicly because of the stigma—and the stigma comes straight from William Bennett."[6] Bennett's "crime" was the mere suggestion that users actually made a decision to continue taking drugs.

Traffic contains scene after scene of subtle and not so subtle suggestions that drug use should be destigmatized and medicalized at the same time. In fact, in one memorable moment, a recovering addict proclaims his drug addiction to be not just a general disease, but rather, quite a specific malady, an "allergy of the body."[7] Throughout the film, "responsible" adults—especially the conservative drug czar played by Michael Douglas—are shown as needing constant education by those involved in the illegal drug trade. At one point, in fact, a teenage dealer arrogantly advises the drug czar on the economics of neighborhood drug sales and addiction. Seemingly astonished to learn about the inner workings of the drug trade, the bewildered bureaucrat appears to be realizing for the first time that an inner-city underground economy actually benefits from the illegal drug market. In an emotional meeting with his daughter at a support group for recovering addicts, he finally understands addiction, realizes the futility of the war on drugs, and decides to resign from his government position.

The concept of the addict-as-expert is a consistent theme in both the news and the entertainment media. A PBS series hosted by Bill Moyers entitled *Moyers on Addiction: Close to Home* focused on the need to move away from "moralizing" on addiction, toward listening to addicts, among them the host's own son. Addiction, said Moyers, is not a character issue nor a criminal justice issue, but rather a health issue "that affects all of our families." Indeed, Moyers chose the *Close to Home* title to stress that everyone's family is vulnerable—even his own. Introducing the documentary, Moyers likened his son's drug and alcohol addiction to his own heart condition. "No one got mad at me when I went off my diet after my heart attack," he said. "No one blamed me for putting my life at risk because of my diet."[8]

This message is compelling in its emotional appeal. Yet the lack of dissenting voices from scientists and researchers who disagree with the medicalization movement is disconcerting for those who still maintain that drug abuse is a decision and not a disease. Through the entire series, no one was invited even to mention the moral issues involved in choosing—if indeed it is a choice—to abuse drugs and alcohol.

Moyers' views on the "science" of addiction were reinforced in the second part of the series, entitled "The Hijacked Brain." This program featured the director of the National Institute on Drug Abuse, Dr. Alan Leshner, lecturing to middle school students on the biology of drug and alcohol addiction. Surrounded by posters featuring enhanced images of the brain, Leshner advised the students that "addiction is essentially a disease of the brain."[9] He cautioned them that drugs alter the brain, "hijack its motivational systems, and even change how its genes function." The seventh- and eighth-grade students were told that addicts are "sick" and that their drug-taking behavior is simply the way their brains respond to the chemicals.

Dr. Leshner has been one of the most prominent promoters of the addiction-as-disease theory. A *Newsweek* cover story on addiction in 2001 (with the obligatory picture of Robert Downey Jr. on the front) featured Leshner in an article entitled "How It All Starts inside Your Brain." Never acknowledging that "it" is the initial decision to take drugs, Leshner uses the "hijacked brain" metaphor in the article to ensure that readers understand that once drugs enter the user's being, he is forever changed—a chemical casualty. Just as a hijacker takes control of an airplane, this theory maintains, drugs take over an individual's life and behavior so he is no longer at the controls. Thus, Leshner says, "Addiction is a brain disease. It may start with the voluntary act of taking drugs, but once you've got it, you can't just tell the addict to stop, anymore than you can tell the smoker, Don't have emphysema. Starting may be volitional. Stopping isn't."[10] But he is oblivious to the logic of his own analogy: smokers can and do stop.

WHETHER DRUG ADDICTION IS really a disease is a question that has surfaced in this country periodically throughout the last one hundred years. In the late nineteenth century, drug use was associated with a decline of moral character. Because of their drug use, Chinese immigrants and American blacks became the objects of extensive social and legal restraints. The Chinese opium smokers were viewed as a threat to American society, while cocaine became especially feared in the southern states because of concerns that blacks would become "unmanageable" once they experienced its euphoric and stimulating properties.[11] There was little movement toward medicalization during this period; the fear of drugs and addiction was powerful enough to permit the most profoundly punitive methods to be employed in the fight against addicts and suppliers.

Yale professor of medicine David Musto, an authority on the history of drug use, writes that as we look back over the "waxing and waning popularity of mood-altering substances, it is difficult to escape the suspicion that, although drug abuse is a real and deeply embedded social problem, attempts to solve it are sometimes nearly overwhelmed by wars of words."[12] The contest is waged by opposing camps of fiercely committed partisans. As times change, and as concerns about drugs escalate or decline, new laws are demanded and passed, old ones are abolished, and sometimes still older ones are retrieved and reimplemented as innovations.

A study of drug laws and policies, which tend to reflect how people typically perceive drug use at a given time, reveals that certain drugs, at certain times, carry negative stereotypes, while others do not. In the 1940s, for example, most people in the United States shared the assumption that marijuana users were immoral and dangerous.[13] This view was reinforced in the popular culture by films such as *Reefer Madness*, which portrayed marijuana users as sexually promiscuous, out of control, and prone to committing violent crime. These strong negative perceptions about marijuana lasted until the mid-1960s, when social attitudes about marijuana began to change, especially among the young and college-educated. In a short time, the use of marijuana sky-rocketed. In 1965, 18,815 people were arrested for violations of state and local marijuana laws; by 1973, the number rose to 420,000.[14] Meanwhile, *Reefer Madness* became a comic cult favorite.

As the number of marijuana users increased—and the demographics changed from those Howard Becker called "outsiders," to people with more social and political power—there was tremendous pressure to remove the harsh punishments for their "experimentation." Powerful advocates were eventually successful in lessening the penalties for marijuana use, and for those who experienced "problems" with it, treatment was increasingly advocated.

Indeed, throughout history drug policy has been driven more by the demographics of drug users than by concerns about the virulence of a specific drug. When marijuana began to be abused by people with status or power, the behavior became medicalized instead of criminalized. As a result, the federal government became heavily invested in treatment in the 1970s, and there occurred what David Musto describes as an "explosion in treatment facilities." From 20,000 clients in federally funded treatment programs in October 1971, the number climbed to over 60,000 by December 1972, and to more than 80,000 the following year. The medicalization movement had a tremendous effect on federal drug abuse laws, with psychological treatment and flexible sentences replacing the punitive sentencing of the past. This was accompanied by a parallel movement toward tolerance. Musto documents that tolerance toward what became defined as "drug experimentation" instead of "drug use" peaked in 1978 as treatment programs proliferated to accommodate the growing population of "addicts."

Yet a powerfully negative reaction began to emerge by 1980, when drugs and drug users again began to be viewed as a serious threat to American life and values. By the mid-1980s, increased fear of drugs, especially worries about crime and violence related to the use of crack cocaine in the inner city, resulted in the creation of harsh mandatory sentencing laws and a rapid rise in the incarceration of drug offenders. The advent of the "crack baby" was particularly significant in heightening the perceptions of deviance surrounding the crack cocaine user.

Fears also mounted over the virulence of powder cocaine when people began to realize that it was not only a recreational drug, but one with lethal consequences that threatened our "best and brightest."

Tragic deaths like that of college basketball superstar Len Bias, who died in 1986 of a powder cocaine overdose three days after being drafted by the defending NBA champion Boston Celtics, became what one noted sports sociologist called "the most important drug event of the last 20 years."[15] Within three months of Bias's death, the National Collegiate Athletic Association instituted a mandatory drug testing policy, and the NBA and the NFL increased the penalties for violation of their drug policies.

The tolerance of the 1970s was replaced by draconian drug sentencing practices in the 1980s—for some. Because crack cocaine was regarded as more dangerous than powder, federal law required judges to impose a five-year prison sentence on any defendant convicted of possessing 5 grams (much less than an ounce) of crack. To receive the same sentence, a defendant found guilty of powder cocaine possession would have to be caught with at least 500 grams (more than a pound). Civil liberties groups have argued that the hundredfold difference makes the law inherently discriminatory because it is typically poor minorities who use crack and are disproportionately sent to prison under the more stringent sentencing guidelines.

Scientists have determined that crack is actually no more addictive than powder cocaine, and that crack users are no more likely to behave violently than those who take the powder form of the drug.[16] Still, a double standard in sentencing continues. There is a strong tendency for the courts to recommend medical treatment for affluent, generally white drug users with good jobs (and medical insurance). On the other hand, crack cocaine users, or those without a strong advocacy community—generally poor blacks and Hispanics—continue to face long prison sentences.[17]

According to Justice Department estimates, more than half of the growth in the prison population since the mid-1980s is due to the increased penalties and mandatory sentences for drug offenses. The number of people in custody in the United States rose from 744,208 in 1985 to 1,630,940 in 1996—an increase of nearly 100 percent. Between 1990 and 1995 alone, the number of those arrested for drug violations rose 27 percent.[18] Yet while such figures suggest a draconian policy, it is also true that overall drug use in the United States has fallen by half since the harsher mandatory sentencing strategies began in the 1980s.[19] Surveys of college athletes reveal that while 14 percent reported having used cocaine during the 1985–86 academic year, the rate dropped to 5 percent by 1989, and to 1 percent in 1998, the year of the latest survey. Athletes are seldom linked to cocaine use these days;

most suspensions are now traced to performance-enhancing drugs or marijuana.[20]

The move to medicalize drug abuse has already had far-reaching effects on the shaping of public policy. Under a law passed by Congress in 1994, federal inmates convicted of nonviolent crimes can reduce their sentences by up to one year by claiming "addiction" and completing a substance-abuse program in prison. While the intention of such a law may be noble—to promote treatment for substance abusers—the reality of the law is that "addicted" inmates are rewarded with early release while inmates without drug or alcohol addictions end up serving significantly longer prison sentences.

The implications of this federal law became clear in California when, as a result of their enrollment in a prison drug treatment program, two high-profile federal inmates had their release dates moved up by more than a year. Former judge Dennis Adams and lawyer Patrick Frega, both key players in a case that exposed how gifts were exchanged for judicial favors, were rewarded in 2001 with early release dates for confessing to substance abuse. According to press reports, neither had documented (or ever mentioned) any history of drug or alcohol abuse prior to incarceration. In press interviews, a longtime colleague of one of the defendants identified him as a "teetotaler." Convicted of racketeering, conspiracy and mail fraud, Judge Adams was scheduled to be released to a local halfway house to serve his last six months, but he requested to be allowed to serve the remainder of his sentence under house arrest at his ex-wife's beachfront Hawaiian home. In December 2001, after serving less than half of his three-year sentence, Adams was released from federal prison and flown at taxpayer expense to Hawaii, to complete an additional six-month halfway-house sentence (a compromise).[21]

Intentionally rewarding alleged substance abusers by designing such inequitable public policies not only minimizes the deviance of drug abuse, but punishes those prisoners who do not abuse drugs. As the stigma for substance abuse continues to diminish, we can anticipate a growing number of individuals making the rational choice to adopt the label of "addict" for the benefits it confers. Some are already realizing that the rewards can be significant. This is especially true in federal policy on disability, in which addiction has been defined by policymakers as something independent of and beyond volition—and therefore a disability. Seen as medically disabled, addicts are entitled to the rights, privileges and protections afforded to those with other forms of disability. Even "drug-disabled" pregnant women are not held responsible for their drug use during pregnancy, despite the harm that it does to the unborn child. In our zigzagging effort to deal with drugs, we have moved far from the 1980s panic over "crack babies," and tolerance has now replaced outrage over drug abuse during pregnancy.

IN *PC, M.D.*, PSYCHIATRIST and public health expert Sally Satel describes the ways in which public policy has been shaped by the medicalization of what were formerly seen as individual decisions. Focusing particularly on the role of the federal government in actually exacerbating the problem of drug abuse, she explains how the new worldview has enabled women to continue abusing drugs throughout pregnancy.

Against the grain of this status quo, Satel cites the example of an innovative prevention and treatment program for drug-abusing pregnant women initiated by concerned doctors and nurses at the Medical University of South Carolina in collaboration with Charleston's police chief and county attorney. This program involved a drug-testing protocol to identify those who were abusing drugs during pregnancy, and instead of treating these women as victims of forces beyond their control, it imposed stigmatizing sanctions, including a law enforcement response. Satel writes that "a woman could be arrested and charged with child neglect or delivery of drugs to a minor if she was using drugs just prior to delivery, or tested positive for drugs and refused or missed an appointment with the substance abuse or prenatal clinic."[22] While some might consider this too harsh, it was successful in reducing the incidence of drug abuse among pregnant women who would deliver their babies at the South Carolina hospital.

Despite the program's success, however, advocates for the pregnant addicts assailed the Charleston plan. The Center for Reproductive Law and Policy filed a $3 million class action suit against the City of Charleston on behalf of ten women who tested positive for drugs. The defendants in the suit included the university hospital as well as individual nurses and doctors who implemented the drug-testing program. The allegations included violation of the women's privacy and reproductive rights, and, because eight of the women were black, racial discrimination. Federal intervention made things worse when administrators at the U.S. Department of Health and Human Services warned that unless the South Carolina hospital abandoned what the agency called a "punitive policy" of drug-testing pregnant women, it would lose the federal funding that comprised 60 percent of its budget. Likewise, the Office for Civil Rights advised the hospital that federal funds may not be used to support a program like theirs which "discriminates" against minority female substance abusers.[23] Under these pressures, the successful drug-testing program was quietly closed.

In attempting to discourage drug abuse during pregnancy, the Medical University of South Carolina was following a useful tradition of challenging destructive behavior. But as Satel points out, the war waged against the University Medical Center, first by women's rights organizations and later by civil liberties advocates and the federal government, demonstrates the enormous power of advocacy groups in redefining deviance. The right of the individual to take drugs competed with, and ultimately defeated the hospital's clinical imperative to treat drug-abusing mothers-to-be and defend the health of the near-term fetus.[24]

Instead of being seen as deviant behavior, substance abuse by pregnant women was viewed as a right—and also a symptom of the pain suffered by women living in an oppressive, patriarchal power structure. Satel cites the 1994 documentary film *Women of Substance*, in which producers Rory Kennedy and Robin Smith criticize programs like the South Carolina plan and depict the drug-abusing women as courageous victims of disease. Satel points out that with no censure of destructive actions and little regard for responsible behavior such as finding work, taking care of their children and staying away from drugs, the documentary clearly conveys the message: "These women are victims of a disease—they take drugs to medicate themselves." Lynn Paltrow of the Center for Reproductive Law and Policy affirmed this point when she told Ted Koppel on ABC's *Nightline*, "Everybody's ready to call these women selfish, when the real problem is that they are not selfish enough. Though they expose their unborn children to potentially dangerous substances, the ones harmed first and foremost are themselves."[25]

Bill White, a senior research consultant at Chestnut Hill Health Systems in Bloomington, Illinois, insists that sanctions like those used in the South Carolina program simply do not work. White claims that even threatening drug-abusing women with loss of their children will not deter their drug use. To illustrate his point, White said in an interview with Bill Moyers, "We found that when we knocked on doors and threatened to take the children, substance-abusing women would readily say, 'Which one do you want, or do you want them all?'"[26] Neither White nor Moyers questioned whether a drug-abusing mother who is so eager to give up her children in the service of her addiction is providing the best home for her children. The right to abuse drugs and yet retain the cushion of victimhood (as well as the claims of parenthood) seems to be fully recognized in the treatment industry.

As a preview of things possibly to come in the United States, Dr. Satel notes that the acceptance of drug use as a "right" has reached its apotheosis in the Netherlands, where addicts have formed a union called the Federation of Dutch Junkie Leagues. This advocacy group lobbies the government for services including housing, health benefits and welfare payments to addicts. Activist addicts and their supporters maintain that drug use is a human right and that the government has a responsibility to make it safer to be an addict.[27] Some churches, for instance, have provided an environment that supports and encourages drug abuse. The pastor of a Dutch Reformed congregation in Rotterdam invites dealers into his church to sell discounted heroin and cocaine to addicted parishioners, who are allowed to use the church basement rooms to inject or smoke the drug.[28]

The Netherlands has embraced a philosophy of "harm reduction" which holds that drug abuse is inevitable and that the proper role of society should be to minimize the damage that it does. Advocates of harm reduction present it as a rational compromise between the alleged futility of the drug war and the extremism of outright legalization. But as Satel points out, "Since harm reduction makes no demands on addicts, it consigns them to their addiction, aiming only to allow them to destroy their lives in relative safety, and at taxpayer expense."[29]

In the United States, the growth in needle exchange programs can be viewed as a first step toward a strategy of harm reduction. Advised that there is a catastrophic spread of AIDS and hepatitis by contaminated needles, the public is presented with a simple choice: Should a drug addict shoot up with a clean needle or a dirty one? Whether addicts should stop abusing drugs is not part of the question posed. To build support for needle exchange, advocates of this policy present the public with "airtight" evidence that it reduces the rate of HIV transmission. But a number of studies have pointed out that research supporting needle exchange has been characterized by serious design errors. More rigorous research has been much more cautious in its claims for decreasing HIV infection.[30] Studies published in the *American Journal of Public Health* concluded that the more rigorous investigations "simply do not support the effectiveness of needle exchange programs as a mean of reducing the spread of HIV." In one of the articles in the journal, Dr. A. R. Moss of the Department of Biostatistics and Epidemiology at San Francisco General Hospital stated, "It becomes very uncomfortable to point out the data supporting needle exchange are not as good as you thought they were." Calvina Fay, director of the Drug Free America Foundation, argues that "most needle exchange programs do little or nothing to steer people into treatment. Instead, they end up becoming social clubs for drug users and a magnet for prostitution and crime, often in neighborhoods that are already on the margins."[31]

Undeterred by such data, San Francisco in 2001 became the first city in the United States to mandate that all of the drug and alcohol treatment agencies serving the city must have harm reduction programs in place. An article in the *San Francisco Chronicle* reassured readers that "no one is suggesting that San Francisco open up spaces for addicts to inject drugs—yet."[32] Instead, the *Chronicle* said that as a preliminary step, needle exchange programs would be expanded to include free medical care for addicts offered by San Francisco's Department of Public Health at each of the city's needle exchange sites. This harm reduction strategy would be supplemented by a series of "addict-education" programs. Addicts soon to be released from jail would be taught how to perform CPR on their friends who may be overdosing on drugs. A pilot project would put the prescription drug naloxone, a heroin antidote, into the hands of addicted couples so they can administer it to each other in case of an overdose. Like the Netherlands, San Francisco will now define "success" in a drug program as helping to maintain addicts "safely" in their drug habit.

Dr. Joshua Bamberger, San Francisco's director for housing and urban health at the Department of Public Health, claims that "Harm reduction opens the doors to honesty and allows providers to move addicts one positive step at a time toward better health." But Bamberger does not indicate how an active heroin addict can ever be viewed as "moving toward better health." While San Francisco has no immediate plans to establish safe injection rooms, a recent city conference on harm reduction cited the "success" of such rooms and prescription heroin in the Netherlands, Switzerland, Germany and Australia. No one at the conference mentioned the squalid conditions of Switzerland's open-air shooting gallery in Platzspitz Park (the notorious "Needle Park"), or the syringe-littered Letten railway station. Nor was there any discussion of Holland's tremendous increase in heroin addiction, property crime, gun-related deaths and organized criminal activity, or of the consequent need for one of the largest per capita police forces in the world.[33]

In Massachusetts, the *Boston Globe* reported that nearly six hundred doctors and nurses called on the governor's office to expand access to needle exchange. The public appears to agree. A statewide poll by the University of Massachusetts at Boston found that 62 percent of the people supported such a policy. In fact, when the *Globe* reported on these harm reduction strategies under the title "Saving the Sinner," the paper was criticized by angry correspondents charging that the reference to "sin" perpetuated old stigmas. One letter from the "furious" executive director of an area drug treatment advocacy organization complained that the headline was "completely inappropriate for a health article—Addiction is a chronic disease that demands a medical and public health response—it is not a moral lapse."[34]

The message has been received and apparently embraced by the public, the politicians and the physicians that addiction is not a moral issue, but rather a medical condition. One reason for this development is simply that "treatment" seems like the humane solution to a complex problem. For stakeholders of a destigmatized attitude toward drug abuse, medicine represents a nonjudgmental alternative to the ideological pull of religion or morals in defining deviance.

MEDICALIZATION LIFTS THE burden of responsibility for drug abuse from the shoulders of the abuser. In fact, in some "treatment" programs, such as methadone maintenance, the addict is enabled to "live with" his or her addiction. Methadone is a synthetic drug, first devised by German chemists seeking new pain-relief medication for soldiers in World War II. In the 1960s methadone was found to blunt cravings for heroin without providing the same sense of euphoria. Today, with heroin use becoming more widespread, especially among young people and the more affluent who increasingly snort or smoke (rather than inject) the drug, methadone therapy has become a profitable industry subsidized by hundreds of millions of taxpayers dollars each year. In California, for instance, 148 clinics dispense methadone to tens of thousands of patients every day. The state spent more than $55 million on methadone therapy in 1999.[35]

From the earliest days of methadone maintenance—which is simply using one narcotic to control another—critics of medicalization have asserted that such treatment simply "authenticates the doctors' expertise about habit-forming and habit-curing drugs, and has legitimized doctors as pharmacological miracle workers—and in the end, has made them steadily more indispensable as the suppliers of new controlled substances."[36]

Yet such medical empowerment is appealing because it holds a promise for a biological solution to what we are no longer willing to treat as a moral problem. Articles like *Newsweek*'s "Can This Pill Stop You from Hitting the Bottle?" offer hope for an easy pharmaceutical "cure" for drug and alcohol abuse.[37] A controversial clinic in the Caribbean has had success with a botanical "drug" called ibogaine. A natural hallucinogen that is still illegal in the United States, this botanical masks withdrawal symptoms and seems to help cocaine addicts. One researcher called it a "slam dunk" for detoxing from opiates, cocaine and alcohol.[38]

For heroin, there is increased interest in "rapid detox," a practice invented at the University of Vienna in the late 1980s. It involves a four-hour medical procedure in which naloxone is injected intravenously into the veins of the addict in what the promoters call an effort to "pry off the billions of opiate molecules that have been clinging to the addict's brain cells and wash them away."[39] Introduced in the United States in 1996, rapid detox was initially offered at only a handful of hospitals, with limited success. In 1999, seven patients died soon after rapid detox was performed by one New Jersey doctor who had conducted more than 3,000 procedures. Despite these concerns, "patients want it," according to one practitioner, "because it gives them a compassionate and comfortable way to get clean."[40] Because of the ease of detoxifying the addict, there is growing pressure to extend the practice. While only about 1,000 procedures a year are done in the United States, Europe has administered rapid detox to more than 12,000 addicts each year. The numbers are expected to rise in the United States if clinical trials show that the procedure is safe.

Of course, these "cures" do little to prevent people from relapsing. Dr. David Cullen, an anesthesiologist at Tufts University, said that the high relapse rate led him to stop doing rapid detox. He had performed the procedure on forty-three patients, but within a year or two, more than 80 percent were either back on heroin or dead from an overdose.

While the promise of a quick cure is appealing, the fundamental attraction of the disease theory of addiction is that it protects individuals from blame for their own behavior. Because alcoholism is no longer considered a moral weakness, for instance, alcoholics are no longer sanctioned for public intoxication. They are instead referred to treatment in medical settings. If alcoholism is a "disease," the only truly therapeutic response is medical rather than moral.[41] What has happened to Darryl Strawberry, Robert Downey and any number of other alcohol or drug abusers is not their fault, but the fault of their genetics or disordered body chemistry or hijacked brain. The addict is "sick," a label without moral judgment or implications of deviance. The designation of sickness also reduces the guilt of the families. Parents bear no responsibility for their child's involvement in substance abuse when the deviant, in essence, is granted a medical excuse.[42]

Indeed, we now glorify the addict in treatment in the same way we would a patient who fought off cancer. A struggle with addiction has been transformed from a stigma to a savvy career move—especially for media celebrities. When actress Melanie Griffith was released from drug treatment, she published a "recovery journal" on her website.[43] It shows beautiful pictures of Griffith in a flowing white dress, stepping into a blossom-strewn world she calls Avalon. In her breathless voice, Melanie sends her "newly detoxified light to everyone who had helped in the healing."

ALTHOUGH IT MAY SEEM humane to conceptualize deviance as sickness rather than badness, sociologists have been warning for decades about the costs of such a redefinition to society and the individual. As far back as 1972, Talcott Parsons wrote that medicalizing deviance still requires the individual to recognize that "Illness itself is an undesirable state, to be recovered from as expeditiously as possible."[44] Parsons pointed out that the medical excuse for addiction is valid only when the patient-deviant accepts the inherent undesirability of his or her "sick" behavior and submits to a subordinate relationship with an official agent of control (the treatment expert) for the purpose of changing it. This, of course, opens the door for the patient-deviant to endure whatever treatment modality the expert demands.[45]

A two-tier citizenship is created: those who are deemed responsible for their actions and those who are not. The "not-responsible" sick person, who is "sick for life" under the medicalization model of addiction, also becomes a second-class citizen, dependent on the fully responsible. The newly labeled ill are subject to potentially powerful agents of social control with the authority to oversee the illness and confer all labels pertaining to illness and recovery.[46] And since one is never "cured" from addiction, the addict receives a lifetime sentence of social control by treatment experts with no possibility of parole to a world of personal autonomy.

Sociologist Peter Conrad warned of these consequences more than twenty-five years ago when he published a prescient article on the "discovery" of hyperkinesis in children.[47] Conrad predicted that this development would eventually involve the dislocation of responsibility from children and parents, and promote the domination of "expert control" within the treatment industry. He also predicted that under this new dispensation, potent medical techniques would be used to control the "sick" individual.[48] The ever-expanding treatment industry for hyperkinesis, or attention deficit disorder, as it became known, and its growing clout in the worlds of education and childrearing are evidence of the accuracy of the predictions made by Conrad and other sociologists.

The current movement not only to decriminalize but also to destigmatize drug abuse could actually increase it by making it cost-free. In fact, psychologist and addiction expert Jeffrey Schaler, author of *Addiction Is a Choice,* asserts that instead of being told they cannot control their habit, addicts should be encouraged to take charge of their lives once again. "The more people believe in their ability to moderate their consumption of drugs and alcohol, the more likely they will be to moderate," he writes. "The converse is also true: the more people believe in their inability to control their consumption of drugs and alcohol, the less likely they will moderate."[49]

Some psychologists also maintain that an important concept to help us understand behavioral choices is "self-efficacy"—people's confidence in their ability to achieve a specific goal in a particular situation. Schaler reminds us that although self-efficacy is an academic concept, it is also common sense to acknowledge that when you think you can do something, you are more likely to be successful than when you believe you cannot.[50] Teaching addicts that they are not responsible and that they are powerless over their addiction destroys self-efficacy.

Schaler and a growing number of other maverick drug and alcohol researchers believe that negative sanctions and stigmas can indeed work in reducing substance abuse, and that the movement to medicalization and harm reduction is a dangerous one. While there is no enthusiasm for returning to the dark days of mistreating drug addicts or for the present policy of incarcerating large numbers of drug offenders, these researchers say that holding substance abusers responsible for their behavior can be effective. They point out that no studies— including those searching for an "addiction gene"—have proved that a factor other than the self is responsible for the individual's choice to abuse drugs or alcohol. Despite the consistency of this data, however, there is a constant demand for more addiction treatment. The public is rarely told just how utterly ineffective most of these treatment programs actually are—especially those that stress the model of addiction-as-disease instead of personal responsibility.

In study after study, we learn that what is occurring "outside a person's body is much more significant in understanding drug and alcohol abuse and recovery than what goes on inside the body."[51] The best predictor of treatment success, according to Charles Schuster, former director of the National Institute on Drug Abuse, is not the treatment program itself but whether the addict has an especially good job that would be lost if there was a relapse. Journalists, politicians and the general public not only ignore a tremendous body of literature on the failure of medicalized treatment modalities, they also pay little attention to the rigorous academic studies indicating that drug abuse is a function of individual choice, not biology.

To understand the impact of environment on substance abuse, it is helpful to compare drug use and abuse among various groups within society. Those with the lowest rate of drug use are those in the military. While some sociologists might claim that there is a self-selection bias—people who enter the military are less likely to abuse drugs anyway—it is also true that many young recruits have indeed used marijuana and other drugs prior to their entry into the service, but fearing the certain punishment of expulsion, stopped once they entered. Other critics might say that the reason for the low rate of drug use is simply the threat of drug testing. And there may be something to that. Yet clearly the most important reason why military personnel abuse drugs at a relatively low rate is the authority and consistent discipline of a military regime. Military leaders are pragmatically concerned with stopping drug abuse, not through arrest and incarceration but through stigmas and sanctions. Barry McCaffrey, former director of the Office of National Drug Policy, asserted that the reason that members of the armed forces have such a low rate of drug use (less than 2 percent) is because of this discipline:

> We've got sergeants and sergeants act like parents are supposed to act—they set standards, and they treat people with respect. But, they also put high demands on them. They say, hey kid, you want to use drugs on this ship, in this squadron, in this battalion—we will separate you from us. We won't lock you up. But, you can't stay with us any longer. As a result, drug abuse rates in the active armed forces remain low. The same kids who are out on the streets smoking a joint or two during their adolescent years, don't use drugs when they enter the military.[52]

This statement illustrates the value of calling deviant behavior by its right name. Drug laws are important, but they are a last resort. The first resort must be social stigmas against such behavior.

Yet the effort to strengthen anti-drug norms has elicited a fierce reaction from the treatment industry. When asked about President George W. Bush's effort to enlist "faith-based" organizations in the rehabilitation of drug abusers, for instance, Bill McColl, spokesman for the National Association of Drug and Alcohol Counselors, charged that this would "put us back when people thought you were an alcoholic merely because you didn't accept Jesus as your personal savior."[53] Despite the success of faith-based treatment programs in states like Texas and Florida, there has been bitter opposition to any attempt by the federal government to begin similar programs. This is not because of the establishment clause, although the Constitution is always cited, but because faith-based programs look at drug abuse and addiction as a moral problem requiring a moral solution. Opponents of this approach ignore the fact that the most effective programs for aiding people in fighting addiction continue to be the Alcoholics Anonymous and Narcotics Anonymous programs. These succeed because they require an "admission of shame and a commitment to right conduct that are, in their intensity and justification, little different from any moral obligation."[54]

In *The Moral Sense*, James Q. Wilson notes that "in Aristotle's language, most people become temperate as their natural sociability—a desire to please parents and friends—leads them to value the deferred pleasures of respect, friendship, the absence of punishment, lasting happiness, that come from subordinating their immoderate passions to moderate habits." Most people control themselves, in other words, because they see self-control as an important dimension of their own morality. Wilson describes this self-control as "a fundamental feature of their social nature: the respect for and the obligation toward others with whom we spend our lives or from whom we expect important benefits. For this reason, it is a profound error to say that one should not be moralistic or judgmental about the more serious addictions."[55] Judging them morally, in fact, is the responsible response.

Too often, however, people are frightened of being accountable; they want someone else to take over the responsibility for their lives—a parent, a warden, a doctor, a drug. Medicalization messages are appealing because they seem so nurturing to those who have this fear. Yet medicalizing deviance not only removes responsibility, but takes away any opportunity for authentic relationships and the support systems these relationships provide. Assuming the "sick role," the addict will never achieve equality in any relationship.

Some sociologists view the rapid rise in medical treatment for erstwhile deviant behaviors and emotions as an attempt to compensate for our deteriorating families and communities.[56] Regardless of the cause, it is probable that the antidote to addiction is not a better prison or, for that matter, a better doctor. Successful treatment programs emphasize the importance of values and hold the individual responsible for his or her behavior, at the same time that they establish a moral atmosphere that clearly discourages the behavior, enhances alternative coping mechanisms, and relies on community disapproval and support.[57] Attempts to define down the deviance of drug abuse have resulted in moral confusion and personal disorder, leading to a no-man's land where no one is responsible and nothing works.

TWO

REMOVING THE STIGMA

FROM MENTAL ILLNESS

During the Middle Ages, many of those identified as "insane" were thought to be possessed by the devil and were burned as witches. Even after this barbarism passed, the mentally ill lived on the edges of society. Increasingly regarded as troublesome, they were incarcerated indiscriminately along with vagrants and criminals.[1] The establishment of mental asylums in the eighteenth century was purely for social control—protection of the sane from the insane—rather than any attempt to provide the mentally ill with care. The most famous of the early mental institutions was St. Mary of Bethlehem in London, commonly known as "Bedlam," a word that soon became associated with chaos or craziness. From the middle of the nineteenth century, more and more patients were identified as mentally ill and committed to state institutions. This led to problems with overcrowding, as well as degrading and inhumane living conditions that lasted well into the twentieth century.

We assume that we have moved far from the days when aristocratic elites visited the mad in Bedlam Hospital and called it entertainment. But as a recent magazine article points out, in a way we haven't moved far from that scenario at all: "In twentieth century New York, professional elites now visit the mad in the streets and call it homeless outreach. The results in both cases are the same: the objects of attention are left to rot in their own filth, perhaps to lose a limb or two to gangrene, or to die."[2] We seem to have returned to the uncivilized days when the mad, left to their own devices, were allowed to roam the streets—frightened and confused, and sometimes creating havoc. Yet unlike the eighteenth century, when such chaotic figures were stigmatized as outcasts of society, advocacy groups have tried to redefine today's mentally ill homeless population as rebels or noncon-formists who refuse to be co-opted by an oppressive society. In honoring the civil liberties of an entire population of mentally ill homeless individuals, we have in turn managed to deny their very real needs and contribute to their degradation.

To understand how the mental health advocacy movement suc-ceeded in defining down the deviance of the mentally ill homeless, it is helpful to look back at the efforts of the advocates from the 1960s who began lobbying for the rights of the mentally ill. Inspired by University of California at Berkeley sociologist Erving Goffman's book *Asylums*, those in the advocacy community began to claim that institutional treatment for mental illness targeted primarily the marginal and pow-erless, and that it actually exacerbated the bizarre behavior of those labeled mentally ill. Once hospitalized, Goffman maintained, these patients became even sicker because of the oppressive patterns of social control to which they were subjected.

Goffman helped persuade social scientists that deviance and con-formity result from the response of others, not from any defect in the individual regarded as deviant. For Goffman, people internalize what others think of them. Simply being seen as mentally ill can make some act accordingly. By this theory, deviance occurs as a conse-quence of acquiring a stigma, a powerful negative label that fundamentally changes a person's social identity and begins to operate as a master status.[3] Accordingly, the person so labeled is blameless in his or her destructive behavior, while those labeling the behavior are actually causing the deviance.

Psychiatrist Thomas Szasz joined Goffman in the 1960s in writ-ing about the role that majority group members, or "the powerful," play in categorizing persons or groups like the mentally ill as deviant. Szasz believed that an elite in effect creates deviance in order to set the mentally ill apart as inferior beings and to justify their social con-trol.[4] Szasz wrote in his 1961 book, *The Myth of Mental Illness*, that there is actually no such thing as mental illness; the behavior denoted by this term is simply a protest of the marginalized against their oppression by the dominant culture. The sometimes bizarre behaviors of psychotics are, he said, "messages" about our social world that the elite culture has tried to repress. The mentally ill have had to resort to signs or symptoms of psychosis so as to make themselves heard.[5]

Szasz claimed that the concept of mental illness undermines the principle of personal responsibility for one's behavior. But few of those who made his book a bestseller were interested in this aspect of his argument. Instead, *The Myth of Mental Illness* was use primarily to provide support for the movement to destigmatize mental illness and deinstitutionalize the mentally ill.

Szasz believed that hospitalization or involuntary treatment should never be allowed for what was, in effect, an imaginary illness. This outlook received strong support from Michel Foucault, who asserted in *Madness and Civilization* that modern conceptions of mental illness were "socially constructed" at the critical moment in the nineteenth century when bourgeois society prevailed and demanded greater conformity to its behavioral norms. From Foucault's postmodern perspective, notions of madness and increased institutional warehousing were the result of the elite's decreased tolerance for those who refused to conform.[6]

British psychiatrist R. D. Laing, another cult intellectual of the 1960s, gave the "myth of mental illness" a new twist. In books such as *The Divided Self*, *Self and Others* and *The Politics of Experience*, Laing drew upon existentialist philosophy in rejecting what he called the "absurdity of normal." In *The Politics of Experience*, for instance, he wrote: "Society highly values its normal man. It educates children to lose themselves and to become absurd, and thus to be normal. Normal men have killed perhaps 100,000,000 of their fellow normal men in the last fifty years."[7] Given such statistics, it is little wonder that Laing romanticized the mentally ill as "more sane" than normal people. Like Szasz, he refused to view mental illness in biomedical or clinical terms, and he believed that psychotherapists should act as "shamans," exorcising the "illness" through a process of mutual catharsis. One example of Laing's therapeutic approach comes from an incident related in his biography, *R. D. Laing: A Divided Self:*

> Laing was invited by some doctors to examine a young girl diagnosed as schizophrenic. The girl was locked into a padded cell in a special hospital and sat there naked. She usually spent the whole day rocking to and fro. The doctors asked Laing for his opinion. What would he do about her? Unexpectedly, Laing stripped off naked himself and entered her cell. There he sat with her, rocking in time to her rhythm.[8]

Like Szasz, Foucault and Goffman, Laing maintained that the mentally ill were simply reflecting and rebelling from the evils of the true deviance—the social pressure to conform and be normal. In one memorable vignette from *The Divided Self*, Laing recounts how "a little girl of seventeen in a mental hospital told me she was terrified because the Atom Bomb was inside her. That is a delusion. The statesmen of the world who boast and threaten that they have Doomsday weapons are far more dangerous, and far more estranged from 'reality' than many of the people on whom the label 'psychotic' is affixed."[9]

Influenced by the work of these intellectuals, mental health advocates in the 1970s began to challenge the efficacy of traditional approaches to mental illness. In the earliest days of this movement, the goal was noble: to bring public attention to the horrible conditions faced by the mentally ill. Popular culture played an important role in this zeal for reform throughout the second half of the last century. In 1948, *The Snake Pit* became the first film to bring attention to the suffering and inhumane treatment of the institutionalized mentally ill. Other films decrying the harsh conditions in asylums increased awareness of the plight of the mentally ill. In 1967, Frederick Wiseman's documentary *Titicut Follies* presented such an alarming exposé of the treatment of patients at Massachusett's Bridgewater State Hospital that it was officially banned by the state.[10]

By the time Ken Kesey's *One Flew over the Cuckoo's Nest* was released in 1975, there was a ready-made audience for the idea of the mental institution as the ultimate agent of social control, and for the parallel notion that insanity is really a sane response to an insane world. Kesey's mental patients are portrayed as healthier than their keepers because they are able to recognize the inauthenticity of the normal world and they refuse to be co-opted by it. The mental patients in *Cuckoo's Nest* are generous and creative and they always operate from a higher moral ground than the craven and emotionally blunted hospital personnel with whom they do battle. While the hero, McMurphy, attempts to bring life and optimism to the dreary hospital, the evil Big Nurse triumphs in controlling and humiliating him—much as society always oppresses those who rebel.

Such ideas had consequences in the real world. By the mid-1970s, social scientists and policymakers so thoroughly embraced the concept of mental illness as a myth that they began to deny the therapeutic needs of many of the mentally ill—even those with severe psychoses and histories of violence. Eventually, any social scientist who viewed mental illness as a form of deviance was on the defensive.

IT WAS IN THIS CLIMATE that the Supreme Court ruled in 1975 in *O'Con-*

nor v. Donaldson that mental patients who pose no obvious danger to anyone cannot be confined against their will. As a result, thousands of men and women were released from mental hospitals throughout the nation. As a substitute for the institutions, "therapeutic communities in non-institutional settings" were supposed to provide support for those who continued to be afflicted by psychotic episodes. Unfortunately, money was never found to build these therapeutic communities, and many severely mentally ill patients ended up on the streets, where they eventually joined the homeless in a dreary quest to survive. Despite the obvious need many had for intensive treatment and continued hospitalization, a series of subsequent court rulings mandated that mental patients must be treated in the "least restrictive setting possible." This meant that unless the mentally ill posed an imminent danger to others, they must be allowed to live as they wished—outside state hospital walls. Believing that even an actively psychotic mental patient would know what was in his or her best interests, the courts ruled that a psychiatric patient could refuse treatment at any time.

As part of the robust movement to provide the mentally ill with all of the rights and privileges possible, an Alaska state appeals court recently ruled that "general concerns" about mental illness cannot play a role in deciding whether an individual may have a permit to carry a gun. Recent changes in the Alaska law require applicants for gun permits only to disclose whether they have ever been committed to a mental hospital or found mentally incompetent by a court. In the application process, those wishing to carry concealed weapons are no longer asked whether they are "mentally ill" or have been treated for mental illness. The latest challenge to the Alaska law arose when a man entered a store in Anchorage, dripping wet, and told a clerk he was trying to soak away chemicals in his body before "they" killed him. He also said that a computer chip had been implanted in his head. When the police arrived, they found that the man had a loaded .358, several bags of bullets—and a permit to carry the gun. When a judge attempted to take away the man's permit, the appeals court ruled that he was entitled to carry a concealed weapon.[11]

The social cost of such rulings has been high. It is difficult to read the daily newspaper in any major city today without being confronted with news of yet another episode of violence by someone described as having a "long history" of mental illness. In a 1999 shooting rampage in Los Angeles, a delusional Buford Furrow, believing that he was under attack by a Jewish conspiracy, killed a postal worker and injured five at the Granada Hills Jewish Community Center, including three young children attending a day camp there. In describing his decision not to seek the death penalty, the U.S. attorney prosecuting the case revealed that Furrow had been attempting for more than a decade to obtain treatment. Government prosecutors read through more than two thousand pages of medical records indicating that he had checked himself into psychiatric hospitals several times, and had made dozens of trips to various hospital emergency rooms, complaining of everything from panic attacks to urges to kill himself and others. In each instance, Furrow was given medication and released without support or follow-up treatment. During his final hearing, as he was sentenced to five life terms for the shooting rampage, Furrow said sadly, "I wish I had been kept in the hospital."[12]

The logical conclusion that might be drawn from stories like Furrow's has been blocked by an elaborate network of advocacy groups whose focus remains on removing the stigma from mental illness. As part of their efforts, they have enlisted help from the highest levels of government.

In 1999, the first-ever White House Conference on Mental Health, organized by Tipper Gore, wife of the Vice President, reaffirmed the idea that those who suffer from mental illness should be supported and maintained within their communities—and must never encounter discrimination in employment, housing, access to health care or education.[13] Conveying the message that the severely mentally ill are no more dangerous than anyone else, this conference was the culmination of more than three decades of federal efforts to remove the stigma from mental illness.[14]

Despite all this, however, Clinton administration surgeon general David Satcher's 500-page *Report on Mental Illness* acknowledged that the majority of U.S. citizens remain "fearful" of the mentally ill. To address these fears, Satcher recommended that the mental health advocacy community "needs to be more dedicated to educating the public about mental illness."[15] The message was that if people are given more information about mental illness and reassured about the efficacy of treatment, they will be less fearful. Generously supported by federal funds and private donations, the National Mental Health Association's "Stigma Watch" program backed up this view, functioning as an ever-vigilant watchdog ready to attack any attempt to enlist stereotypes or link violence to people with mental illness.

Worries that citizens might try to block housing for the mentally ill in their neighborhoods led to a national media campaign to convince the public that it had nothing to fear. In New York City, the National Mental Health Association displayed hundreds of subway posters that proudly proclaimed, "Mentally Ill Persons Make Good Neighbors." The problem with the poster campaign was that it became increasingly difficult to reassure New York subway riders when they were confronted daily with an aggressive homeless population, most of whom were severely mentally ill or substance abusers, or both. How could New Yorkers believe that the mentally ill would be good neighbors when they had to deal with what the *New York Times* has called a "nether world" of more than a thousand mentally disturbed homeless persons living in the subway system?[16] To its credit, the *Times* has always been honest about the problem of the mentally ill homeless in the city. Unlike some newspapers and television documentaries that promote a sentimental view of "homeless families" caught in an unjust economic system, the *Times* has acknowledged in its reporting that the causes of homelessness are more complex and perhaps intractable. In a celebrated 1992 series, the *Times* concluded that New York had become a place where seriously disturbed—and disturbing—people had retreated to the underground to live.

Although it mirrored the day-to-day reality perceived by those who actually rode the subways and walked on the city's streets, the *Times* series was denounced by the mental health advocates and those who provide services to the homeless. Described as "mean-spirited," with little regard for the needs of the poor, the newspaper became the target of the advocacy community's ire. Nonetheless, in many ways the deviance described in the 1992 series paralleled the deviance that Senator Daniel Patrick Moynihan referred to in his speech before the American Sociological Association that same year.

In *The Future Once Happened Here*, urbanist Fred Siegel goes into greater detail about how New York City officials helped define deviancy down by refusing to address the problems posed by the mentally ill street population. Siegel recalls that when Governor Mario Cuomo was asked in the early 1990s about the problems of violent mental patients on the streets of New York, his first response was to deny that there was any such violence. When reminded that several attacks by mentally ill homeless people had been documented in the newspapers and in the courts, Cuomo responded, "The Constitution says you cannot lock up a person just because he is a nuisance, urinating in the street." When asked about changing the law, Cuomo replied that "it couldn't be done."[17]

For Cuomo and many of New York's other elected officials, the civil liberties of the mental patient were paramount. Those the average New Yorker might have regarded as disruptive vagrants were redefined by public officials and advocacy groups as "nonconformists" who should not be oppressed by middle-class values or subjected to the social proprieties that might intrude upon their independent lifestyles. As a result, Siegel says, "An unparalleled set of utopian policies produced the dystopia of day-to-day city life."[18]

The consequences of having an increasingly disorderly homeless population whose deviance is embargoed from discussion are supported by data in Myron Magnet's *The Dream and the Nightmare.* Magnet reveals that 65 percent of the homeless singles in New York City shelters tested by urinalysis showed positive results for drugs or alcohol. Of that group, 83 percent tested positive for cocaine. A startling number of them were convicted felons with outstanding warrants for their arrest. Magnet found that when police checked the records of homeless men arrested for misdemeanors in New York's Pennsylvania Station, they found that most had outstanding warrants—some for murder and assault. Nationally, at least 40 percent of the single homeless population has been in prison for an average of two years. While some were jailed for crimes committed after they became homeless, the majority, 63 percent, were criminals first and homeless later.[19]

San Francisco, whose liberal policies have made it a mecca for the homeless, shows the problem in microcosm. During the 1990s, the number of prisoners, most of them homeless, requiring mental health treatment increased by 77 percent, according to San Francisco jail officials. In 2000, 5,600 inmates were treated at a cost of more than $3 million. More than 80 percent had substance abuse problems and many had been jailed more than once.[20] The *San Francisco Chronicle* estimated that the city now spends about $22,000 every hour on homeless people. In a November 2001 series on the homeless problems in the city, the *Chronicle* documented the daily routines of some of these individuals:

> Horrified passersby encounter Joe Dinovo, a one-legged drug addict, naked from the waist down, lying in his own vomit at high noon last summer on the sidewalk near 16th Street and South Van Ness Avenue. Dinovo, an Ohio native who has been periodically homeless in San Francisco for six years was old news to paramedics called by one concerned citizen. "We see him eight or 10 times a week." Awakened, Dinovo cursed bystanders, ate from a trash can, then urinated and gushed diarrhea into the street.[21]

While Mayor Willie Brown continued to declare that he "will not make being poor a crime," San Francisco citizens began to question the more than $51 million spent annually on the homeless. The tally includes the more than $41 million spent on health care bills, $3 million in paramedic costs, $3.8 million for public crews to clean streets and parks of urine, excrement and other leavings, and more than $3 million on psychiatric services to those incarcerated in local jails.[22]

Changing public perceptions of the problem in San Francisco parallel those in New York during the 1990s. The 1993 New York mayoral race began with an attempt by Mayor David Dinkins to brand his challenger Rudolph Giuliani as someone who would "criminalize homelessness." National politicians and celebrities came to New York to help reelect Dinkins, including Senator Ted Kennedy, President and Mrs. Clinton, Tipper Gore, Barbra Streisand and Danny Glover. As Fred Siegel says, "The parade of celebrities and politicians who came to support Dinkins spoke as though they were freedom riders of sorts who had come to rescue the city from its customary mores."[23] However, in the midst of the contentious campaign, a mentally ill homeless man named Jeffrey Rose diverted attention away from the celebrity visitors when he grabbed a baby away from its mother on a busy street and began stabbing the child in the face with a pen. Eight years earlier, Rose had been arrested for pushing a man through a glass counter at an East Side deli.[24]

Giuliani was elected because of the frequency of such incidents and because he promised to address the conditions that the voters knew were contributing to the degradation of the public space. And, to a great extent, Giuliani became successful as mayor by refusing to allow deviancy to be defined further down. By addressing minor disorder on the streets—personified by the notorious "squeegee men" who coerced motorists into paying for unneeded and unwanted window washing—the city attracted new businesses and tourists once again and was in many ways restored.

Continuing attacks on subway riders by violent mentally ill individuals supported Giuliani's views and did little to convince New Yorkers that these seriously disturbed people would ever "make good neighbors." In 1995, Reuben Harris, a mentally ill man with a long history of drug and alcohol problems, pushed a sixty-three-year-old woman to her death from a Manhattan subway platform. Witnesses described Harris as appearing to be waiting until the train approached the station before he shoved the unsuspecting woman onto the tracks. Afterward, Harris was described as "laughing and babbling gibberish" while he walked away from the subway stop.[25] A paranoid schizophrenic with twelve admissions to state hospitals in the last eighteen years, Harris had simply walked out of the Manhattan Psychiatric Center on Wards Island at least four times during the previous year. Officials said they didn't know how long Harris had been living among the homeless before this crime. They confirmed that he had a history of violent behavior, having been convicted of slashing a subway panhandler in the face with a razor six years earlier. Nevertheless, a Manhattan jury found him "not guilty" by reason of "mental defect" in the death of the sixty-three-year-old woman. His attorney congratulated the jury for being "brave" enough to understand that Harris was a "sick man" and that "we don't put our sick and our frail in jail."[26]

By 1999, when Edgar Rivera was pushed onto the tracks by a violent homeless man just as a train entered the Lexington Avenue station at 51st Street, any remaining sympathy for those capable of such behavior had evaporated. Although Rivera, a thirty-seven-year-old father of three young children, survived the attack, both of his legs were severed. The anger toward the perpetrator, Julio Perez, a homeless man with a history of mental problems and substance abuse, was evident in the response from the media. At the time of the attack, Perez was living in a shelter for the homeless in Washington Heights and being treated for a twenty-year history of schizophrenia at a program run by New York Presbyterian Hospital. Rivera, his victim, is now suing the hospital and the homeless shelter in civil court, contending that they failed to take adequate steps to protect others from an obviously unstable mental patient.

This type of civil litigation, designed to hold responsible those who care for the violent mentally ill, is becoming more common, and in itself is a backdoor way of reestablishing such behavior as deviant. Patricia Webdale, whose young daughter Kendra was killed when she was pushed in front of a New York City subway train in January 1999, sued seven medical institutions for negligence in releasing Andrew Goldstein, the man who committed the crime. Webdale filed a $70 million lawsuit against psychiatric staff members of the various Manhattan and Long Island area hospitals that had repeatedly sent Goldstein home even though they knew he was dangerous and unlikely to take the medication that stabilized him. Goldstein had been hospitalized thirteen times in 1997 and 1998, and had committed more than a dozen assaults, many on hospital staff, during the two-year span. In addition to hearing imaginary voices, according to an article in the *New York Times*, Goldstein variously asserted that "someone had removed his brain, that he was six or eight inches tall, that his penis had grown from eating contaminated food, and that someone named 'Larry' was stealing his feces and eating them with a knife and fork."[27]

The Goldstein case was an important one because it finally led the New York State legislature to allow courts to require the involuntary hospitalization of mentally ill individuals who are found to have stopped taking their prescribed medications. But the law pertains only to those who have been mandated by the court to take medication, not to people like Paul O'Dwyer, another homeless man. In May 2000, O'Dwyer tried to push three women and a man onto the tracks of the West Fourth Street and Broadway Lafayette stations. But unlike many of the other subway criminals in the city, the clearly disturbed O'Dwyer had no mandate for medication to control his violent aggression, and hence the courts could not act.

Although the fund of compassion for the mentally ill homeless is being depleted as a result of incidents like these, organizations such as the National Alliance for the Mentally Ill still try to deny that the people they champion for constitute a threat. Following the subway attack on Kendra Webdale, for example, this organization rallied to the defense of the perpetrator, saying that he too was a "victim." The alliance's executive director, Laurie Flynn, wrote in a media release, "We grieve for Andrew Goldstein, whose promise was stolen by schizophrenia over a decade ago." Flynn told readers, "It is important to remember that schizophrenia is a cruel, chronic, and disabling brain disorder that affects approximately two million Americans each year." But she also insisted that "with appropriate medication and support, the treatment success rate for schizophrenia is 60 percent higher than the treatment success rate for heart disease." This analogy fails to note that when treatment fails for heart patients, no one dies except the heart patient. In a mantra repeated by many mental health advocates, Flynn claimed that "studies have shown that individuals who receive appropriate treatment for schizophrenia are no more prone to violence than the rest of the population."[28] While this may be true, the problem is that patients suffering with schizophrenia cannot always be relied on to continue their own treatment. Flynn concluded her press release with a plea for others to join the alliance's Stigma Alert Listing Service so that "you can have all of the latest stigma updates delivered to your e-mail account."

Indeed, NAMI's Stigma Alert as well as the Stigma Watch of the National Institute of Mental Health pay careful attention to any sign of negative portrayals of the mentally ill in the news or in popular culture. When one of the nation's most popular television dramas, *ER*, depicted the violent murder of one of the show's most beloved characters by a young college student with schizophrenia, the NIMH Stigma Watch alerted other mental health advocates, urging them to complain to their local television station, the sponsors and the show's producers.[29] Likewise, when the short-lived ABC series *Wonderland* featured a young rampage killer who claimed that he had received his instructions to kill from Greek gods, Stigma Watch wrote to ABC and to Peter Berg, the creator and executive producer, charging that the show's tone would "discourage viewers from seeking treatment for mental illness."[30] One sponsor of *Wonderland*, a pharmaceutical company, withdrew its support for the show after this first episode as a result of pressure from advocacy groups for the mentally ill.

WHILE THE OVERWHELMING majority of people with diagnosed mental disorders are not violent, research indicates that there is a complex but real connection between mental illness and violence, and to deny it is disingenuous. The factors that appear to be associated with an increased likelihood of violence by the mentally ill are exactly what common sense would suggest. A history of violence is a significant risk factor. Violence is most likely to occur when an individual is experiencing active symptoms of a mental disorder, the low of a depressive jag, or the panic of an anxiety attack, rather than while the disorder is dormant.[31] But the highest risk is associated with substance abuse: Individuals who are diagnosed with milder forms of mental illness but who abuse drugs or alcohol are the most likely to turn violent. Nearly all of the attacks on innocent subway riders and pedestrians in New York City involved substance-abusing, mentally ill, homeless persons.

The most systematic and extensive study of the relationship between mental illness and violence was completed in 1996 by the National Clearinghouse on Family Violence, in Ottawa, Canada. Computerized databases covering the scientific literature in the areas of psychology, sociology, criminology, law, medicine, philosophy, psychiatry, forensic psychiatry and epidemiology were searched for any articles dealing with mental illness and violence. The analysis by the Canadian research team revealed that while a "causal connection" between violence and mental illness cannot be claimed, when substance abuse is brought into the equation there is a "significant risk factor for violence and criminality."[32] The report also claimed that the incidence of violence among those hospitalized with mental illness in the past is increasing. However, the study's authors asserted that only a small number of these mentally ill persons, typically those with acute psychotic symptoms or those with a history of prior violence, are responsible for the majority of violent incidents. They maintained that most violent incidents by the mentally ill occur in the home, and the victims are relatives. The report warned that mentally ill individuals who are younger are at highest risk of violence and criminality.

For a series on "rampage killers," the New York Times recently examined one hundred multiple-homicide incidents that occurred in the United States over the last fifty years. Reporters gathered extensive information on all the cases and looked even more closely at a subset of more than twenty-five of them. The analysis included reviews of court cases, news coverage and mental health records, and interviews with families and friends, psychologists and victims. In some cases, reporters questioned the killers themselves.

Based on this information, the Times investigation revealed a high association between violence and mental illness. Nearly half (47) of the 100 rampage killers had a history of mental health problems before they killed, 20 had been hospitalized for psychiatric problems, and 42 had been seen by mental health professionals. Psychiatric drugs had been prescribed to 24 of the killers at some point before their rampages, but most of them were not taking their prescribed medication when they committed the crimes. Before their homicides, 23 of the killers had displayed signs of serious depression, and 49 had expressed paranoid ideas.

Robert Smith, one of the case histories described in the Times series, believed he was God when he herded five women and two children into the back room of a beauty school in 1966, forced them to lie in a circle and methodically shot each person in the head. More than thirty years after the horrific crime, Mr. Smith related in a letter to Times reporters from prison, "The sole thing I have learned worth telling is the ironclad necessity of retaining control over one's bodily fluids." He blamed sexual self-stimulation for his decision to kill his victims, and had used the pull-tab from a can of diet soda to try to amputate his own penis while in prison.

The Times analysis found that in 63 of the 100 cases of public rampage killings, the perpetrators had made general threats of violence to others in advance of their crime. It found that 55 of the killers had regularly expressed explosive anger or frustration, and 35 of the killers had a history of violent behavior and assaults. Most interesting, the Times reporters found that the killers were so noticeably unstable that even in their own circles they had been awarded nicknames like "Crazy Pat," "Crazy John" or "Crazy Joe."[33] The series reported that "more than half" of the 100 rampage killers had histories of serious mental health problems, including 48 with some kind of formal mental health diagnosis.[34]

Although in many cases frightened co-workers independently sensed something disturbing about the person, most believed that they would be safe if they just kept their distance. Friends laughed off homicidal talk. Parents and siblings claimed to have nowhere to turn, praying that the irrational fury was merely a phase. But as the *Times* pointed out, most of the killers had spiraled down a long, slow slide, mentally and emotionally. The reporters claimed that "most of them had left a road map of red flags, spending months plotting their attacks and accumulating weapons, talking openly of their plans for bloodshed. Many showed signs of serious mental health problems for years." Yet in case after case, "the warning signs were missed by a tattered mental health care system; by families unable to face the evidence of serious mental turmoil in their children; by employers, teachers and principals who failed to take the threats seriously; and by the police who, when alerted to the danger by frightened relatives, neighbors or friends, were incapable of intervening before the violence erupted." The laws enacted in the 1970s to protect the mentally ill from institutionalization or forced treatment in effect prevented others from obtaining help for the seriously disturbed individual.

Most of the workplace rampage shooters studied by the *Times* had been fired or disciplined precisely because they were already threatening violence, getting into fights or behaving bizarrely. James Davis, whose co-workers had nicknamed him "Psycho," had been hospitalized with schizophrenia. He had picked fights repeatedly at the tool warehouse where he worked in Asheville, North Carolina, and had warned his colleagues, "If they ever decide to fire me, I will take two or three of them with me." Co-workers knew that he lived alone, that he owned a .44 Magnum and that he practiced firing it in his basement. His family noticed him acting strangely. When Davis was fired, his bosses were so anxious about his reaction that they broke the news to him in a room where they could use a table to deflect an attack. Some employees had planned escape routes when they heard of his firing. The next morning, he stormed the warehouse and shot seven people, including the two supervisors who had fired him the day before.

Anyone who lives in a major metropolitan area is familiar with frequent reports on the evening news about assault or murder growing out of "enraged" or "disturbed" behavior. One especially tragic story unfolded during the spring of 2001 when an out-of-control freshman at the University of California at Santa Barbara gunned his similarly out-of-control car down a street filled with partying Santa Barbara students. Four were killed in the ensuing crash. The driver of the careening car, who had been known on the Santa Barbara campus as "Crazy Dave" because of his increasingly bizarre behavior, was immediately charged with four counts of murder. Evidence indicated that he had deliberately driven his car into a crowd of strolling students. Witnesses at the scene claimed that when the car finally was disabled by the crash, the driver began yelling, "I am the angel of death," and claiming that those he had hit "deserved to die."

Newspapers related that the driver of the car had been "troubled" for years. Before his arrival on the Santa Barbara campus that fall, he had attended a small, "self-contained" Santa Monica high school of fewer than a hundred students. Portrayed in the *Los Angeles Times* as a "nurturing, highly personalized learning environment," the high school was characterized more bluntly by one former student as "a school for kids with problems."[35] Once the troubled student arrived for classes on the Santa Barbara campus, he became overwhelmed by the demands of the rigorous curriculum and social setting. He was allegedly abusing drugs. Eventually his behavior deteriorated to the point that several students described him as "wacked out."[36] Dorm mates interviewed for the *Los Angeles Times* claimed that they "did all they could to avoid him." Even his own roommates reportedly had asked him to move someplace else.[37] During the weeks before the collision, students recalled that the clearly disturbed young man had begun telling anyone who would listen that "he was a prophet who wanted to spread good through the world. He spoke of God, the devil, the supernatural, and said he was afraid he was going to die."[38] Despite all this, not a single student, administrator, dorm advisor, professor or counselor on campus believed that anything should be done to help the troubled student.

MENTAL HEALTH ADVOCATES help create a cloud of unknowing around these disturbing episodes. It is difficult to make moral judgments on those who cannot control their behavior, we are repeatedly told. These killers were violent because of factors beyond their control. Drugs, bullies, patriarchal husbands made them do it. Biology was destiny. The nightly parade of psychological practitioners on the television news suggest that there are "uncontrollable hormonal factors" behind the types of mental illness that cause mothers to kill their newborn babies. "Biochemical causes" are said to lead teenagers to shoot their classmates. Television documentaries like the award-winning **PBS** *Mind* series propose that the violence associated with mental illness is often the result of uncontrollable neurochemical factors.

As a result, we are now encouraged to see violence as the result of biochemical determinism. At the same time that partisans of this viewpoint reassure us that the mentally ill make good neighbors and should be allowed to carry concealed weapons, they admit that we can never predict what these unstable individuals might do, nor control their outbursts of savage behavior. These advocates avoid being caught in a contradiction by asserting that if only the "troubled" individuals had been properly treated and medicated, none of the mayhem would have occurred.

Although the consequences of redefining intractable mental illness as semi-normalcy are everywhere apparent, the movement for destigmatization continues. Paul Fink, past president of the American Psychological Association, says that the first and most important step in this process is to address the "misuse of the terminology of mental illness." Fink believes that in large part, stigma results from the misapplication and popularization of terms, and that words like "crazy, or maniac create a tremendous misunderstanding of mental illness and must be eliminated from people's vocabulary."[39]

Other advocates believe that a "more practical" way to remove stigma is a national mental illness reeducation campaign, beginning at the elementary school level. A recent bill in Congress, for instance, would require all schools "to teach students to recognize the symptoms of depression, schizophrenia and other mental illnesses, and to emphasize that they are common, inherited and treatable conditions."[40] This kind of "education" continues in the adult world through similar "workplace initiatives." Thus does the destigmatization movement envision a cradle-to-grave campaign to accomplish its objectives.

THREE

EXPANDING THE MARKET

FOR MENTAL ILLNESS

W hen the deviance of mental illness was being downgraded, it was inevitable that the definition of mental illness would be expanded, and the condition would even be celebrated. Each fall, in fact, Canada observes "Mental Illness Awareness Week." The theme for 2000, "Working with Mental Illness," was designed to reduce the stigma associated with mental illness, and to encourage employers and corporations to adopt workplace education strategies to change attitudes about mental illness and foster appreciation for the significant contributions of the mentally ill.[1]

American businesses have long struggled with mandates requiring them to accommodate their mentally ill employees. There is realistic self-interest in such programs. Depression, one of the most common mental illnesses, primarily hits workers in their most productive years, and has taken its toll on business. More than $70 billion in medical expenditures, lost productivity and other costs are now attributed to depression. Sales of antidepressant medications have risen more than 800 percent, to $10.2 billion, since 1990, and a large percentage of the costs is borne by employers. In a national survey conducted in 2000, 70 percent of large employers said they worried about surging psychiatric claims.[2] Employers are especially concerned about complying with the demands made by their mentally ill employees, because of costly lawsuits that can arise over federal requirements for accommodating their demands—no matter how unreasonable.

Recently the Ninth Circuit Court of Appeals in San Francisco ruled that a woman who was fired in 1995 because her excessive primping and dressing rituals interfered with her work could sue her employer for a violation of her rights under the Americans with Disabilities Act.[3] The court found that Carolyn Humphrey's elaborate grooming practices stemmed from an obsessive-compulsive disorder, a mental illness that is protected under the ADA. The court overruled a federal judge who earlier had issued a summary judgment in favor of the hospital that employed her, on the basis of its "reasonable accommodations" for Ms. Humphrey. (In response to Humphrey's grooming obsession, her employer had given her a flexible schedule, allowing her to start work at any time of the day, in an effort to accommodate her need to wash, brush and then rewash her hair for up to three hours each morning if it "didn't feel right.") The Ninth Circuit ruled that when the hospital eventually fired her, it was "without cause."

Obsessive-compulsive disorders are among the top five reasons that businesses consult government services for help on navigating disability laws. Accommodating this condition has placed a heavy burden on employers. But mental health advocates maintain that employers will make the accommodations willingly once the stigma is removed and mental illness is recast as "normal."

As we normalize mental illness, we should not be surprised when behavior that was once called "assault and battery" is now identified as "rage"—a condition something like temporary insanity. Newspapers across the country now print stories about "road rage," a concept that first appeared in the United States in the summer of 1996 following outbreaks of freeway mayhem. Road rage quickly became a "serious social problem," and by 1997 there was a congressional hearing on the subject, as the media cited surveys to the effect that nine out of ten drivers had experienced this emotion.[4] Attorneys for motorists charged with road rage have blamed their outbursts on urban sprawl.

In a new twist on road rage stories, newspapers have reported eruptions of "surf rage" in southern California, when groups of surfers attack each other to see who controls the waves. In a surf rage case in San Diego in 2001, witnesses reported that one wave rider lost his temper and assaulted a second who apparently had cut in front of him. The aggrieved party repeatedly pushed his long board into the other surfer and then tried to hold him under the water while punching him in the head. None of the other surfers who saw this intervened to help the victim. Police were finally summoned by a nonsurfing witness. When the matter came to trial, the defense suggested that surf rage is a "real problem," resulting from the overcrowded conditions at

San Diego's beaches and from pollution that has closed formerly favored surfing spots. As a consequence, surfers just "snap."[5]

Just as hyperactive children are now considered to have an illness rather than simply to be disruptive or disobedient, adults who erupt in rage when their surf space is invaded or another driver cuts them off on the highway are increasingly viewed as suffering from mental disorders—presumably neurological in origin and amenable to treatment by the medical profession.[6] A recent book entitled *Shadow Syndromes* takes the redefinition process even further by contending that nearly *all* of the behavioral problems we formerly blamed on character flaws are instead "due to mild versions of full blown mental disorders."[7]

In this book, psychiatrist John Ratey and co-author Catherine Johnson claim that "neuropsychiatry has discovered that a great deal of (normal) craziness is, in fact, heavily influenced by the genetics, structure, and neurochemistry of the brain." Ratey and Johnson believe that every troublesome personality trait has its roots in a formerly "unsuspected brain dysfunction," and that each of these personality or behavioral problems can and should be addressed through therapy and medication. The authors maintain that the loner, the gifted person who cannot seem to live up to his or her potential, the obsessive neighbor you can't get off the telephone, the confirmed bachelor, the man who cannot talk about his feelings, or even the husband who throws tantrums like a four-year-old—all are actually mentally ill. For Ratey and Johnson, "The normal problems of so-called normal people are gray and silver shadow versions of full color mental illnesses."[8] Adults who "tantrum" or experience road rage, surf rage or air rage, in other words, are all suffering from hidden or partial mental disorders, which derive entirely from faulty brain function.

When character flaws become brain dysfunction, the inclination to hold people responsible for their disruptive or destructive behavior diminishes. As Ratey and Johnson say, "the profound and corrosive sense of shame we may feel over our behavior begins to lift when we understand that it is created by subtle differences in the brain." Throughout their book, the authors provide examples of these shadow syndromes. Many of their examples come from case histories of those they have identified as "tantruming adults" whose enraged episodes result from "biologically based behaviors that occur through no fault of the out-of-control adult." For instance, Gary, an adult patient "who averaged more than 40 tantrums a month," claimed to have exhausted almost every available means of mastering his temper by the time he went to see a psychiatrist. He had been a sober member of Alcoholics Anonymous for ten years, and he regularly attended a men's group to discuss feelings and relationships. Yet none of this worked. Gary continued to have such out-of-control tantrums that his second marriage was on the brink of collapse and his daughter was terrified of his frightening outbursts.

A "solution" was found for Gary. He had diagnosed his own mental disorder after reading about the symptoms and realizing that he, too, most likely suffered from a neurological impairment. He found a psychiatrist who confirmed his self-diagnosis for attention deficit disorder and prescribed the psychotropic medication desipramine. According to Gary, this quieted the "brain noise" produced by "random firings of the brain stem." Ratey and Johnson claim that tantrums—even adult tantrums—often result from "An excess of mental noise from this lower brain region which connects the brain with the spinal cord. When there is too much mental noise in the brain, the noise can overwhelm the higher brain centers—the seat of reason found in the frontal lobes of the cortex that allows the lower emotional brain to take over."[9] None of this "noise" has been confirmed through scientific research, yet once the medication was prescribed, Gary seemed to improve.

THE MOVEMENT TO MEDICALIZE disordered behaviors is especially evident in the ways we now view what used to be considered normal behavior problems in children. In particular, there is the alarming increase in the medication of children with Ritalin, the psychotropic drug of choice for those diagnosed with attention deficit hyperactivity disorder.[10]

ADHD, as it is now commonly known, was determined to be a mental illness by a vote of American Psychiatric Association members at their annual meeting in 1987, and the new definition was then added to the *Diagnostic and Statistical Manual of Mental Disorders*. Children (and increasingly adults) who exhibit behaviors such as inattention, distractibility, trouble in follow directions, a tendency to lose things, and difficulty awaiting their turn to speak or participate in activities are now seen as victims of ADHD. In the past, these behaviors were labeled as achievement-ability discrepancies, poor impulse control, or perhaps simply unruly classroom behavior, but they are now redefined as a type of mental illness requiring treatment rather than self-control.

Relieved to find that their children's behavioral problems are the result of a neurobiological disorder rather than a failure of discipline, large numbers of parents have willingly allowed their children to be diagnosed and medicated—with no scientific confirmation of the origins of ADHD, and even less information about the side effects of the medication. A report by the National Institute of Mental Health in 1998 admits that "after years of clinical research and experience with ADHD, our knowledge about the cause or causes of ADHD remain largely speculative."[11] Even the NIMH cautions that "further research is necessary to establish ADHD as a brain disorder."

Yet despite the lack of compelling scientific evidence about ADHD, there continues to be a significant increase in the diagnosis of children as suffering from this "mental illness." Some states have adopted practices that will identify the disorder even before children begin to attend school. A bill approved by the California Assembly requires that each child be screened for poor self-esteem, depression, abuse, exposure to violence in the media and at home, and access to guns during their pre-first-grade physical examination.[12]

Not surprisingly, the use of Ritalin in the United States has increased by more than 700 percent since 1990, as more than six million children between the ages of 3 and 18 have been labeled mentally ill and medicated with the psychotropic drug. No other country in the world diagnoses its children with mental illness in this way. Only American children appear to be suffering from an epidemic of "brain dysfunction" that has not yet begun to affect the children of Europe or Asia or Africa. Today, more than 90 percent of the world's supply of Ritalin is being used on American children.[13]

When Lawrence Diller, author of *Running on Ritalin*, reviewed the National Disease and Therapeutic Index of IMS Health, the survey used by pharmaceutical companies to report on medication usage, he found that in addition to Ritalin, there has been an increase in the use of other psychotropic drugs on children. Between 1995 and 1999, stimulant drug use went up 23 percent. The use of Prozac-like drugs for children under 18 went up 74 percent; in the 7–12 age group it rose 151 percent; for children under 6 it climbed up an astonishing 580 percent. For children under 18 the use of mood stabilizers is up 4,000 percent and the use of new antipsychotic medications such as Risperdal has grown nearly 300 percent.[14]

The labeling and medicating cycle is beginning at an ever earlier age. The July 1998 issue of *Clinical Psychiatric News* revealed that in Michigan's Medicaid program, 223 children three years old or younger

were diagnosed with ADHD and treated with one or more psychotropic drugs including Ritalin, Prozac, Dexedrine, Aventyl and
Syban. Of these toddlers, 33 percent were medicated with two or more
of these drugs.[15] The children enrolled in the Medicaid program are
among Michigan's poorest and are primarily racial minorities.

Increasingly, parents are actually requesting a diagnosis of mental illness for their children. Unlike parents of the past, who would
have tried to avoid such a label for their children, parents now have no
stigma to fear. Today's "neurological impairment" carries no shame or
disgrace. Indeed, in a domesticated version of the *Cuckoo's Nest* worldview, many parents have become convinced that their children who
are diagnosed with attention deficit disorder are probably brighter and
more creative than the children who pay attention in class, don't act
out, and do their work responsibly. Parents are advised that large
numbers of educated people—some of them very talented and
famous—have suffered from such "neurological impairments." A diagnosis of a brain dysfunction, moreover, removes any responsibility for
the child's behavior from the parents. It is not their fault that their
child is unhappy, is doing poorly in school, and cannot sit still in class;
it is the child's faulty brain function. And so parents embrace a chemical shortcut to the behavior modification that in the past was
recognized as a family duty.

Advocacy groups like Children and Adults with Attention Deficit
Disorder (CHADD) have played an important marketing role by
extolling the value of medications. Predictably, these efforts have been
well rewarded by the pharmaceutical companies. In fact, these companies have subsidized CHADD with more than $1 million to promote
the idea that attention deficit disorder is neurobiological in nature and
can be successfully addressed with medication.[16]

By allowing their children to be labeled "mentally ill" and medicated when they have trouble paying attention in school, however,
parents are not only refusing to allow them to learn strategies of self-
control and personal responsibility, but also endangering their kids'
future.

Immediately prior to the Columbine High School shootings in
1999, Eric Harris, one of the two students involved, had received news
of his rejection by the Marine Corps because of his history of using
psychotropic medication. In 1998, a fifteen-year-old sophomore from
Idaho named Shawn Cooper was taking Ritalin when he fired two
shotgun rounds at his high school, narrowly missing students and staff
members. T. J. Solomon, a fifteen-year-old student at Heritage High

School in Conyers, Georgia, was also being treated with Ritalin when he opened fire on his classmates and wounded six. Kip Kinkel, a fifteen-year-old student in Springfield, Oregon, who murdered his parents and then proceeded to school where he fired on students in the cafeteria, killing two and wounding twenty-two, had been prescribed both Ritalin and Prozac.[17]

There is no necessary causal relationship between the violent actions and the drugs. Yet the drugs were prescribed to control anxiety and alleviate depression, and the fact that violence erupted after their use raises serious questions about the indiscriminate resort to psychotropic medications to control the behavior of children in schools and in institutional settings. Could old-fashioned discipline have done any worse?

This issue is finally beginning to gain some attention from the legal community. Recently, lawsuits have been filed in California and New Jersey alleging that the maker of Ritalin conspired with the American Psychiatric Association to "create" the disease of ADHD and later exaggerated the drug's benefits.[18] The lawsuit also names advocacy groups like Children and Adults with Attention Deficit Disorder, which received generous funding from the company that manufactures Ritalin. The cases seek billions of dollars in damages and are likely to be followed by suits on behalf of consumers in other states.[19]

Meanwhile, the diagnosis of mental illness keeps expanding and the use of medication continues to grow. The medicalization movement has gained such momentum that it now attempts even to alter the behavior of the family pet. Encouraged by a major pharmaceutical company, many veterinarians now post flyers in their offices advising the "canine patients' family" to "give your dog the gift of good behavior." Interested pet owners are advised to complete a ten-question survey to determine whether their animals would be good candidates for the pharmacological management program. The questions on the survey include these: "When left alone, does your dog destroy, chew or dig at your walls or furniture? Does he follow you when you go from one room to another? Does your dog beg you for attention? When you are leaving, does your dog become agitated? When you return, does your dog greet you with excessive excitement? Does your dog ever seem hyper?"

Once the survey is completed, pet owners are advised to discuss their dog's "problem behavior" with the veterinarian. When the answer to any of the questions is "yes," one southern California veterinarian suggests "Clomicalm" as a "behavior modification strategy" for the dog now labeled as mentally disturbed. Manufactured by Novartis Pharmaceuticals (coincidentally, also the maker of Ritalin), this drug will theoretically offer a new generation of dog owners a perfectly behaved pet requiring little training effort on their part. Novartis promotional materials advise owners not to be concerned if their dog seems drowsy and not quite itself, but to administer the medication in the early morning so the dog will sleep while they are away at work. And just as parents are cautioned not to discontinue the use of Ritalin by their children—even when they head off to college—the Novartis canine materials provide similar warnings that "while some dogs may be fine without the continued use of Clomicalm as a behavior modification technique, it is more helpful to continue these techniques indefinitely."[20]

NOT ONLY HAVE WE convinced ourselves that there is no stigma associated with a diagnosis of mental illness in our children, our pets and ourselves, but we also wonder increasingly whether mental illness may actually be a positive sign of creativity or greater intelligence. This perspective is certainly not a new one. What is new is the credibility it has now acquired—as the film *A Beautiful Mind* so clearly shows.

This film depicts the life of John Nash, a brilliant Nobel Prize–winning mathematician, whose career was cut short at age thirty-one by the sudden and completely debilitating onset of paranoid schizophrenia. Ignoring the fact that in reality, severe mental illness led to a thirty-five-year period in which Nash was unable to work or even think clearly, *A Beautiful Mind* is filled instead with suggestions that the paranoid delusions helped and even inspired the brilliant mathematician. The film was criticized by Dartmouth mathematics professor Daniel Rockmore, who had been a mathematics major at Princeton in the early 1980s and had many recollections of the real Professor John Nash. Rockmore's memories of a troubled individual differed greatly from the film's portrayal of an "avuncular John Nash now happily teaching freshman calculus there." What troubled Rockmore most in the movie's conflation of fact and fantasy was its "roasting once again that favorite chestnut of madness equals genius."[21]

In *Touched by Fire*, a best-selling book on manic-depressive illness and the artistic temperament, Kay Redfield Jamison asserts that some of the most creative work by poets, novelists, composers and artists is inspired by, or partially executed in, a "psychotically manic state." Jamison, a professor of psychiatry at the Johns Hopkins School of Medicine, believes that the superior product that is created in this psychotic state can later be "significantly shaped or partially edited while its creator is depressed and then put into final order when he or she is normal."[22]

As evidence of the madness-creativity link, Jamison offers psychological and biological arguments to demonstrate that creative activity emerges from "extreme emotional states." The tension and reconciliation of "naturally occurring" emotional and cognitive states in artists with manic-depressive illness is key to the creative process, she argues. Because of the valuable contributions of mental illness to the arts, Jamison worries about the implications of future gene therapies and possible early prevention of manic-depressive illness. For her, the disappearance of mental illness would be a tragic loss, and she asks, "Does psychiatric treatment have to result in happier but blander and less imaginative artists?"[23]

To support her claims about the relationship between creativity and mental illness, Jamison draws upon research showing that children who have been diagnosed with manic-depressive illness demonstrate an unusually high incidence of outstanding artistic, verbal and mathematical abilities. She also points to studies finding that higher academic and creative performance is associated with greater psychological disturbance and increased use of mental health facilities.[24] And she provides readers with names of hundreds of artists, poets, writers and composers who have shown symptoms of mental illnesses. The list includes famously troubled individuals like Sylvia Plath, Anne Sexton, Edgar Allen Poe, Ernest Hemingway and F. Scott Fitzgerald, but also some who have commonly been viewed as stable—Rupert Brooke, Robert Burns, Gerard Manley Hopkins and Alfred, Lord Tennyson among them.

Jamison co-produced a concert program with the Los Angeles Philharmonic based on the lives and music of manic-depressive composers, including Robert Schumann, Hector Berlioz and Hugo Wolf. The concert was so successful that it led to the creation of a series of similar concerts devoted to the accomplishments of the mentally ill that were performed across the country. These concerts provided the foundation for a series of public television specials that Jamison has produced on the contributions of manic-depressive illness to the arts.[25]

Some feminist literary critics are also zealous in adding names to the list of the famously mentally ill, although their aim is not to link mental illness to creativity, but rather to show these women as victims of a patriarchal society. Many feminists now maintain that Emily Brontë, Emily Dickinson and Virginia Woolf all suffered from anorexia nervosa, a form of mental illness that in its most serious form causes sufferers to starve themselves to death.[26] This diagnosis is based on "suggestive" anecdotal evidence found in the biographies or writings of these women, leading to the conclusion that they were "silenced" by men and pushed into illness.

Such theorizing might be called "mental illness chic." Celebrity bulimics like actress Jane Fonda and that most famous of all anorectics, Princess Diana, contributed greatly to diminishing the deviance of these eating disorders. They are hailed as courageous heroes whose confessions helped other women recognize eating disorders. Yet some social scientists have documented that these testimonials actually encouraged similar behavior.[27] In large part because of the positive attention given it, anorexia became an epidemic in the 1980s. Alarmed researchers recognized that the publicity accorded to anorexia and bulimia, rather than preventing these disorders, was actually creating a secondary wave of patients. The deviance of starving oneself was tempered by the glamour of high-profile sufferers. The cases increased and new sufferers were then "normalized." Under intense pressure from eating disorder advocacy groups and mental health professionals, insurance companies are increasingly being required to provide long-term psychiatric care to those with anorexia.

UNIVERSALIZING MENTAL ILLNESS has produced a kind of higher psychobabble, exemplified in an *American Scholar* article by James Trilling, son of the literary critic Lionel Trilling. The younger Trilling, an art historian who says he has attention deficit disorder, claims that his father was "emotionally distant, prone to fits of rage, and often unable to write." He attributes these oppressive personality traits—along with the critic's famous love of literary complexity—to an undiagnosed mental illness. The publication of this article so angered Dr. Paul R. McHugh, director of psychiatry at the Johns Hopkins Medical Center, that he resigned from his position on the editorial board of the *American Scholar*. Calling the essay "abominable" and "mean-spirited," Dr. McHugh said he feared that such thinking did damage to psychiatry, taking the field back to a time when it was used "to get at people who were defenseless."[28]

Casual—and punitive—application of the "mentally ill" label can be seen on college campuses as well as in score-settling memoirs. While the mentally ill on the streets "make good neighbors," according to activists, such generosity of perspective does not always stretch to some politically outspoken students.

At Temple University, for instance, a student was involuntarily committed to a psychiatric ward when he attempted to organize an event to counter a university-sponsored play that mocked Christianity. The controversy began during the fall semester of 1999 when Michael Marcavage, a senior at Temple University, learned that the play *Corpus Christi*, which portrays Jesus Christ as a homosexual who has sexual relations indiscriminately with his disciples, would be staged on campus. Marcavage tried to protest because "it was very upsetting that my classmates would be mocking who I believe to be God."[29] He appealed for permission from university administrators to present a counter-event featuring gospel singers, speakers and the presentation of a biblically based play about the life of Christ, to be performed by members of the Temple University chapter of Campus Crusade for Christ. Marcavage claimed to have received written permission for the event from the administration, but at the last minute, administrators retracted their promise. The ensuing brouhaha ended with Marcavage, a dean's list student who had served as a White House intern, being handcuffed, put in a police car, and forcibly detained in a psychiatric ward at Temple University Hospital.

The designation of politically incorrect views as "mental illness" has begun to reach beyond the college campus. When John Rocker, the now-notorious relief pitcher, made derogatory remarks about foreigners, homosexuals and minorities, major league baseball commissioner Bud Selig implied that such talk was a symptom of mental illness, and he mandated psychological testing and counseling.* While few defended what Rocker said, there were some who viewed the incident as an example of the press now functioning as the nation's Red Guard, redefining the recalcitrant as mentally ill and helping to channel them into reeducation camps.[30]

Sociologist Thomas Scheff decries the way diagnoses of mental illness have been proliferating.[31] Unlike diseases in other branches of medicine, most psychiatric diagnoses still have no proven link to causes and cures. Scheff cautions that the most dangerous outcome of

---

* But when black boxer Mike Tyson made similar anti-gay, anti-white comments at a national news conference early in 2002, there was no similar furor.

the medicalization of deviance goes far beyond the threat to the individual. His real concern is that the medicalization of deviance legitimates powerful and efficient methods of social control through medical institutions that threaten individual freedom. It is ironic that in a time when we are told that the mentally ill are "normal" (or at least ubiquitous), we are also told that those with whom we may disagree are "crazy"—and perhaps should be locked up.

Despite these concerns, the rate of diagnosis and treatment for mental illness continues to grow. In one report, Surgeon General David Satcher claimed that more than half of the entire population has suffered from a diagnosable mental disorder at least once during their lives. Worse, Satcher warned that more than 20 percent of all children show symptoms of a diagnosable mental disorder in any given year.[32] The message was clear: we are all vulnerable to a diagnosis of mental illness. Even a former President of the United States, Bill Clinton, seems to have jumped on the bandwagon. At the 1999 National Prayer Breakfast immediately following the Monica Lewinsky scandal, the President implied that his behavior resulted from a mental disorder. After thanking the clergy, his family, the American people and God for forgiving his sins, he proceeded to remark about how men are reluctant to ask for help on mental health issues: "Men are still really hung up about asking for help. I know about that. That's a hard thing for men to do. I know about that."[33]

There was little reaction to the President's remarks, and even less to similar statements from his wife when she implied in an interview published in *Talk* magazine that her husband's "problems" stemmed from abuse he endured during his childhood years in Hot Springs, Arkansas. While neither the President nor the First Lady ever specifically acknowledged that they were referring to mental illness per se, the use of phrases like "childhood abuse causes of these problems" suggested that they were seeking absolution through such a diagnosis.

THE CORRESPONDENCE BETWEEN political correctness and presumptions of mental illness is also evident in the legal defenses of female criminal defendants, particularly those involving "battered women's syndrome." Data from the Department of Justice indicate that in spouse homicide cases, female defendants receive significantly lower conviction and incarceration rates than male defendants—despite the similarity of the crime and the surrounding circumstances.[34] The Department of Justice study was based on a sample of spouse murder cases handled in the 75 most populous counties in the nation, which were targeted for study because they are the locations where more than half of all spouse murders in the nation occur. Analysis of these data revealed that on average, convicted wives receive prison sentences about 10 years shorter than convicted husbands. Excluding life or death sentences, which are overwhelmingly imposed on men who kill their wives, the average prison sentence for killing a spouse was 6 years for wives, but 16.5 years for husbands. Among those wives sentenced to prison, 15 percent received a sentence of 20 years or more, while more than 43 percent of all husbands received such lengthy sentences. If the study had included the life or death sentences imposed on men, the gender discrepancy in sentencing would have been much higher.

While self-defense (wives defending themselves from abuse by husbands) might be assumed to explain the dramatic differences in prison sentences by gender, the Justice Department data indicate otherwise. The average prison sentence was 7 years for unprovoked wife defendants and 17 years for unprovoked husband defendants.

Of the 100 wife defendants tried by either a judge or jury, 31 percent were acquitted. By contrast, of the 138 husband defendants tried, only 6 percent were acquitted. Of the 59 wife defendants tried by a jury, 27 percent were acquitted, but of the 91 husband defendants tried by a jury, not a single one was acquitted.

The Justice Department study reveals, moreover, that the time in custody from the day of the murder, to arrest, indictment and final disposition was significantly longer for female than for male defendants. For husbands tried by a jury, 12 months was the average elapsed time from the day of the murder to the conclusion of the jury trial. For wives tried by a jury, the processing time was more than 18 months. In many of these cases, the additional processing time gave the defense the additional time needed to build the "battered women's syndrome" or "post-traumatic stress syndrome" defense.

Recently, Sara Dean, a San Diego woman convicted of manslaughter for killing her husband to "escape his terror," was spared a prison term by a judge who said he was "moved" by what a local newspaper described as the "litany of horrors" she endured during her three-year marriage. As a result, the defendant's request that she serve no prison time and instead be placed on probation was granted—even though she had been convicted on a charge that usually carries mandatory prison time of up to eleven years. In media reports on the case, Judge Alvin Green explained that he was swayed by Dean's allegations of "the horrors she had suffered at the hands of her 39-year-old husband." Tales of psychological, sexual, mental and physical abuse filled the emotional sentencing hearing in the San Diego court-house. When asked why she had neither reported the abuse nor sought help—despite the fact that there are a number of battered women's shelters throughout San Diego, and many free clinics for counseling—Dean maintained that she was afraid that if she sought help, her husband would kill her.

In an interview with a local reporter, Dean's defense attorney said that a psychiatrist and psychologist had documented that Dean suffered from post-traumatic stress syndrome, a condition that is most commonly associated with soldiers returning from war. "She was a prisoner who killed her captor to escape punishment," according to the attorney.[35] The defense lawyer failed to mention to the reporter that Dean had moved to Florida and briefly begun a new life—far away from her abusive husband—the year before the murder. However, missing her friends and her San Diego home, she decided to return to live again with the man her attorney later described as her "captor."

Post-traumatic stress was first brought to the nation's attention by the media shortly after the war in Vietnam ended. In the mid-1980s, CBS television aired a special entitled *The Wall Within*, which claimed that a million veterans suffered from post-traumatic stress. The men portrayed on the CBS special included one who had killed his mother, one who spent years on drugs, one who defended his mountain home with a gun. Likewise, the *New York Times* warned that the war in Vietnam, which had ended more than a decade earlier, was "being recalled with increasing frequency and vividness in courtrooms throughout the country as veterans charged with crimes cite their traumatic Vietnam experiences as their prime defense. Because of their war experiences, hundreds of Vietnam veterans have said that they should not be held accountable for such crimes as murder, rape and drug dealing."[36] In many cases, these men in fact were absolved from all responsibility for their crimes.

Since this time, post-traumatic stress syndrome has been used as a defense by people with no connection to the Vietnam War. As in the Dean case, judges and juries now believe that post-traumatic stress syndrome can cause individuals to commit violent and premeditated crimes—including the sales and distribution of illegal drugs—decades after the initial trauma. It is now suggested that simply witnessing a traumatic event can cause such stress. Of course, as Stanton Peele

EXPANDING THE MARKET FOR MENTAL ILLNESS

points out in *Diseasing of America*, it is difficult to imagine someone in a violent subculture filled with killing and drug dealing who cannot cite some deep trauma in his or her defense. For Peele, post-traumatic stress offers an excuse for perpetual violence without any attempt to reduce violence or the conditions that lead to it. He believes that medicalizing deviance in this way "muddles the moral picture," creating a host of psychological and clinical defenses that desensitize us to killing and the loss of life.[37]

Battered women's syndrome as a defense for the murder of husbands led to the inclusion of "masochistic personality disorder" in the *Diagnostic and Statistical Manual III*. However, under pressure from feminists who wanted to retain the option of using the syndrome for legal defense purposes but did not want to "blame" women who stay in abusive relationships, the American Psychiatric Association voted to delete masochistic personality disorder in upcoming revisions. In 1987, it was changed to "self-defeating personality disorder," which is included along with premenstrual syndrome (PMS) as a proposed diagnostic category needing further study. Although no longer classified as a mental illness, the benefits of the battered women's syndrome remain available to those who choose to avail themselves of the diagnosis. Many psychologists and psychiatrists are willing to testify to the "post-traumatic stress" aspect of this "syndrome" in defense of those who maintain that they killed their husbands or partners to escape abuse.

The popular culture has played an important role in the redefinition of violent behavior by females. Long before someone like Sara Dean ever thought of using the post-traumatic stress defense, there was the television movie *The Burning Bed*, featuring Farrah Fawcett's stellar performance as the battered-wife-turned-avenger. In what Stanton Peele calls a "pioneering case" of the battered women's syndrome, *The Burning Bed* suggested that Francine Hughes was "justified" in setting her sleeping husband on fire in 1977, after allegedly enduring twelve years of abuse. Portraying Hughes as a loving mother to her three children and a helpless victim of her abusive husband, Fawcett generated enormous sympathy for all female victims of abuse. Viewers could not help but cheer when Hughes was exonerated by a jury on the grounds that she was "temporarily insane" when she poured gasoline on her sleeping husband's bed, lit it on fire, and fled from the scene with her three children as he burned to death.

Despite the "happy ending" to the cinematic homicide, which portrayed a triumphant and vindicated Francine Hughes, Peele points

out that the real-life Hughes continued to lead a debilitated and troubled life.[38] Still, the film's portrayal of the battered women's syndrome
led to what has become a standard defense for the increasing number
of women who kill their husbands or boyfriends.

There is a perverse justice in the mental illness defense being
applied to crimes of violence by women. From the earliest days of
medicine, mental illness—especially hysteria—has been regarded as a
women's syndrome. The very term "hysteria" comes from *hystera*, the
Greek word for uterus. Classical healers described hysteria as a female
disorder characterized by convulsive attacks, random pains and sensations of choking. In her historical analysis of hysteria, Elaine
Showalter notes that these early healers believed the influence of the
uterus traveled randomly around the body—Monday in the foot, Tues-
day in the throat, Wednesday in the breast. A myriad of symptoms
were produced, including choking sensations, pains in various parts of
the body, paralyses, seizures and sexual longings. As advances in medicine demonstrated that the power of the uterus did not migrate,
doctors relocated the center of hysteria to the nervous system. Women
were described as a "nervous sex" suffering from the vapors, spleen
and fainting fits, or eroticized as hysterical nymphomaniacs.

Showalter writes that eventually hysteria became identified as a
"wastebasket diagnosis" to explain any random physical or psychological symptoms women might have exhibited.[39] By the late nineteenth
century, the celebrated Parisian neurologist Jean Martin Charcot published more than one hundred case histories of hysteria. Likewise, the
French physician Auguste Fabre wrote in 1883 that "what constitutes
the temperament of a woman is rudimentary hysteria." Such theories
came in handy as European society in the late nineteenth century was
hit by the first great wave of modern feminism. Women could not be
granted the vote, opponents said, because they were hysterical by
nature.[40]

Today, similar claims are being made by pharmaceutical companies who, with psychiatrists, are now treating premenstrual syndrome
as a mental illness. In television ads, drug maker Eli Lilly is promoting
the drug Sarafem to treat the problem, now dubbed "premenstrual
dysphoric disorder," or PMDD. But the pink and purple pills are not
new at all. They are simply repackaged and color-enhanced versions of
the popular antidepressant Prozac.[41] Although the American Psychiatric Association includes PMDD in its appendix to the current
Diagnostic and Statistical Manual of Mental Disorders, the part of the
manual reserved for issues needing further research, the FDA has

approved Sarafem to treat PMDD as a mental illness. Helping in the transition from syndrome to disorder are television advertisements for Serafem that show an agitated woman wrestling with a shopping cart, with a voice-over, "Think it's PMS? It could be PMDD." Subsequent ads show one woman arguing with her husband, and another frustrated because she cannot button her pants.

Some find it alarming that having trouble with a shopping cart or arguing with one's husband can be grounds for a diagnosis of mental illness. Paula Caplan, a psychologist and affiliated scholar at Brown University, suggests that "instead of labeling women as mentally ill, physicians should instead urge diet changes, exercise, less caffeine and even calcium supplements. But, no one makes much money off calcium tablets."[42]

MENTAL HEALTH PRACTITIONERS in conjunction with the mental health advocacy community and the pharmaceutical companies appear to have gained control over the conceptualization of mental illness. Because of the power we have given to "experts" to redefine deviant behavior as medical problems, our lives are increasingly controlled by a medical elite. Dr. Paul McHugh is among the few psychiatrists who have decried this development. As he says, "Whether treating the bored little boy in a crowded classroom, the oppositional teen, or the overworked and angry adult, today's psychiatrists are like 'mental cosmetologists' ever ready to chemically normalize any example of human psychological diversity that exceeds the current limits of social tolerance."[43]

Last year, doctors wrote more than 96 million prescriptions for serotonin reuptake inhibitors, a class of antidepressants including Paxil. The practice of medicalizing deviance has encouraged the dangerous fantasy that life's every passing imperfection can be clinically diagnosed and alleviated, if not eliminated, by pharmacological intervention through pushbutton remedies. Practitioners like McHugh, at the risk of being called "old fashioned," maintain that a model focusing on growth, maturity and responsibility is the only rational response to the disease model of deviance that threatens to diminish us all.

FOUR

MORAL PANICS AND THE

SOCIAL CONSTRUCTION OF DEVIANCE

W hile some forms of deviance like mental illness have become so broadly defined that the concept loses its meaning, other behaviors are considered so threatening to one interest group or another that a hysterical overreaction emerges. Sociologists refer to this phenomenon as "moral panic." First used by British sociologist Stanley Cohen, the term now refers to a form of collective behavior characterized by widely circulating rumors that greatly exaggerate the danger posed by some newly identified form of deviance.[1] In a moral panic, there is a heightened level of concern over the behavior of a certain group and a greater than normal fear about the consequences of this behavior for the rest of society. Sociologists describe the sentiment generated by the newly identified threat as a "kind of fever—characterized by heightened emotion, fear, dread, anxiety, hostility, and a strong feeling of righteousness."[2] Those tagged as deviants become the personification of evil, or what sociologists call "folk devils."

The classic historical example of a moral panic is the European witch-hunt, during which more than one hundred thousand people were executed because they were believed to possess evil powers.[3] Moral panics occurred in America during our own Salem witch-trials, and to much a lesser extent, in the "reefer madness" of the 1930s. In each case, harsh sanctions were applied to designated deviants: death sentences for those identified as witches in Salem, and draconian prison sentences for drug offenders in modern America.

Perhaps the most extreme recent instance of a moral panic involved the "recovered memories" of children in day care centers throughout the country beginning in the early 1980s. The first allegations of child sexual abuse were leveled against the McMartin Pre-School in Manhattan Beach, California, where a fabricated claim by the parent of one student expanded into panic-driven estimates that at least 1,200 children had been sexually molested. The panic spread so quickly that within a short time, hundreds of preschools throughout the country were closed and dozens of day care workers were stigmatized and imprisoned.[4] Most of these allegations of abuse involved (as is typical in a moral panic) nearly identical stories—in this case, of children being molested by day care workers dressed up as satanic priests or fearsome clowns, wielding knives and other instruments of torture in secret rooms and underground tunnels.

The alleged behavior of day care workers was portrayed as so strongly evil and so universal that it became an overnight "social crisis." Soon the media was presenting "experts" on Satanism to help educate the public. (One woman who claimed to have bred three children for sacrifice to Satan became a popular guest on daytime television talk shows.)[5] A wave of panic over the sexual abuse and satanic ritual sacrifice of children swept across the country.

Looking back at this outbreak of hysteria, it is impossible to understand what happened without looking at the role that advocacy groups and the federal government played in fomenting it. The passage of the 1974 Child Abuse Prevention and Treatment Act gave federal funds to states that identified abused children and prosecuted abusers. This provided a windfall—and an incentive—to those states with large numbers of abuse cases. As additional cases were identified, more funds became available. This federal measure was crucial in what was to come because it justified the creation of elaborate state and local agencies—what some have called a "child sexual abuse industry"—whose sole raison d'être was the investigation of child maltreatment. Mandatory reporting swelled abuse statistics, while the practice of basing investigations on confidential and anonymous reports opened the way to a high volume of groundless or malicious charges.[6] A huge bureaucracy evolved with the expansion of child protection agencies and staff who were ready, willing and anxious to conduct child abuse investigations on a grand scale.

But the campaign against day care workers could never have emerged without a powerful advocacy community of unlikely allies—

religious fundamentalist groups and radical feminists—both receptive to any allegations of sexual abuse of children.

Fundamentalist groups, ever vigilant to the possibility of satanic influence, provided a ready audience for accusations of abuse connected with satanic rituals, especially when it was associated with another of their worries: the misuse of day care by working parents. Feminists, on the other hand, helped inspire the moral panic because of the rape issue and their belief that America is rife with sexual abuse as a result of patriarchal power.[7] It was a small step from seeing women as the targets of predatory males, to seeing children as the targets of predatory adults. Indeed, by the early 1980s there was an explosion of feminist-inspired books on the sexual exploitation of children, including *The Sexual Assault of Children and Adolescents, Sexually Victimized Children, Betrayal of Innocence, The Best-Kept Secret* and *Father-Daughter Incest*.[8] Television movies and news documentaries on this subject proliferated. The feeding frenzy stimulated official investigations and reporting of abuse, some authentic but most not, and allowed the panic to reach critical mass.

Sociologist Philip Jenkins found that there were fewer than 2,000 sexual abuse cases reported in 1976, but almost 23,000 in 1982. In 1990, the Child Welfare League of America ran a full-page advertisement in the *New York Times* announcing that "since 1981, child sexual abuse is up 277 percent."[9] In this supercharged statistical atmosphere, wild exaggerations of sexual abuse and incest were accepted as fact. In 1984, "incest survivor" Katherine Brady told a congressional committee led by Senator Arlen Specter that there is "an incest epidemic in America.... One out of four girls, before she reaches thirteen in America, is sexually molested by fathers, stepfathers, uncles."[10] Fathers in the midst of custody hearings frequently became targets of incest charges. Once launched, such allegations ended any hope for equitable settlement or custody resolutions.

Celebrities began to come forward with their own tales of incest or sexual abuse, tearfully dramatized on *Larry King, Sally Jessy Raphael* and *Oprah*. LaToya Jackson, a former Miss America, and even Oprah herself all revealed that they too had been sexually molested as children. Some claimed to have developed multiple personalities or "alters" in response to the abuse. Roseanne Barr, for example, disclosed that she had unearthed twenty-one personalities in herself, including such bizarrely named alternate personalities as "Piggy, Bambi and Fucker."[11] Case studies of child sexual abuse victims were packaged and presented to the public in best-selling books and television movies-of-the-week. On the popular soap opera *One Life to Live*, one of the heroines, "Vicky," developed an "alter" by the name of "Nicky," which in turn led to a rash of real-life multiples with the same name. According to a *New Yorker* article on the hysteria over multiple personality disorder, "Nicky" quickly became the most common name for "alternate personalities" identified by those diagnosed with the disorder.[12]

Given the government's financial incentives and the expanding sexual-abuse practitioner base created by feminists anxious to prove that we live in a "rape society," it is not hard to see how a moral panic about day care workers could emerge. Convinced that pedophiles were using day care centers to practice their perversions, hysterical parents began to pressure prosecutors throughout the country for convictions, relying solely upon testimony by preschool children. Many of the children's stories were prompted by sexual abuse therapists invested in the now discredited "recovered memory" syndrome. In ritualized and homogeneous stories, children spoke of being stabbed, raped and forced to perform unspeakable sex acts on adults. They told preposterous tales of elephants and tigers populating the hidden tunnels underneath the day care centers, and a variety of other animals offered in ritual sacrifice to Satan. (Quite remarkably, no child ever showed any injury in any of the high-profile day care sexual abuse cases.) Every aspect of this story strained credulity, but this did not keep it from developing into a media avalanche in which day care workers everywhere were presumed guilty.

The hysteria created demands for long sentences for the convicted sexual abusers. The criminal justice system responded. In the trial of the childcare workers at North Carolina's Little Rascals Day Care Center, one of the alleged perpetrators was sentenced to twelve consecutive life sentences. In Boston's Fells Acres Day Care Center case, convictions resulted in a 30-to-40-year sentence for one of the several childcare workers convicted of the sexual abuse of children in their care. The families of the victims in the Boston case shared a $20 million settlement.

Few journalists and not a single social scientist questioned the lack of evidence or the credibility of witnesses. The *Wall Street Journal*'s Dorothy Rabinowitz was virtually alone in suggesting that the case entailed a moral panic, in which evidence was fabricated and citizens' rights were violated. Charges of sexual abuse in day care were growing feverishly, and dozens of innocent people embarked on long prison sentences, awaiting appeal of their cases. Deviance among day care workers was thought to be pandemic, and was inflated into the greatest deviance of all. During the years when the day care providers at Fells Acres were imprisoned, the State of Massachusetts commuted the sentences of eight women convicted of killing husbands or mates who allegedly had battered them. Yet the day care workers, trapped in exactly the opposite spiral, remained in prison.[13] Killing one's husband was becoming more understandable, while the alleged sexual abuse in day care had suddenly become a crime worse than murder.[14]

In the early 1990s, new research cast doubt on the interrogation techniques favored by prosecutors and therapists in the satanic cult abuse trials. "Recovered memories," like those by which the preschool children implicated their caretakers, were proven to be, generally, false memories. Appeals courts began reversing the ritual abuse convictions, and parole boards began recommending that sentences be commuted. As new findings discredited the fabricated testimony, the panic subsided and the courts began the slow process of overturning the preposterous charges against imprisoned day care workers in Massachusetts, California, Florida, North Carolina, New Jersey and elsewhere.

Nearly all of these innocent day care workers have been exonerated, yet their stories have not always had happy endings. As Dorothy Rabinowitz notes, "For those falsely charged and imprisoned for long terms, freedom is, at best, complicated—harder than anything they imagined in the years behind bars, and different in a thousand ways, most of them disturbing."[15] And for the parents of the "victims," the nightmare continues, as many keep looking for evidence that their children were indeed abused in satanic cult activities. Even today, parents from the discredited Fells Acres prosecution continue to search for the underground tunnels and the evidence of ritual animal sacrifices to Satan.

This moral panic illustrates the old maxim that the charge and conviction are always on page 1 of the newspaper but the retraction, exoneration or commutation is on page 34. In Massachusetts, journalists from the *Boston Herald*, the *Boston Globe* and local TV, eager to participate in what had quickly become a national story, closely followed the Fells Acres prosecution. Yet today, as Rabinowitz points out, "only silence reigns on the Fells Acres case, and on the great abuse trials that occasioned so much fevered reporting.... As was true of the witch trials of an earlier Massachusetts, this prosecution will, in time, be the source of amazement and horror."[16]

THE MORAL PANIC OVER satanic abuse of preschool children was the product of feverish imaginings. But a different kind of moral panic surrounds the issue of pedophile priests in the Catholic Church. Both panics involve allegations of sexual misconduct. But unlike the preposterous claims of ritual abuse and animal sacrifice occurring in the secret tunnels under day care facilities, accusations against Catholic priests continue to be confirmed. As cases in Dallas, San Francisco and Boston reveal, there are indeed priests who have molested young boys. There have been convictions and major compensatory damage awards to those victimized. And there is evidence that in a misguided attempt to rehabilitate these priests, the Catholic Church has furthered the panic by transferring priests from treatment centers back into parishes where they have resumed the cycle of abuse. A recent cover of *Newsweek* angrily trumpets: "Shame, Sex, and the Catholic Church."[17]

As a result of the publicity that has accompanied these high-profile cases, even those who had remained skeptical about satanic abuse in day care centers have accepted the notion that sexually abusive priests are part of a pandemic. Indeed, a few years ago, in what began as a casual conversation with colleagues in the faculty dining room, I was surprised by the consensus at our lunch table that it is foolish, even dangerous, to allow a child to be an altar server within the Catholic Church. It was a typical Monday, and we were talking about our family weekends when one of those at the table mentioned that her young son had assisted at an elaborate funeral Mass for a local politician. She was beginning to tell us about the ceremony when one of our colleagues interrupted: "I hope you never leave him alone with one of those priests! Don't you realize that most of them are pedophiles?"

The response was surprising because not long before, we had all been scoffing about the furor over day care providers, which we all agreed qualified as a typical moral panic. But when it came to the "crisis" of the pedophile priests, my usually skeptical colleagues accepted uncritically the idea of an "epidemic" of sexual abuse within a complicit Catholic Church. They regaled each other with stories they had seen in the media of "cover-ups" perpetrated by bishops in a futile effort to protect the Church from scandal, and spoke of the huge monetary settlements that had been paid to what they believed were the "thousands" of victims. One of them cited a $119.5 million jury award to eight former altar boys in Dallas, Texas. Rudy Kos, the priest at the center of the scandal, had since left the priesthood and moved from Dallas to San Diego, so when the Dallas civil suit began, the details from the case were broadcast each evening on the local television news programs. Nightly updates on the scandal provided graphic details of the alleged sexual abuse of teenage boys by Kos between 1987 and 1992.

The Dallas abuse story dominated San Diego's print and broadcast media for more than a year. On many days, the daily chronicle of priestly abuse was the lead story on local newscasts. Savvy producers "framed" the story by showing decade-old file footage of religious events at one of San Diego's most beautiful and elaborately adorned churches. While completely unconnected to the Kos case, this footage was calculated to universalize the crisis: It was not just a single deranged former priest, but the larger institution of the Catholic Church that was implicated. Every time a newscast employed the stock images, focusing on the ornate vestments, incense, candles and crucifixes, it promoted a subliminal association, implying that pedophilia was part of a much greater sickness hidden in the rites and appurtenances of the Catholic Church.

In recent years, priestly pedophilia has been described in the national media as an "ecclesiastical Watergate" and the "greatest threat facing the Church since the Reformation."[18] Television documentaries have chronicled the Catholic crisis on *60 Minutes, Dateline* and *20/20,* while shows like *Oprah* and *Geraldo* have introduced viewers to several of the victims of predator priests. Even a PBS documentary on the life of Pope John Paul II could not resist devoting a major portion of the broadcast to this issue.[19]

As a result of such media overload—and the real, if often numerically exaggerated, revelations of abuse—public views of the pedophile priest and a complicit Catholic Church have developed into a moral panic. Indeed, the "sins of a few" have now been extended generally to what the media continues to call the "sins of the Fathers." And as a result of the panic, all priests are now vulnerable to guilt by ecclesiastical association. Harvey Silverglate, a board member of the American Civil Liberties Union, recently expressed concern that "we're in an atmosphere now where there's a substantial chance of accusations against, even conviction of, an innocent priest. The problem with witch hunts is that everybody accused is suddenly found guilty."[20]

Sociologists have viewed moral panics as characterized by an inordinately fearful or emotional response to a deviant threat, both in media representation and in political forums. They have also noted that a panic is often based on a single case or a few high-profile cases. Isolated instances of sexual abuse by priests like Rudy Kos or John Geoghan, the serial abuser who caused a crisis in the Archdiocese of Boston, are combined with advocacy data that are reported endlessly, thus leading to the manufacture of "facts" about an "epidemic."

One of the most revealing signs that a moral panic is under way is when the statistics cited by those invested in its spread cannot be confirmed—and seem far out of proportion to reality. In the case of pedophile priests, a favorite source of advocacy data is "The Linkup," a support group for victims of clerical abuse. Until recently, the organization was headed by an ex-Catholic and former seminarian named Tom Economus (who died in March 2002 at age 46). Apparently angry at the Church for its resistance to change on issues like abortion, homosexuality, married priests and the ordination of women, he was the perfect inquisitor.

Linkup (formerly known as VOCAL, Victims of Clergy Abuse Linkup) asserts that 16.3 percent of all 50,000 priests in the United States are pedophiles. No data exist to confirm this figure. In fact, advocates from Linkup arrive at a figure of more than 8,000 pedophile priests in American parishes, and 2,092,440 children who have suffered abuse at their hands, by estimates rather than hard data. Only the panicked atmosphere surrounding the priesthood could give authority to this statistical subjectivity.[21]

The distortion of data (Linkup claims that victims of priestly abuse would "fill a city the size of Boston") and wild exaggeration of specific cases are typical of a moral panic. For example, at the height of the day care panic, newspapers were reporting the incredible statistic that more than fifty thousand children had been murdered in satanic sacrifices throughout the country. A 1994 national survey reported in *Redbook* found that 70 percent of Americans believed those who claimed to have been abused by satanic cults as children but to have repressed the memories for years. An additional 32 percent said that the FBI and the police ignore evidence of ritual abuse because "they don't want to admit that the satanic cults exist."[22] In these cases, the information documented by those with an interest in fueling the moral panic was effective in constructing a phantom threat from imaginary evildoers.

The ongoing crisis in the Catholic Church offers another window onto the nature of moral panics. Social scientist Philip Jenkins, author of *Pedophiles and Priests*, says that "the panic reaction does not occur because of any rational assessment of the scale of a particular menace." Rather, it arises as a "result of ill-defined fears" that eventually find a dramatic and oversimplified focus on one incident or stereotype. This stereotype later provides a visible symbol for discussion and debate.[23] Jenkins sees the crisis of the pedophile priests as socially constructed in large part, and the evidence as inflated and over-defined in an effort to transform the Catholic Church itself into a site of deviance.

Jenkins' research has led him to conclude that "in reality, Catholic clergy are not necessarily represented in the sexual abuse phenomenon at a rate higher than or even equal to their numbers in the clerical profession as a whole."[24] However, he believes that there are structural and organizational reasons that the Catholic Church should have produced a disproportionately high level of nationally reported scandals. Unlike a scandal in a Baptist congregation, for instance, which would remain strictly localized because of the church's decentralized structure, a scandal in a Catholic parish, because of the hierarchy in which it exists, is immediately viewed as a generalized "Catholic" scandal. There are now national agencies within the Church whose functions include the recording and tabulation of all formal accusations against priests. As instances of abuse come to light, zealous attorneys routinely subpoena diocesan archives, which can be used to expose and litigate allegations, and this in turn creates a network effect. Jenkins claims that it is because the Catholic Church, unlike less centralized churches, keeps records of isolated cases of abuse that it has faced this moral panic.[25]

In contrast to its fixation on Catholic priests, whose vow of celibacy is itself increasingly seen as deviant in an era of sexual candor and promiscuity, the media often ignores sexual abuse by non-Catholic clergy. Jenkins points out that one of the most egregious clerical molestation cases of the 1980s concerned a Pentecostal minister named Tony Leyva, who abused more than one hundred boys in various southern states over a period of several years. Within the Pentecostal community, independent preachers like Leyva are subject to few or no hierarchical controls and no centralized record-keeping. This lack of bureaucracy, combined with the highly mobile nature of itinerant ministers, makes it unlikely that they will remain in any one area long enough to generate sufficient complaints to merit investigation.[26]

As the reaction to pedophile priests shows, reports of the "death of deviance" have been greatly exaggerated. There are still many who regard some behaviors as seriously deviant, and the activities of the stereotypical pedophile priest certainly fall into that category. However, the problem has become so overblown and confused that it is difficult to assess how extensive it really is. Philip Jenkins does not deny that sexual abuse by clergy has occurred, or that the hierarchy of the Catholic Church has made some serious mistakes in clumsily trying to cover up the issue. What he finds puzzling, however, is why charges of clerical sex abuse became so exaggerated so quickly. And why has the Catholic Church been singled out for vilification and charges of institutionalized deviance when similar behavior has also occurred in other denominations?

To UNDERSTAND HOW THE PANIC has evolved, we must acknowledge that some abuse by clergy has indeed occurred. Moreover, psychiatric centers in Connecticut, Maryland and New Mexico where priests from throughout the United States were sent for treatment released them prematurely as "rehabilitated." Yet the Church itself must admit that it minimized the risk these priests posed to the children in their parishes, as part of an attempt to wish the problem away. On the other hand, we must also recognize that there are stakeholders who have promoted the panic in an effort to propagate their own negative views of the Church.

Anti-Catholicism has always been present in America: the Ku Klux Klan, in fact, originated as an anticlerical even more than an anti-black organization. Suspicion of the Catholic Church abated somewhat in the middle of the last century, as Catholic immigrants became more fully integrated into American society and in the melting-pot narrative. But anti-Catholic sentiments revived after the 1960s because the Church continued to take conservative positions on hot-button issues such as abortion, homosexuality and female priests. High-profile art exhibits, films and plays that mock the Church provide numerous examples of anti-Catholic attitudes. Hostility toward the Catholic Church is apparent even in the U.S. legislature, where in debates over proposed school voucher plans, opposing lawmakers sometimes fret that this would enable religious organizations "to use public funds to settle court cases involving pedophile priests."[27]

While anti-Catholic prejudice outside the Church certainly has played a role, it is clear that the pedophile priest panic has been more strongly driven by the resentments of former Catholics and of dissidents within. Philip Jenkins remarks:

As in other historical periods in which there has been intense hostility to the Church and its clergy, it is not necessary to suppose that the frequency or gravity of clerical misdeeds has increased significantly in recent years. What has changed however, is the moral perception of the public, and crucially, of some within the Catholic laity themselves, who now provide a hungrily receptive audience for claims of priestly atrocities. As the media and various interest groups present sensational stories to feed the emerging market for anti-Catholic sentiments, the attitudes and expectations of the audience become ever more skeptical of clerical value and authority.[28]

Moral panics are most likely to erupt when traditional norms and values no longer appear to have much relevance to people's lives, but there is little to replace them. People's awareness of this vacuum makes them all the more susceptible to panic-mongering.[29] Since Vatican II, when the Catholic Church "opened its windows to a dialogue with the modern world," the traditional centralized authority that had organized Catholicism for centuries came under challenge from within.[30] In the flux that followed the ecclesiastical changes of Vatican II, the liberal wing of the Church has attempted to defeat what some persist in viewing as its "clericalism, legalism and triumphalism." Conservative Catholics are often regarded as "the party of reaction and the traditional wielders of the anathema."[31] And although there is little truth in either of these caricatures, the ideological disagreements that accompanied many of the changes of Vatican II helped to open the door to the moral panic surrounding pedophile priests. In fact, Jenkins believes that if this crisis had not come to the foreground of the Church, some other problem would most likely have emerged, because an attack on the priesthood—and the authority structure of which it is a part—was inevitable in the climate of change following Vatican II.

Jenkins sees the Church as being caught in a sort of ecclesiastical pincer movement. Although it may seem counterintuitive, traditionalist and conservative groups within the Church have publicized and sometimes exaggerated the pedophile problem in an effort to counter what they regard as "a homosexual subversion of the Church."[32] Pointing to the fact that most cases of sexual abuse by priests have involved sexual liaisons between priests and boys in their teens or young seminarians in their early twenties, some of these conservative critics identified such sexual relationships as evidence of a growing homosexual culture within the priesthood.[33] In many ways, they are correct. "Pedophilia" may be a misnomer. The overwhelming majority of cases of sexual misconduct involve gay priests who have been sexually active with teenage male seminarians.* While such homosexual relations with minors are criminal offenses, and are of course immoral, they are not examples of pedophilia or child molestation.

Philip Jenkins points out, "As the priest shortage became acute during the 1970s, the Church became willing to accept homosexual clergy on the understanding that they remained strictly celibate on the model expected of their heterosexual counterparts."[34] But this understanding came in conflict with the movement to redefine homosexuality as "normative," and soon gay priests were finding support for homosexual activity in gay advocacy groups associated with the Church. For example, Dignity, a liberal Catholic organization, lobbies for change in the official Church teachings on homosexuality. Decrying the Vatican's reaffirmation that homosexual behavior is "disordered," such activists support gay priests and in fact encourage them to express their "sexual nature." And the behavior that results has played a considerable role in the Church's current crisis over "pedophilia."

The conservative faction of the Church may have had some impact in exacerbating the pedophilia panic, but a far greater hostility to the priesthood exists on the ecclesiastical left. For more than three decades, the liberal-activist wing of the Church has been engaged in a battle with the hierarchy over issues including sexual morality, academic freedom, priestly celibacy, divorce and remarriage, reproductive freedom, and the role and the status of women. Disgruntled former priests and feminist dissidents within the Church have a powerful incentive to exaggerate the claims of abuse by priests. Academic appointments at Catholic universities and colleges have provided a platform for their criticism.

Catholic feminists, many of them teaching in theology or religious studies programs on university campuses or functioning as activists in the women's movement, have exploited the moral panic to criticize what they regard as the deviance of the Church's patriarchal hierarchy. For example, following the recent disclosures about molestation by priests in the Archdiocese of Boston, Lisa Sowle Cahill, professor of theology at Boston College, published an opinion piece in

---

* After a sex scandal in the early 1990s, the Archdiocese of Chicago opened up its records for all 2,252 priests who served there over a period of forty years. Only one of the priests had allegedly assaulted a preteen; the most common complaints of sexual contact involved teenage boys who were 15 or 16. See Lisa Miller and David France, "Sins of the Father," *Newsweek*, 4 March 2002.

the *New York Times* asserting that the "pedophile scandal exposes the weaknesses of a virtually all-male decision-making structure." Cahill claims that the Church needs a "more open and collaborative model of governance—including women and lay men at the highest levels." Finally, she suggests that the way to "force the church bureaucracy to listen is for all Catholics to withhold funds from all diocesan and Vatican collections and organizations."[35]

Philip Jenkins writes that "Feminists advanced beyond the mainstream construction of clerical abuse in their assertion that sexual exploitation should be defined more broadly than simply priestly pedophilia. In this feminist perception, the problem is one of clergy exploitation directed against adult women as much as children."[36] From the dissident feminist perspective, "the pedophilia scandal is a new and powerful weapon in the arsenal of reformers anxious to restructure the Church away from the traditional concepts of hierarchy, male dominance, and clerical elitism."[37]

Some Catholic feminists, including most notably Boston College theologian Mary Daly, have attacked what they call a "Theology of Abuse." Daly's hostility to the Catholic "patriarchy" has spilled over into her classroom at the Catholic college. For more than thirty years she has refused to allow males to enroll in her undergraduate and graduate courses, claiming that her classroom must be maintained as a "space on the boundary of a patriarchal institution."[38] Other feminist theologians agree with her that sexual abuse and violence can be eliminated from the Church only by an overthrow of the patriarchy.

A text called *Christianity, Patriarchy and Abuse* goes beyond attacks on priests and Church leaders to suggest that in Catholicism it is God himself who is the "ultimate abuser." This book describes God as "the patriarchal prototype of the molesting father or priest, and the atoning sacrifice of his son is an act of monstrous tyranny." One feminist writer even challenges the theology of the crucifixion on the grounds that it is indicative of "an abusive act of a father toward a child."[39]

Within this emotionally charged context, Catholic feminist groups have had an interest in accepting charges of priestly pedophilia whether or not they are true. To strengthen their position, and to gain greater visibility in the fight against the patriarchal Church, feminist speakers at a recent Linkup conference, for example, argued that "the Church's child sexual abuse crisis stemmed from its patriarchal nature" and asserted that "the solution was to be found in making domination a sin rather than a right."[40]

The relationship between pedophilia, patriarchy and feminist advocacy becomes explicit on the Linkup website, where we read that "four in ten United States Catholic nuns report having experienced sexual abuse," an assertion made nowhere else, and with no scholarly substantiation here. The website also presents similarly unsourced data saying that "40% of the nation's 85,000 nuns have experienced *sexual trauma*, ranging from rape to exploitation and harassment."[41] A panic based on homosexual abuse, therefore, is extended into the heterosexual world as well.

Women have also been the audience for the media barrage about the pedophile priests, which has included articles in *McCall's*, *Ms.* and *Redbook*. Typically the stories devote a few sentences to a specific allegation of abuse, and then parlay this into a criticism of the Church hierarchy and its presumed patriarchal policies. The connection between these stories and the growing power of the feminist movement is not tendentious. In a content analysis of the computerized database *Newspaper Abstracts*, Philip Jenkins found that prior to the late 1980s there were almost no references to sexual abuse by clergy. From 1989 through 1991, there were 130 such items, or about 40 each year. By 1992, the number of stories rose dramatically, to more than 200 annually.

The following year, 1993, was a watershed year for this moral panic. In perhaps the most notorious of the allegations of priestly abuse, former seminarian Steven Cook testified that he had been sexually victimized in the 1970s by Chicago's Cardinal Joseph Bernardin. Cook's charge attracted sensational media coverage and brought forward other alleged victims and their families onto television talk shows and documentary programs. By the following year, however, Cook had withdrawn his charges, stating that he realized that the "recovered memories" he had relied upon in his accusation were actually not at all reliable, and that the abuse could not possibly have occurred.[42]

In his book *The Gift of Peace*, Cardinal Bernardin devoted an entire chapter to Steven Cook. His description of the fabrication of charges and the later recantation sheds light on the way a moral panic is promoted. Cook recalled that as a young seminarian he had become involved in a homosexual relationship with his seminary teacher. After the relationship ended, Cook grew embittered and eventually left the Church. Many years later, when he saw allegations of priestly misconduct multiplying in the press, he contacted a lawyer with a reputation for bringing financially lucrative legal actions against priests accused of sexual abuse. Although Cook was pursuing a case only against his seminary teacher, he claimed that his "advisors" urged him to name the cardinal—very big game indeed—along with the seminary teacher in the legal action. Eventually, Cook began to actually believe that he had "recaptured memories" of being sexually abused by Bernardin—despite the fact that he had never actually spoken with the cardinal.[43]

Philip Jenkins points out that clerical abuse has been the most discussed item of religious news in the lay press since the doctrinal upheavals in the Catholic Church during the 1960s. Some magazines have used a single case to represent the scandals of a given city or diocese, as when the *New Yorker* described the problems of the Diocese of Worcester, where several priests were accused of "homosexual activities" with minors. The group nature of these cases was especially damaging to the Church because it implied that homosexual activity with teenage boys had acquired a sinister institutional or subcultural status within the Church. Reporting like this reached a peak in 1992, when more articles on priestly pedophilia appeared during this single year than in the previous ten years combined.[44]

Ever hungry for more salacious stories of priestly abuse, some media outlets have actually solicited victims. The *San Francisco Examiner* and local radio station KGO, for instance, assigned teams of reporters to ferret out clerical wrongdoing. KGO created a "clerical abuse hot line" to solicit complaints, and the *Examiner* ran a three-day exposé, accompanied by a series of blistering editorials including "An Archdiocese in Denial: Sex, the Church, and the Cops."[45]

THE ABUSE STORY HAS GIVEN legitimacy to calls for reform by many left-leaning Catholics who had been demanding changes in the rules and authority structure of the Church for decades. In response, fed by the growing public concerns and demands, the media has also offered "solutions" to the abuse crisis which typically involve a major reform of aspects of traditional Catholicism—most notably the elimination of priestly celibacy. A recent headline in the *Seattle Times* made the connection between these two issues explicit: "Pope Deplores Pedophilia, But Won't Lift Priests' Celibacy."[46] Once seen as the foundation of spiritual commitment and a sacrifice that a young seminarian makes in his quest for holiness, celibacy is now viewed as a form of deviance in an age of sexual liberation—a "cause" of pedophilia. Few in the media ever acknowledge the logical inconsistency of assuming that a married priesthood would solve the problem: child abusers are not interested in adult sexual relations.

The media has certainly played an important role in transforming a serious problem into a panic. Perhaps the alliterative phrase "pedophile priest" was just too irresistible for writers not to use it—over and over again. Likewise, punning titles like the *New York Times* headline "Priests Who Prey" spice up (and trivialize) the subject.[47] "Just Following Orders" was the title of an article on the abuse scandal that appeared in the liberal Catholic periodical *National Catholic Reporter.* Longtime critics of the Catholic Church hierarchy, the *NCR* editors may have used this title to reassure readers that the deviance of the "traditionalist" Church is finally being exposed. For Philip Jenkins, the title "Just Following Orders" evokes "shades of Nazi Germany and those who undertook vicious or illegal acts in their unquestioning obedience to superiors."[48]

In addition to these sinister allusions, there have been several attempts to equate the Catholic Church with the activities of organized crime. Indeed, some have drawn an implicit analogy with the Mafia's code of secrecy in describing the purported "code of silence" surrounding pedophile priests. In a 1993 television documentary, Andrew Greeley, a Catholic priest, sociologist and best-selling author, explicitly compared the Church's closed structure to that of the Mafia—but said the Church was worse: "Even the Mafia has sanctions.... The priesthood doesn't."[49] In 1993, Greeley issued a fictionalized criticism of the Catholic Church in a novel about an evil pedophile priest named Father Greene. Entitled *Fall from Grace*, the best-selling novel describes Greene as "a sadomasochist and multiple child molester." Worse, Greene, whose seminary nickname was "Lucifer," is required by satanic cults to perform blasphemous and homicidal rituals, including a "Black Mass." In one of the most ludicrous yet graphically violent scenes in the book, there is a bloody and horrific ritualized human sacrifice to Satan within a Catholic rectory.[50]

While Greeley, a longtime and outspoken critic of traditional Catholicism, has attacked the way Rome has handled allegations of sexual abuse, his attacks are mild in comparison with those from the liberal wing of the Church—especially those from the *National Catholic Reporter.* Contributors to *NCR* have been relentless in drawing attention to the clergy sex scandals by presenting the cases as part of a systemic problem caused by the celibacy requirement. Jenkins points out that it was *NCR* that "pioneered" the term "pedophile priests."[51]

NCR writer Eugene Kennedy, a former Maryknoll priest, has

devoted himself, like other contributors to the paper, to excoriating the Church's "traditionalist" policies—especially the celibacy requirement for men and women in religious orders. Kennedy comments on the failure of "official Catholicism" to investigate abuse and other problems that he believes have arisen from the rule of celibacy. He writes that the root causes of the pedophile crisis (in particular, the celibacy requirement) are "so much a part of the weave of overall ecclesiastical culture that they cannot be teased out without tearing the cloth itself."[52] And indeed, it is hard not to conclude that ripping up the entire institutional garment of Catholicism is what such critics desire.

In a series on the "crisis of soul" of the American priest, Kennedy laments, "The pedophile crisis exploded like an anti-personnel mine in the mid-80s as heavily publicized stories documented the rending of the temple veil that once shrouded incidents of the sexual abuse of boys by priests."[53] He longs for a "post-clerical, de-centered priesthood, in which the adjustments to celibacy are varied." The priesthood, says Kennedy, must be changed to include "the love and understanding of a specific woman or, in some cases, a certain man."[54]

Likewise, in the wake of the recent Boston scandal, journalist Andrew Sullivan, himself a professing Catholic, blames the "onerous burden" of celibacy that "can easily distort a person's psyche." He accuses the celibate priesthood itself of attracting pedophiles by promising to "put a straitjacket on their compulsions and confusions," and argues that in such a restrictive environment, "alas, that straitjacket can often come undone." Sullivan believes that when constrained by celibacy, "the presence of large numbers of gay priests—forced to preach against their very identity and to fight against their own need for love and relationship—only intensifies the psychological pressure."[55]

CARDINAL LAW'S DECISION TO remove more than eighty Boston priests in a zero-tolerance policy for as-yet-unsubstantiated charges of abuse fanned the flames of what some regarded as a fading panic. Because of this, the Church remains at risk for lawsuits—most of them as a result of abuse allegations going back more than twenty or thirty years. Indeed, it sometimes appears that the Church itself has internalized the panic, as children and teenagers are now barred from serving at Mass in some parishes because of the "risk" they create. Fearful of the potential for additional lawsuits, for instance, Archbishop William Levada of San Francisco instituted a policy that banned teenagers from working as office or clerical assistants in parish rectories. Maurice Healy, spokesman for the archdiocese, explained in an interview with the *San Francisco Chronicle*, "We believe it is a prudent measure, which removes all possible appearances of improprieties in the rectory setting."[56]

The Church has been profoundly damaged by this crisis, just as day care centers and workers were stigmatized by the panic triggered by "recovered memories." A *New York Times* article in 2000 suggested that Catholic parents have become less likely to encourage their children to consider a life in the priesthood. The article reminded readers that "the prestige of the priesthood has been shaken over the last decade with each news report of child abuse by priests." As one parent remarked, "You get a tremendous amount of stress, bad press, and bad publicity, and to top it all off, you get no grandchildren from it. From a parent's point of view, it doesn't seem like a very promising career."[57] Now, the many good priests are painted with the same pedophile brush as the few serial molesters who were allowed to serve in parishes across the country.

In 2001, the North American College, the major seminary in Rome for some of the "best and brightest" American seminarians, had the largest entering class in thirty years. While some call this "an augury of a bright future for the Catholic Church," there are persistent concerns that the priesthood has been seriously injured.[58] The alliteration of "priest" and "pedophile" has become so much a part of our culture that "grandmothers who used to pray that at least one son would become a priest now warn their grandchildren never to be alone with the men we still call Father."[59]

It is likely that the panic surrounding the pedophile priest will continue—not because there will be more cases, but rather, because there are so many within the Church who can gain so much by keeping the panic alive. For feminists lobbying for women's ordination, the image of the pedophile priest surely points to the need for women to fill priestly roles. For conservatives still decrying the reforms of Vatican II, the pedophile panic proves that the changes have gone too far and that a tolerance of stealth homosexuality in the clergy has caused this problem. And, for gay rights activists intent on denouncing what they view as the Church's hypocrisy on gay sexuality, the pedophile crisis offers proof that the sexual repression of gay priests has led directly to the molestation of children. The confluence of so many players with so much to gain has created what has become indeed the "perfect panic."

FIVE

POSTMODERN

PEDOPHILIA

U nlike the psychologist, the sociologist's main objective in studying deviance is not to classify a specific behavior simply as either deviant or conforming, but to position that behavior on a continuum ranging from negligible to serious in terms of the reaction it evokes.[1] If behavior is considered unacceptable, inappropriate or morally wrong by the majority of the members of a community, it is regarded as "deviant." What is judged to be "mild" deviance is often ignored, while those acts viewed as "very deviant" elicit demands for severe sanctions. When a behavior warrants and receives condemnatory or punitive reactions, sociologists assert that it has seriously violated the prevailing behavioral standards.

As the previous chapter indicates, the very word "pedophilia" brings forth such an emotional response from most people that in the past there was never a question about where it was on the continuum. Because of the corruption of innocence involved in the use of children for adult sexual gratification, this violation has elicited such strong aversive responses that the public demand for severe negative sanctions has been unrelenting. Indeed, pedophilia has historically been so stigmatized that we have implemented laws which now demand that convicted sex offenders be publicly identified to the community for the rest of their lives—long after they have served their sentences in prison.

Still, we are presently confronted with what looks like a paradox.

The furor over the day care panic suggests that norms concerning the sexual abuse of children are fully intact. Yet at the same time that the day care crisis was reaching its denouement, a movement to redefine pedophilia as the more innocuous "intergenerational sexual intimacy" was gaining strength. While "priestly pedophiles" were being vilified in lurid exposés, open pedophilia—the intentional use of children for pleasure—was on the verge of being normalized.

As in the case of the medicalization of substance abuse, this movement to reevaluate pedophilia resulted from the efforts of a powerful advocate community supported by university-affiliated scholars and published case studies. While much of this academic support for adult-child sexual activity originated in European universities, there are a growing number of researchers and publishers in the United States who also are willing to question the taboo of pedophilia.

One of the most often-cited sources justifying the relaxation of sanctions against this behavior is *Male Intergenerational Intimacy: Historical, Socio-Psychological, and Legal Perspectives.* This collection of essays by American, Dutch, German and English scholars, many with university teaching positions, provides a powerful argument for "intergenerational intimacy." The book is explicit in its aims: "To go beyond the usual narrow views to shed critical light on the broad spectrum of man-boy love and its place in ancient and contemporary societies."[2]

Several of the essays are geared to assisting readers "to gain an understanding of childhood sexualities." A chapter by Professor Ken Plummer claims to draw upon the theoretical work of the new social historians, the socialist-feminists, the Foucauldians and "constructionist" sociologists in order to build a "new and more fruitful approach to sexuality and children."[3] Plummer writes, "Rather than viewing sex as a unitary essence with a common meaning, this new definition searches for the multi-layered complexity, historical diversity and situational ambiguity of sex."

Drawing upon the language of postmodern theory, Plummer maintains that "childhood" is not a biological given, but rather "socially constructed—an historically produced social object." If this is true, it follows logically that childhood can also be deconstructed. And so, Plummer says that we should no longer assume that childhood is a time of innocence simply because of chronological age. In fact, he writes, "A child of seven may have built an elaborate set of sexual understandings and codes which would baffle many adults."[4] Within this perspective, there is no assumption of linear sexual development—no real "childhood," only a definition externally imposed, presumably by the dominant power arrangements. Plummer concludes that there should be "greater flexibility than is usually thought" regarding sex with very young children.

Plummer decries "essentialist views of sexuality." Essentialist thinking about childhood is problematic for him because it helps to create essentialist thinking about pedophilia—in particular, the idea that it is essentially immoral. On the other hand, Plummer writes, "By adopting a constructionist perspective, I suggest the need to examine the changing and highly variable contexts in which children come to build and negotiate their different sexual worlds. When the complexity of such worlds can be better understood, the complexities of intergenerational sexuality will become more apparent."[5]

Knowing that most readers will question whether seven-year-old children actually build and negotiate sexual worlds on their own, Plummer engages in what sociologists describe as "neutralization techniques": questioning the "abnormality" of adults who seek sex with children, and suggesting that not necessarily all but some children may be precociously ready, willing and able to have sex with adults. Removing the "essentialist" barriers of childhood enables apologists to cast pedophilia as part of the "politics of transgression"—which in postmodernist lingo is not a matter of sin. Pedophiles in this view are not deviants, but merely what Michel Foucault calls "border crossers."

Gerald Jones, another contributor to *Male Intergenerational Intimacy*, also claims that sexual contact with minors does not necessarily constitute abuse. He begins with the seemingly innocuous premise that "children and adolescents can experience close one-to-one friendships with adults, and many actually do so." Such "intergenerational intimacy" includes "all non-coercive, two-way interactions in which a physically mature adult and a pre-adult in mid-adolescence or younger share interests, communicate with, and trust each other, share power in the relationship, spend time together, and feel mutually fond of one another. Sexual contact is not assumed, but if present, is regarded as adjunct rather than essential."[6] Adding sex with minors onto a list of desirable aspects of friendship normalizes it. For Jones, the sex of "intergenerational intimacy" is different from sexual abuse, defined as "an unreasonable, unilateral imposition by the adult of unwanted behavior upon the other person, or unwanted sexual behavior that may be induced by trickery, coercion, or physical force." Intergenerational intimacy, on the other hand, entails "mutuality and control," and creates an environment for "sexual activity between an adult and a child or an adult and an adolescent which allows each to exercise choice."[7]

From such a perspective, "homosexual intergenerational intimacy" is not just morally neutral but actually good because it is "developmentally functional." As Jones writes, "It is widely assumed, though not well documented in empirical research, that children tend to make use of older persons of their same sex outside the family as role models and heroes."[8] Thus, an adult who uses a same-sex child for sex contributes to his moral growth in much the same way as a good father who is active in community life. Jones concludes his chapter by suggesting that the study of intimate intergenerational relationships, pedophilia and child sexuality will be effective only to the extent that professionals involved resolve to identify and "reject emotionality" in all its forms and influences: "Terminology must be neutral and each researcher and author must acknowledge the probability that society's emotional reactions are affecting the results or interpretations."[9] In other words, professionals must give up the bias against pedophilia—which is itself a loaded word to be strenuously avoided—and be willing to entertain the possibility that it is actually normal.

For most of the contributors to *Male Intergenerational Intimacy*, achieving acceptance for adult-child sex begins with neutralizing the harshly critical language surrounding pedophilia. By placing intergenerational sexuality in an antiseptic context where the very concept of childhood is called into question (is it a state of innocence, or a state of sophisticated desire?), advocates seek to destroy the taboo against what used to be deviant sexual behavior. They try to give the movement to normalize pedophilia a powerful theoretical base that will legitimate what had been considered unspeakable.

Enlisting credible academic authorities in this redefinition process—some of the contributors to *Male Intergenerational Intimacy* are respected professors at well-regarded institutions—has been an effective strategy for this movement. Concepts of deviance rely primarily on a group evaluation that is amenable to change—especially when trusted individuals register their opinions on behalf of a redefinition. While pedophiles have been making the same argument for years—that the coerced child "liked" the sexual activity, or actually initiated the sexual foreplay—it is only recently that the "experts" have purported to validate many of these claims. Their endorsement gives these claims standing as "scientific fact," which can be used by advocates working to change perceptions.

MALE INTERGENERATIONAL INTIMACY includes writings of activists as well as scholars. David Thorstad, former president of New York's Gay Activists Alliance and a founding member of the North American Man/Boy Love Association (NAMBLA), provides a chapter chronicling the history of intergenerational intimacy within the American gay rights movement. Thorstad writes, "In present day America it is all right to talk or publish books about boy love in Ancient Greece or the pederasty of great men like Byron. But, it is quite another matter to leave the academic ivory tower and acknowledge that boy-love goes on in every neighborhood today." The author believes that "the pendulum of history swings—lurches forward and back, not an incremental advance, characterize the struggle for social change."[10] A phrase like "struggle for social change" links acceptance of pedophilia to the "liberation" movements of the 1960s.

The North American Man/Boy Love Association was created in 1978, when 150 persons attended a conference on "Man/Boy Love and the Age of Consent" in Boston's Community Church. Coordinated by leaders of the gay movement in Boston, this attempt to legitimate pedophilia gained instant credibility—and a "sense of urgency," according to Thorstad. Following the meeting, thirty charter members formed NAMBLA, the first activist organization to promote adult male sexual relationships with young boys.[11]

Since its earliest days, NAMBLA has been involved in controversies both inside and outside of the gay community. Writing of the discrimination within the gay community that he faced as a member of NAMBLA, Thorstad recalls, "In 1980, following a heated debate, the Coalition for Lesbian and Gay Rights called for my removal as a keynote speaker at a gay rights rally on the steps of the state capitol in Albany." He also recollects that soon afterward, a lesbian group attempted to get NAMBLA out of a gay rights march in New York City. Speaking of censure from the National Organization for Women, Thorstad recalls: "When a boy from Gay Youth of New York spoke at the rally in Sheridan Square to defend the right of under-age males to participate in the movement, he was booed by representatives from NOW."

Not surprisingly, NAMBLA has drawn even more criticism from outside the gay community. The Federal Bureau of Investigation launched its first probe into the group in 1981, resulting in several arrests. In response, the media began to pay attention to NAMBLA activities, and suggested in news reports that the organization had ties to prostitution, kidnappings, and the production and distribution of child pornography. In an effort to defend NAMBLA, a "Stop the Witch Hunt" committee co-sponsored a forum with New York University's Libertarian Student Association entitled "An Introduction to the Man/Boy Love Issue."

NAMBLA remains a visible—if still ambiguous—presence in the gay community, participating in Gay Pride marches, and working to normalize pedophilia. In 2000, NAMBLA was a major supporter of the first "International Boy-Love Day," an event whose purpose was "to remind men who love boys that we are good and loving people and not the monsters that we are portrayed to be." The event was promoted on several Internet sites and advised "men who love boys" to light blue candles and leave them in public places as a mark of solidarity on December 21, the first day of winter. The night of the winter solstice was chosen for the commemoration because it is the longest night of the year, and also the turning point toward longer daylight hours. Candles represent this coming victory of light over darkness—symbolic of the time when boy-lovers are finally accepted as good people.

While NAMBLA has continued to build momentum, there have been obstacles along the way. In the spring of 2000, the organization found itself embroiled in a $200 million wrongful death and civil rights lawsuit filed in U.S. district court in Boston. The suit claims that the writings on NAMBLA's website led NAMBLA member Charles Jaynes to torture, rape and murder Jeffrey Curley, a ten-year-old Cambridge boy. According to prosecutors, NAMBLA publications were found among the belongings of Jaynes, who, along with his lover, Stephen Sicari, allegedly had an obsession with the boy. The prosecution claimed that Jaynes and Sicari led Curley from his neighborhood with the promise of a new bike and then smothered him with a gasoline-soaked rag when he resisted their sexual advances. According to the Boston Globe, the two men packed the boy's body in a cement-filled container and dumped it in a river in Maine.[12]

While groups like NAMBLA organize politically around the claim that "boy-lovers are simply men who only care deeply about children," more explicit Internet sites that serve the pedophile population show a different perspective. Most of these sites give pedophiles an opportunity to share strategies on how to find and seduce young boys; some give suggestions about how to track boys under twelve in shopping malls or parks. Website instructions advise pedophiles on how to lure the boys by giving them cookies or starting conversations about popular toys like Pokémon and Nintendo games.[13] Often, the writers on these sites describe how they were aroused by these very young boys, and nearly always relate in detail how much the boys allegedly enjoyed their sexual experiences with men.

Participants in chat rooms linked to these websites often try to gain credibility for pedophilia by referring to the ancient Greek practice in which men initiated young boys into maturity through mentoring relationships that sometimes involved sexual relations. There are sometimes instructions for chat-room visitors to check other sites for the latest in "scientific" information supporting the pedophile orientation. The Danish Pedophile Association site, for instance, has "scientific research findings on the benefits of child sex," along with helpful suggestions on how to find and seduce children for sex. The message on such sites is clear: pedophilia is "normal," and those who would suppress this kind of sexuality are the real deviants. The Danish site specifically warns against subjecting the pedophile to any of the modalities associated with mental illness:

> There is a growing trend to put pedophiles into therapy. The thera-pists have a hard time with treatment because it is impossible to change somebody's pedophile orientation, or any other sexual orien-tation for that matter. When interviewing a pedophile who has been charged with what they call a "sexual offense," the therapist often hears a story about a child who enjoyed the sexual affair and partici-pated actively and with enthusiasm. Refusing to believe that this is possible, the therapist may conclude that the pedophile suffers from cognitive distortion. This is a presumptuous claim when the issue is an event of which the patient has first hand experience, while the therapist has only second hand knowledge.[14]

The Danish Pedophilia Association provides its website visitors with an opportunity to differentiate between the "sexual abuse" of children and the more desirable "erotic-sexual contact with children." According to the association, the true sexual abuser is "one whose lust is the only criterion, and the erotic needs of the child are ignored and the child is a passive partner and sex object."[15]

It is easy to ridicule or dismiss the writings of fringe groups like NAMBLA or the Danish Pedophile Association. But it is also true that these stigmatized groups have been given powerful support by some within the academic mainstream. A study released by the American Psychological Association is currently being used by NAMBLA and other advocacy groups to further normalize pedophilia. Published in the APA's *Psychological Bulletin*, the article, entitled "A Meta-Analytic Examination of Assumed Properties of Child Sexual Abuse Using College Samples," concludes that sexual abuse of children does not actually cause harm. As NAMBLA has asserted for more than twenty years, the authors of this study—all college professors—say that the negative effects of such abuse have been overstated: "The self reported effects data do not support the assumption of wide scale psychological harm from child sexual abuse."[16] These authors do not find an overall link between childhood sexual abuse and later emotional disorders or unusual psychological problems in adulthood. The study calls for a redefinition of the term "child sexual abuse," maintaining—in language that could almost have been lifted from NAMBLA's own literature—that if it was a "willing encounter" with "positive reactions" on the part of the child or adolescent, it should be given a different, "value-neutral" name such as "adult-child sex" or "adult-adolescent sex."

NAMBLA quickly posted the "good news" on its Internet site, asserting that "the current war on boy-lovers has no basis in science." Citing the APA's statistics, the website proclaimed: "A recent study showed that 70% of males in the studies of man-child sex reported that as children or adolescents, their sexual experiences with adults had been positive or neutral." While the authors of the *Psychological Bulletin* study claimed that their intention was merely to differentiate between willing and coerced acts with children and between positive and negative childhood sexual experiences, the reality is that their study is now being used by groups like NAMBLA to normalize pedophilia.

Those who criticize the conclusions and recommendations of the *Psychological Bulletin* study have found themselves stigmatized as the deviants. Conservative radio talk-show host Dr. Laura Schlessinger was among the first to bring national attention to the study when she referred to it on her program as "junk science." Later, Schlessinger wrote an opinion piece published by major newspapers throughout the country that castigated the American Psychological Association for providing a forum for such thinking. She took issue with the authors' central conclusions, saying, "Non-coerced sex with a child is a misnomer because there is always an element of coercion, involving a misuse of adult authority to exploit the child's need for affection or attention." Schlessinger concluded by saying that "Psychological research is highly subjective. Combined with powerful political forces for change in attitudes about mothering (radical feminism), sexual orientation (homosexual activism) and sex education (sexual libertarians) that infiltrate psychological associations and universities, the 'findings' can be very dangerous."[17]

Schlessinger was immediately vilified not only for her criticism of the study's methodology and conclusions, but also for her unfortunate coupling of pedophilia with homosexuality. Gay rights organizations accused her of having committed "hate speech" against gays. Fearful of gay reprisals and boycotts, several sponsors withdrew their support.

Although some may find Schlessinger's style abrasive, she was actually reflecting the dominant public attitude. Congress joined her in denouncing the *Psychological Bulletin* article about pedophilia in a 355-0 vote after Rep. Matt Salmon (R-Arizona), sponsor of the resolution, called the American Psychological Association's publication an "emancipation proclamation of pedophiles."[18]

JOURNALIST MARY EBERSTADT has attempted to shed some light on the current movement to downgrade the deviance of pedophilia. In an article entitled "Pedophilia Chic Reconsidered," Eberstadt writes that in order to understand the movement, we need to look closely at the ways in which pedophilia is being redefined, and who is doing the redefining. She points out that among other things, a double standard is being asserted, since only male-to-male pedophilia is being reassessed, not male-female pedophilia: "Publishing houses are not putting out acclaimed anthologies and works of fiction that include excerpts of men having sex with young girls. Psychologists and psychiatrists are not competing with each other to publish studies demonstrating that the sexual abuse of girls is inconsequential; or, indeed, that it ought not even be defined as 'abuse.' "[19]

Moreover, when pedophilia involving mature women with young boys is presented by the media, it is almost always in negative tones. When the teen television series *Dawson's Creek* portrayed a sexual affair between a female high school teacher and her young student, the deviance of the relationship was made clear in the severe sanctions imposed on the teacher. A few years ago, when the story of sixth-grade teacher Mary Kay Letourneau's involvement with one of her twelve-year-old male students hit the newspapers, most people readily labeled her deviant. When Letourneau persisted in the relationship and conceived the boy's child, she was incarcerated.

Eberstadt maintains that the public is being urged to reconsider homosexual pedophilia because certain elements in the gay community have become powerful enough to demand this reconsideration. Recognizing that powerful interest and advocacy groups now hold much of the power to redefine the culture, she remarks that "the more the gay rights movement has entered the mainstream, the more this question has bubbled forth from that previously distant realm into the public square."[20]

While male pedophilia remains contested terrain, woman-girl sex barely registers on the cultural radar screen. A growing body of literature, including fiction and biography as well as screen treatments, focuses on the "coming of age" of young lesbians. *The Vagina Monologues,* for instance, is now part of the standard dramatic repertory in student productions on college campuses. The play explores a young girl's maturation, which begins when the thirteen-year-old enjoys a sexual experience with a twenty-four-year-old woman. *The Vagina Monologues* is clearly controversial for some audiences, yet any attempt to criticize the play is attacked as deviant, and sometimes severely sanctioned.

Robert Swope, a columnist at *The Hoya,* the student newspaper at Georgetown University, was fired after he wrote a critical review of a student production of *The Vagina Monologues.* In his regular column, Swope said he was dismayed that the mostly female crowd laughed throughout the scene in which a young teenager is given alcohol and then subjected to sexual conquest by an adult woman. "If a 24 year old man had gotten her liquored-up and then had sex with her," he wrote, "rational people would consider that rape." Swope also criticized the Catholic university for allowing the play to be performed. Editors of *The Hoya* rejected Swope's column, calling its content "divisive." When Swope objected to what he considered censorship, the paper's editor in chief fired him. Swope then found himself excoriated as a "misogynist" and "book burner."[21]

IN 1994, WITH LITTLE OR NO public outcry, the American Psychiatric Association revised its *Diagnostic and Statistical Manual* (DSM) so that neither pedophilia nor child molestation would, in itself, necessarily be indicative of psychological disorder. To qualify as disordered, molesters must feel "anxious" about the acts or be "impaired" in their work or social relationships. With little media reporting, and even less critical response from the psychological or psychiatric community, the American Psychiatric Association thus took the first step in changing perceptions of what have traditionally been regarded as among the most serious offenses in our society.

As we have seen in the previous chapters, positions taken by the

American Psychiatric Association have generally been predictive of changes in the culture. Even so, whether its pronouncements reflect science or politics is subject to debate. The organization has a long history of succumbing to pressure by interest groups. In 1974, under fire from the emerging gay rights movement, the members of the APA voted at their annual meeting to delete homosexuality from the list of mental disorders in the *Diagnostic and Statistical Manual*—thus removing any stigma from homosexual behavior. Like the subsequent stand on pedophilia, this vote had nothing to do with new research or groundbreaking genetic findings, but was a political response to an already powerful social movement. For years before the APA's reassessment of homosexuality, gay rights advocates had lobbied the association at the annual meetings. There were boycotts of the cities in which the APA held its conventions, and there was a well-planned media attack on the association. Given the intensity of this lobbying effort, it was no surprise when the APA finally bowed to the pressure.

While many have welcomed the decision by the American Psychiatric Association to normalize pedophilia, it must be acknowledged that the more conservative elements of the gay community have joined with others to condemn the pedophile movement. The Log Cabin Republicans, for instance, have publicly criticized the gay rights movement's "leftist leadership" for failing to condemn the North American Man/Boy Love Association.[22]

Pedophilia is a behavior whose status now appears to be in transition. While Internet sites provide men with tips on how to seduce young boys, academics armed with deconstruction theory and "neutralization techniques" defend this kind of activity under the genteel name of "intergenerational intimacy." The revision of the DSM to destigmatize such behavior represents one more round in the semantic and ideological war to determine whether or not pedophilia will remain a commonly recognized form of deviance.

SIX

STIGMA AND

SEXUAL ORIENTATION

While the successful portrayal of racism and discrimination as forms of deviance was a key to the
success of the civil rights movement of the early
1960s, there was little parallel social change for
the gays in that era. This was a time when same-
sex couples faced a disapproving and fearful public, an aggressive
police force and a hostile media. As other minority groups made
significant progress in gaining rights and privileges, members of the
gay community continued to face overwhelming discrimination and
had legitimate fears for their personal safety.

Although most cities did not specifically outlaw gay bars or social
events, gay couples could not socialize freely because of police harassment and fears of arrest. Same-sex dancing couples were commonly
arrested if their bodies were touching. During the 1960s, "police raids
became so routine that they triggered drills at gay bars. When the
lights blinked, it meant that the police were coming in, and couples
knew to separate if they were touch-dancing or to stop what they were
doing if they were involved in heavy petting. The bartenders would
jump over the bar and mix with the customers to avoid arrest."[1]

What was derisively called the "gay lifestyle" was portrayed in
stereotypical ways in both the news and the entertainment media. On
television, the late-night comedy monologues were often laced with
jokes about homosexuality and stereotypical portrayals of effeminate
gay men.

Then, on June 27, 1969, in what is now recognized as a gay Boston Tea Party of sorts, the gay community began to chart a new course. It started with another police raid at a gay bar. Eight New York City police officers raided the Stonewall Inn in Greenwich Village and attempted to arrest the dancing drag queens there. Unlike the docile response to police raids of the past, the besieged gay men fought back. As the couples who had been dancing in the bar were handcuffed and escorted to the waiting police vans, jeers were directed at the police. Someone threw a handful of coins, and in response, the police expanded their arrests to include those milling around outside the bar. In turn, gay men and lesbian women escalated their resistance. Attracted by the growing commotion, the crowd began to grow as gay patrons from nearby Greenwich Village bars arrived on the scene. Beer bottles followed the coins, and then bricks from a construction site were thrown at the arresting officers. Someone dislodged a parking meter and used it as a battering ram on the door of the now-locked Stonewall Inn. Someone else hurled a burning garbage can at a plate-glass window. The riot that fueled the gay rights movement had begun.

In these early days of gay resistance, established homosexual groups like the Mattachine Society, which had pushed for gay civil rights for years, pleaded with the newly empowered liberationists to maintain decorum. But the radical gay rights groups proliferated. Randy Wicker, a highly respected Mattachine leader, said later of the Stonewall riot: "I was horrified that a bunch of queens would kick up their heels at the police and get the attention, after all we had tried for so many years, wearing suits and ties and looking normal. And now, these queens were giving us this image."[2] But few paid much attention to such conservative thoughts. The powerfully angry appeal of the radical gay liberation movement had won the day, and eventually, the decade.

Now, more than thirty years later, the disagreement between conservative gay integrationists and lifestyle radicals remains, but the context has changed. Last year, Vermont's legislators granted gay and lesbian couples the right to civil unions, which offer state-given rights such as inheritance and next-of-kin status. Other states may follow. Workplace discrimination against gay men and lesbian women has dramatically declined, and homosexual employees have successfully lobbied their employers to provide equal benefits to same-sex partners. And, as in the case of other minority groups, there are affirmative action programs in place in major corporations to find and retain gay workers. Some police departments are now making an effort to recruit and promote openly gay and lesbian police officers. The number of self-described gays and lesbian officers in the San Diego Police Department, for instance, grew from five in 1992 to more than fifty in 2001. Gay and lesbian officers are scattered in patrol, investigations, the SWAT team, community relations and training.[3]

Wall Street financial firms also now target recruiting efforts directly at gay and lesbian business students. According to the *Wall Street Journal*, "Goldman-Sachs Group has wined and dined gay M.B.A. students at fine restaurants in New York's Chelsea and Boston's Back Bay neighborhoods. J. P. Morgan and Co. and American Express co-hosted a dinner for gay students in the plush corporate dining room of J. P. Morgan's Wall Street headquarters." Merrill-Lynch formed a network with the goal of mobilizing and attracting gay workers. Some companies like Coors Brewing have gay and lesbian corporate relations managers.

Research indicates that the average gay worker's income is about 25 to 30 percent higher than that of a comparable heterosexual male. Advertisers spend increasing sums to convince the gay community to spend its discretionary dollars on ever-expanding product lines. Prudential Securities has created both gay and lesbian versions of an ad touting its expertise in estate planning and other thorny financial issues for unmarried couples. Fleet Boston Financial Corporation and America Express market financial services that fit the unique needs of same-sex partners. Dozens of small businesses are taking note of the report in the 2000 Census of a 300 percent increase in same-sex households nationwide since 1990, and are marketing to these new gay and lesbian families. Although such households comprised only 0.57 percent of all households in 2000, that is a significant increase from 0.17 percent in 1990. The new entrepreneurs attempting to tap that market niche include Love Out Loud in New York, which sells children's "Rainbow Rompers" embroidered with the words "Love Me, Love My Dads."[4]

The achievement of the gay community in normalizing homosexuality took place against significant resistance. The initial efforts of the radicalized gay community during the Stonewall era did not significantly alter negative public perceptions. The media focus on Stonewall's glitzy drag queens and the leather-clad revolutionaries marching in the Greenwich Village streets did little to dispel public disapproval. During those early days, the movement drew attention because of its entertainment value—not because of any new acknowledgment of the inherent dignity of gays and lesbians. Nor was the cause of normalization served by annual Gay Pride celebrations in cities like San Francisco, traditionally led by the lesbian biker group, Dykes on Bikes, and the cross-dressing bearded "nuns" marching as the Sisters of Perpetual Indulgence.

Throughout the 1970s, the media response to these gay rights celebrations had always been to look for the most colorful or outrageously depraved part of the parade and highlight it on the evening news. As a result, the majority of heterosexuals continued to view the gay community as a site of deviance. Two gay authors, critical of the way the homosexual community was presenting itself in those days, asked, "Why is it that gay men who might otherwise be dressed in Brooks Brothers suits metamorphose into bespangled drag queens one day each year and sashay in pink cha-cha heels through town in the gay pride marches?"[5]

The 1980s brought more unfavorable attention to the gay community, often in the form of fear and loathing over the primary role that gay men played in the spread of AIDS. When epidemiologists and sociologists first proved that AIDS was being spread sexually through the gay community, homosexuals reacted with denial. The gay world rejected risk-reduction guidelines that were based on the growing realization that the disease was spreading through promiscuous sexuality involving anal intercourse with multiple partners.

The bathhouses remained open in the Castro, San Francisco's gay district, and many gay men continued to engage in high-risk sexual behavior throughout much of the decade. Even at the height of the AIDS crisis, when there were no longer any doubts about the origins or risks of AIDS, gay activists in New York, San Francisco, Los Angeles and Boston opposed any attempts to close the bathhouses, which they characterized as "centers of gay culture."[6] Gay bathhouses in Boston remained open, despite the risks, until 1989. Images of promiscuity, the reckless endangerment of others, and the pursuit of pleasure at all costs supported the stigma attached to what was still regarded as a deviant population. Not surprisingly, one-third of all respondents to a 1985 Gallup poll said that AIDS had worsened their opinion of homosexuality.[7]

By the 1990s, however, a major shift occurred among gay leaders, who began to acknowledge the need to understand the public's fears and prejudices surrounding homosexuality. This attitude reflected a growing recognition that the deviant self-presentation of the gay community had been counterproductive. Conservative gay authors like Andrew Sullivan and Bruce Bawer, as well as radicals-turned-moderates like Gabriel Rotello and Michelangelo Signorile, preached a more temperate gay behavior and rhetoric, and worked to convince the public that homosexuals are, as the title of one of Sullivan's books asserts, "virtually normal."

Gabriel Rotello called for "moderation and balance" in gay sexual practices.[8] The real cause of the AIDS epidemic, he wrote, was the high number of sex partners—on average more than a thousand per year—with whom each "fast-lane" gay man had sex. For writers and activists like Rotello, gays and lesbians can diminish the deviance of homosexuality only if they promote sexually safe lifestyles and renounce the belief that promiscuity is essential to gay identity. As protease inhibitors have fought the ravages of AIDS and given the gay male population a new lease on life, incrementalist tactics of reasoned debate and civility have replaced the more revolutionary tactics of the past. Gays and lesbians have become integrated into American normalcy.

AN INFLUENTIAL BOOK WRITTEN at the close of the disastrous AIDS-afflicted decade of the 1980s provides an understanding of how the gay community succeeded in its effort to escape the label of deviance, which threatened to attach itself even more firmly at the onset of the epidemic. *After the Ball: How America Will Conquer Its Fear and Hatred of Gays in the 90's,* by Marshall Kirk and Hunter Madsen, demanded that gays realize that how they were presenting themselves was the most important structural impediment to acceptance. Even more remarkably, Kirk and Madsen suggested that the gay men view the AIDS epidemic as presenting them with a unique opportunity for full acceptance and inclusion.

Kirk and Madsen said that the latent sympathy resulting from the tens of thousands lost to AIDS could actually help the cause of the gay community. Acknowledging that Americans are basically fair-minded, they wrote, "As cynical as it may seem, AIDS gives us a chance, however brief, to establish ourselves as a victimized minority—legitimately deserving of America's special protection and care."[9]

Applying a marketplace metaphor to defining deviance, savvy salesmen Kirk and Madsen showed how the "deviants" of the past could be repackaged as the "victims" of the present. They provided gay activists with a blueprint for what they called a "conversion of the average American's emotions, mind, and will, through a planned psychological attack."[10] To change public opinion, Kirk and Madsen suggested three important tactics of persuasion: *desensitization, jamming* and *conversion*.

Desensitization is an effort to present gays as unthreatening and inoffensive ("They are your neighbors, your friends, your teachers, and your co-workers—they are all around you"). To achieve the goal of desensitization, Kirk and Madsen advised that the gay community needed to inundate the heterosexual world with a continuous flood of gay-related advertising, presented in the least offensive fashion possible, meant to convince the consumer that homosexuals are perfectly—not just virtually—normal.[11] One memorable ad that appeared in major newspapers and magazines pictured a golf club, a fishing rod and a tennis ball. Capitalizing on the "conventional wisdom" within the gay community that 10 percent of the total population is gay, the text of the ad read: "Did you know that more Americans live a normal gay lifestyle than play golf...or tennis, or go fishing? Being gay is natural for millions of people. So why make sport of them?"[12]

Learning from the success of Black History Month, Kirk and Madsen realized that desensitization would be more likely to occur if the heterosexual community knew more about the valuable contributions that have been made by gays and lesbians. They asserted, "The honor roll of prominent gay or bisexual men and women is truly eye popping. From Socrates to Eleanor Roosevelt, Tchaikovsky to Bessie Smith, Alexander the Great to Alexander Hamilton, and Leonardo da Vinci to Walt Whitman."[13] From a marketing perspective, famous historical figures are especially useful because they carry enormous credibility. Their other virtue is that "they are invariably dead as a doornail—hence in no position to deny the truth and sue for libel.... By casting a violet spotlight on such revered heroes, in no time a skillful media campaign could have the gay community looking like the veritable fairy godmother to Western civilization."[14] It is no accident that today, on many college campuses and increasingly within many elementary and high schools, students now celebrate the accomplishments of famous gay philosophers, artists, scientists, poets and authors.

With the assistance of books like Lilian Faderman's *To Believe in Women: What Lesbians Have Done for America—A History*, colleges and universities throughout the country have instituted "Gay Appreciation" weeks (or months, on some campuses) to mark the accomplishments of gays and lesbians throughout history.[15] Faderman lists dozens of women that she believes were lesbian, among others pioneering social worker Jane Addams, early women's suffrage leaders Susan B. Anthony and Anna Howard Shaw, public health pioneer Emily Blackwell, and many other powerful women.*

More and more, elementary and middle school students are introduced to the historical contributions of gays and lesbians. To help future teachers integrate gay and lesbian themes into their classrooms, one West Coast university offered a course in spring 2002 promising to "use adolescent and children's literature, poetry, film and music to investigate what it means to be gay, lesbian or bisexual."[16] Enrollment in the course, entitled "Finding Common Ground: Using Adolescent and Children's Literature to Explore Issues Related to Gay, Lesbian, Bisexual and Straight Identities," would help fulfill the "children's literature" requirement for future teachers enrolled in the University's School of Education.

Across the country, in Newton, Massachusetts, the Oak Hill Middle School posted on a bulletin board, for the benefit of its 11-to-13-year-old students, the photos of fourteen "major gay figures of the ancient and modern world."[17] Included were historical icons like Alexander the Great, Leonardo da Vinci, Michelangelo and William Shakespeare, along with various figures from more recent times, such as Walt Whitman, Marcel Proust, Eleanor Roosevelt, James Baldwin, Andy Warhol—and, of course, Congressman Barney Frank.

An ad in the *Washington Post* pictured Walt Whitman with the words: "Would Walt Whitman Be Allowed to Teach English in Virginia? Walt Whitman was gay. He was also one of America's greatest poets. If he were alive today some people would not let him be a teacher."[18] Kirk and Madsen pointed out that the Whitman ad generated both favorable public reaction and a major increase in donations. Likewise, an ad picturing Leonardo da Vinci described him as "Artist, scientist, inventor, philosopher, probably gay too.... That would make this gentle genius a criminal across much of the United States if he lived today. Homophobia could keep him out of the classroom, the laboratory, even the art studio. That's not genius. That's just bigotry."[19] And a similar ad about Alexander the Great: "They say I was the most

---

* There has even been an attempt to draw in "metaphorically gay" people to support the cause. In the *Chronicle of Higher Education,* Tyler Curtin, queer studies theorist at the University of North Carolina at Chapel Hill, asserted that Bill Clinton was metaphorically not only the first black president, but also the first queer president, "a lover of oral and anal sex, who significantly was compulsive about bestowing on friends and acquaintances that iconic queer text, *Leaves of Grass.*"

brilliant general in history.... But, if I were alive today, the U.S. Army wouldn't even let me enlist, just because I was gay. Before they lose more good soldiers, someone should tell them, they're fighting the wrong war. Stop Anti-Gay Discrimination in the Military."[20]

The strategy has been effective, but it has elicited complaints—some of it from the gay community itself. Lesbian social critic Camile Paglia asks, "Wouldn't students be better off if their teachers fed them facts rather than propaganda? Proclaiming Eleanor Roosevelt gay is not only goofy but malicious. It reduces a bold, dynamic woman whose entire achievement was in the public realm to gossip and speculation about her most guarded private life." Paglia reminds us that those who promote Shakespeare as a homosexual for their own ideological agenda conveniently overlook the fact that not one of his thirty-seven plays addresses homosexuality or alludes to it except in negative terms. "Is Iago, with his evil fixation on Othello, now to be a gay role model?" asks Paglia. Although she writes frequently about the dark romance of lesbianism, she also cautions that "the intrusion of militant gay activism into primary schools does more harm than good by encouraging adolescents to define themselves prematurely as gay, when in fact most teens are wracked by instability, insecurity and doubt."[21]

Desensitization techniques are even more powerful when combined with *jamming*, defined by Kirk and Madsen as moving people to a different opinion about homosexuality through a form of operant conditioning. The "trick" of jamming, according to Kirk and Madsen, is to make the homophobe feel a sense of shame "whenever his homo-hatred surfaces." They wrote that "propagandistic advertisement can depict homohating bigots as crude loudmouths and assholes—people who say not only faggot, but nigger, kike and other shameful epithets."[22] In the redefinition of deviance, then, anyone who dares to question the morality of gay sexual behavior is labeled a "homophobe." The efforts of the "homophobe" to stigmatize homosexuality as deviant will rebound on him and cause him to unlearn such intolerant behavior. Ads to help in the jamming process include those that link prejudice against homosexuals to hate crimes such as lynchings and cross burnings. One ad placed by gay activists depicted Klansmen dressed in white robes with the ironic caption: "Some guys have trouble accepting gay people.... They think we're crazy and we dress funny."

A television advertisement shown during the 2001 Grammy Music Awards presented teenage boys (ostensibly fans of controversial

rap singer Eminem) who were casually using the word "gay" in a pejo-
rative manner. The ad then coupled these ordinary-looking teenage
boys with a shocking image of the brutal slaying of Matthew Shepard,
the young gay man who was "crucified" in Wyoming in 2000. The message was that "hate speech" such as Eminem's song lyrics will actually
kill gays. Likewise, a popular ad that ran in newspapers and magazines in the late 1980s pictured Hitler with the caption: "Madman,
Murderer, Homophobe." Kirk and Madsen suggested that the Nazi +
pink triangle link makes for powerful communication because no one
can plausibly deny that gays in Nazi concentration camps were victims deserving sympathy and protection.[23]

Some advocacy groups have made the willingness to wear or display a pink triangle in support of the gay community a kind of moral
litmus test on college campuses. In the late 1990s, there was an incident at a Catholic University in which a professor's reluctance to meet
the test raised a controversy that apparently contributed to ending his
teaching career. The popular part-time faculty member had taught at
this university for several years. He was a strong presence in the classroom, with the highest student evaluations in his department, yet he
was not offered a contract to teach again. No explanation was given
for this, but those familiar with the case believe that the reason was
his unwillingness to display a pink triangle proclaiming his office "An
Open Zone for Gay, Lesbian, Bisexual and Transgendered Persons."
When asked to post the symbol in the office space he shared with
other faculty, he responded in writing that he would do so if requested,
but that "if the space were mine, I would not post such a sign." This
response was widely circulated on campus. The part that probably
sealed his fate was his assertion that "any institution, especially a
Catholic institution, marginalizes itself with such vapid symbolism."
One senior professor called him a "homophobe" for even questioning
the appropriateness of displaying the pink triangle.

Recalcitrant students are generally much more likely than teachers to be attacked as homophobic—a word which itself redefines
deviance. Upon setting foot on campus, first-year students at many
colleges and universities are subjected to mandatory diversity training
that focuses on homosexuality. In an article for *Commentary,* a young
woman described her freshman orientation at Williams College as
including compulsory "Feel-What-It-Is-Like-to-Be-Gay" sessions in
which students from the Bisexual, Gay and Lesbian Union led tours
through the freshman dorms and required students to state their
names and declare themselves gay—even though they were not—just

to experience what it feels like to "come out." The final session of the Williams orientation was a program on race, gender and identity. In this session the entire freshman class was assembled in a dark auditorium, where, with eyes closed, they listened as "slurs were hurled at the students from all directions" to help them experience what it feels like to be the target of homophobic hate.[24]

The Williams College activities are not atypical. The *Wall Street Journal* reported that freshman orientation on many campuses creates an "official moral agenda for students who arrive with a wide variety of personal ethical commitments."[25] The result can be psychological turbulence. During his first weeks at Harvard, for instance, freshman Samuel Burke found himself in trouble as a result of not understanding the importance of identity politics on campus. While trying to help some strangers find a table at which to eat lunch in a crowded dining room, Burke spotted an empty one, removed the sign that read "Reserved HRGLSA," and invited the visitors to sit there. As it turned out, these initials stood for the Harvard-Radcliffe Gay and Lesbian Students Association, and Burke's casual act became "an ideological offense" against a "protected group."[26] He was promptly called before a "campus court." Although he offered to apologize publicly to the gay and lesbian student group for removing the sign, Burke was "pushed to the brink of tears by the official inquisitors who questioned his motives at every turn and threatened him with severe punishment."[27] Heavy pressure on the now-disgraced freshman continued throughout the remainder of his first semester, and he received disciplinary probation just before he went home for the holidays. Distraught and overwhelmed by the ordeal at Harvard and the stigmatizing sanctions, Samuel Burke committed suicide during Christmas break. Thus did the tactic of "jamming" succeed beyond all expectation in casting shame over the merest hint of "homophobia."

The third and most important approach that Kirk and Madsen suggested to reverse the prejudice against gays and lesbians is *conversion,* that is, "subverting the mechanism of prejudice through the use of associative conditioning." They wrote: "It isn't enough that antigay bigots should become confused about us, or even indifferent to us—we are safest, in the long run, if we can actually make them like us."[28] Conversion aims to achieve this by presenting attractive and unthreatening homosexuals in magazines, on billboards and on television.[29]

Kirk and Madsen warned against using "bull-dykes or drag queens" for this purpose. They criticized one ad promoted by the Alexandria (Virginia) Gay Community Association because it featured a lesbian couple that "reinforces an unappealing stereotype—suggesting perhaps two leathery old dykes from tobacco road who bark at each other with gin-cracked voices, and who first met at a motorcycle roundup."[30] Kirk and Madsen pointed out that when this ad appeared in print, it generated great hostility and decreased donations for the Alexandria association. The authors were similarly critical of an ad portraying two male sailors kissing, for while the ad was intended to portray a loving relationship, most viewers are repelled by such public displays of affection by gay men—especially in uniform.

They contrasted these efforts with successful conversion techniques showing how "normal" gay people are. One appealing ad by the Los Angeles–based Lesbian and Gay Public Awareness Project shows an attractive middle-aged woman flanked by her two attractive daughters. The caption reads: "I'm proud of my lesbian daughter."[31] Likewise, a television ad entitled "Someone You'd Like to Know" pictures an average-looking solid citizen named Steve who tells us that he "works hard, has a bunch of friends, some straight and some gay. We get together and shoot baskets once a week, until it gets too cold. I like to ski too. My folks are terrific—they helped David and me afford our first apartment. Now they drop by a lot."[32]

Viewers of these ads would never mistake Steve for a member of NAMBLA. Instead, we learn that Steve's family is important to him, giving him acceptance and support, and that he is a regular guy who likes regular sports and has a monogamous relationship. There is no subtext of multiple lovers, drugs, AIDS, ball gowns or feathered boas. We are told that Steve lives a conventional life—just like every other gay man.

DESPITE SUCH MESSAGES and the undeniable strides gays and lesbians have made toward acceptance and inclusion, national opinion polls continue to confirm a strong ambivalence toward homosexual behavior. The most recent General Social Survey found that more than 70 percent of the American people still believe that sexual relations between members of the same sex are wrong.[33] Likewise, a major attitudinal survey by sociologist Alan Wolfe indicated that although middle-class Americans are reluctant to make judgments about almost every aspect of other people's behavior, this is not the case when it comes to homosexuality. Wolfe found that among his interviewees, "many were clearly made uncomfortable by the topic and did not want to speak about it; one flat out refused to discuss the subject, while others responded with nervous laughter, confusion or expressions of pity." A large number of respondents, while reluctant to condemn people of different faiths or even atheists, had little trouble condemning gays. Common characterizations of homosexuality that surfaced within the interviews were: "abnormal, immoral, sinful, unacceptable, sick, unhealthy, untrustworthy, mentally ill, wrong, perverted and mentally deficient." Wolfe noted that "both the size of the group willing to condemn homosexuality, and the vehemence with which they did so, indicated that here is indeed the ultimate test of American tolerance."[34]

In other words, after thirty years of "marketing" efforts to portray its lifestyle as part of the mainstream, the gay community is still viewed with suspicion by much of the heterosexual population. Moreover, the advances that advocacy groups make can be undercut by developments such as the rise in new AIDS infections reported in 2000. A front-page headline in the *San Francisco Chronicle* warned: "San Francisco HIV Rate Surges."* The article reported that after years of stability, wrought by strong prevention programs and a safer-sex ethic, city health experts estimated that the number of new infections by the virus that causes AIDS had nearly doubled during the previous year. Multiple partners and the condom-free sexual practice described on the front page of the *Chronicle* as "barebacking" were responsible for the trend.

Researchers at the University of California in San Diego found further evidence of these worrisome trends on a national level. A longitudinal study collected data from people recruited in nine cities, including San Diego, Montreal, Los Angeles, New York, Seattle, Dallas, Vancouver, Birmingham and Denver. These data indicate that a growing number of gay men are infecting others knowingly, with full knowledge of their own HIV status. Researchers discovered that some recently infected study participants have a strain of HIV that is resistant to protease inhibitors.[35] The authors of the study identified a new trend involving "willful and purposeful infection by both partners—a

---

* The concern is based on indicators monitored by San Francisco health authorities in clinics that serve the high-risk gay population. The report is important because until this time, there were no data to confirm new infections. Among the troubling trends in San Francisco are the escalating rate of rectal gonorrhea, which more than doubled in five years, from 20 per 100,000 in 1994 to 45 per 100,000 in 1999. Worse, the proportion of gay men reporting condom use fell from 70 percent in 1994 to 54 percent in 1999; and the proportion of gay men having unprotected sex with multiple partners nearly doubled, from 23 percent in 1994 to 43 percent in 1999.

complex pathology called bug chasing." In fact, there are websites
where uninfected people can solicit sex with those who are already
infected. Called "gift giving," this practice adds to continuing perceptions of deviance within the gay community.

Developments such as these show that the success that gay and
lesbian groups have had in shedding the "deviant" label is provisional
and can be adversely affected by information that calls up old stereotypes. Gay advocates have responded by trying to prevent this
information from appearing in the press. After the lacerating experience of reporting on AIDS, much of the national media, fearful of
seeming homophobic, are reluctant to dwell on the disturbing health
trends. Local reporters have also learned to be cautious about
reprisals. According to court documents filed by the *San Francisco
Chronicle*'s lawyers, gay activists began to make threatening phone
calls to reporters after the latest published articles about the rise of
unsafe sex practices among gay men in San Francisco. In court decla-
rations, reporters claimed that late-night callers to their homes told
them "gay rage has you in its sights," promised to hunt them down,
and mentioned spouses and children by name. The *Chronicle* evacu-
ated its offices on November 11, 2001, after receiving a bomb threat
that the newspaper's lawyers attributed to gay activists.[36] Two city
health officials also reported receiving similar threats.

In what some might view as "reverse gay profiling," law enforcement also appears to have become disinclined to link criminal or
violent behavior by a gay individual to the gay lifestyle, even when
there is a clear relationship. For instance, when "spree murderer"
Andrew Cunanan terrorized the gay community a few years ago, the
FBI and other law enforcement agencies throughout the country were
reluctant to tie his killings to his homosexual orientation. In her book
*Vulgar Favors: Andrew Cunanan, Gianni Versace and the Largest Failed
Manhunt in U.S. History,* reporter Maureen Orth describes the failure
of law enforcement agencies to apprehend Cunanan—despite a
plethora of clues provided by his gay lifestyle. Although four San
Diego friends of Cunanan maintain that they had mentioned to the
FBI that he had known Gianni Versace long before the gay fashion
designer was killed, "Versace's name simply does not appear in any
FBI file prior to his murder."[37] Orth attributes many of these missed
opportunities to an unwillingness to antagonize the gay community by
linking Cunanan's murders to his homosexuality.

Not surprisingly, Orth was denounced for what one reviewer
called her "inability to hide her disgust for the gay community." The

Gay and Lesbian Alliance Against Defamation (GLAAD) placed her name on the "alert" page of their website (along with Dr. Laura Schlessinger and rap artist Eminem), and began publishing inflammatory articles about her writing. GLAAD also criticized the editors of *Vanity Fair* because the magazine gave an article based on Orth's book the title "On the Trail of the Gay Serial Killer," and took aim at *Newsweek*'s report on Cunanan because it contained "voyeuristic details" about his being an openly gay teenager.[38] *Newsweek* was accused of doing a "disservice to gay people, by implying that being openly gay, flamboyant and least likely to be forgotten in high school somehow foreshadowed the current state of affairs."[39]

TO CHANGE THE LINGERING perceptions of deviance that bedevil the gay community, Andrew Sullivan suggests that signs of committed and sustained relationships by "real" gay couples—not marketing artifacts—will be required. Sullivan believes that gays must stop assuming bigotry when confronted with disagreement about their lifestyle, and must live in a way that establishes their common humanity with the majority of Americans.[40]

Sullivan is harsh in his criticism of both the religious fundamentalists of the far right, and the academic cohorts of the Foucaultian "queer left" who enlist a liberationist politics that "seeks only to shock and anger."[41] He believes that the refusal of extremists on the left and the right to engage in the give-and-take of politics has impeded progress, and asks for what he calls the "politics of public equality" for homosexuals. Sullivan suggests that instead of automatically dismissing all who oppose homosexuality on religious or ideological grounds as homophobes, gays should seek dialogue. And instead of demanding special preferences from the state, they should ask only to be treated in the same way as any heterosexual. The politics he pursues would initiate a conversation between homosexuals and heterosexuals that focuses not on what one group owes the other, like a job or an apartment (or a special lunch table in the Harvard cafeteria), but rather on "what each can teach the other in the open context of a civil culture."[42]

Sullivan believes that marriage would provide "role models for young gay people, who, after the exhilaration of coming out, can too easily lapse into short-term relationships and insecurity with no tangible goal in sight." Institutionalizing gay marriage, he says, would reinforce a trend toward monogamy, and would "bring the essence of gay life, a gay couple, into the heart of the traditional family in a way

STIGMA AND SEXUAL ORIENTATION   107

the family can most understand and the gay offspring can most easily acknowledge."[43] The values of commitment, monogamy, marriage and stability are, Sullivan believes, models for homosexual existence.

National Journal writer Jonathan Rauch makes a similar argument that homosexual marriage provides an opportunity to ensure that homosexuality is "pro-social rather than anti-social." Rauch too believes that gay marriage could "transmute love into commitment. Love is often fleeting and crazy-making. Marriage is lasting and stabilizing.... Society stands to benefit when all people, including gay people, have this care and make this commitment."[44]

The movement to legalize marriage of same-sex couples has the potential to transform the debate by blunting the issues raised by promiscuity and unsafe sex. A recent article in the prestigious *American Sociological Review*—the flagship journal of the American Sociological Association—makes a powerful plea for a more flexible approach to marriage and family, while supporting the spread of gay and lesbian parenting. Sociologists Judith Stacey and Timothy Biblarz write, "Knowledge and policy will be best served when scholars feel free to replace a hierarchical model of the family, which assigns 'grades' to parents and children according to their sexual identities, with a more genuinely pluralist approach to family diversity."[45]

Assessing the effects of gay and lesbian parenting, Stacey and Biblarz found that there were indeed differences in outcomes for children raised in what they call "lesbigay" families as against heterosexual families; but they assert that these differences should not be viewed as deficits. They found no outcome differences in anxiety, depression or self-esteem. They did observe, however, that "sons appeared to respond in more complex ways to parental sexual orientation." On some measures, like aggressiveness and play preferences, "the sons of lesbian mothers behave in less traditionally masculine ways than those raised by heterosexual single mothers." Stacey and Biblarz saw major differences in the sexual activity of children raised in the lesbigay families.[46] Relative to their counterparts with heterosexual parents, the adolescent and young adult girls raised by lesbian mothers were "significantly more sexually adventurous and less chaste," whereas the sons of lesbians exhibited the opposite pattern, being "somewhat less sexually adventurous and more chaste." Most revealing, among young adults there were substantial differences in the proportions of those who reported having had a homoerotic relationship: 64 percent of those raised by lesbian mothers reported having considered same-sex relationships, compared with only 17 percent of those raised by heterosexual mothers. Stacey and Biblarz call these findings "provocative."[47] But they do not analyze the implications of such differences.

Gay marriage might be the final step in the effort to redefine the deviance of homosexual orientation. Yet because of the complexity of this issue and widespread resistance to its possible impact on the family and childrearing, this shoe may not drop anytime soon.

SEVEN

CELEBRATING THE SEXUALLY

ADVENTUROUS ADOLESCENT

O f all the contested terrain in the culture wars, the sub-ject of sex has attracted the most attention—and created the most contentious debate. Whether it is dis-agreement over homosexual "normativity," the type of sex education in our children's schools, or the portrayal of sex in popular culture, there seems to be an ongoing, often raucous conversation about sex in America. We seem, in fact, to inhabit a sexu-alized society. In middle school hallways, preteens pose and posture suggestively, while their older brothers and sisters mimic sexual inter-course on the dance floor as they freak dance at their high school proms. On many college campuses, condoms are distributed to first-year students long before they receive their first course syllabus—at the same time that the campus women's center is warning the female students that they, too, may be the "one in four" who will be date-raped that semester.

In *Ready or Not*, Kay Hymowitz suggests that the sex-saturated society we now inhabit is the result of baby boomers who expected they would be able to give their children a "healthy" outlook free of the Puritan hang-ups they believed had plagued their parents and grand-parents:

> They hoped that their daughters would no longer experience the fear and shame that had once shadowed the girl who had "done it," and

that they would be confident enough to admit, to act on, and to own their desire. This generation hoped that they would demystify sex, free it from the control of "church ladies" and what sexual reform advocates had long called the "conspiracy of silence." In this new world, sex would be better, and so would kids.[1]

The goal of liberation must have seemed a noble one at the time, but as with most utopian longings, there was a gap between idea and practice. In 2000, PBS's *Frontline* presented a disturbing documentary on what at one time would have been viewed as seriously deviant behavior among teens in the Atlanta suburb of Conyers, Georgia. Entitled *The Lost Children of Rockdale County*, the program described a syphilis outbreak among teens in this bucolic community. First detected in the spring of 1996 by a Conyers health clinic nurse, the mini epidemic eventually involved more than two hundred teenagers, at their core a group of girls who met together after school and in the early evenings to drink, use drugs and have a variety of sexual encounters, often in groups, with slightly older boys.

Normally, a syphilis outbreak would not be national news. But Conyers, an upwardly mobile middle-class suburb, was not typical of the areas where epidemiologists and social scientists usually find sexually transmitted disease (STD) outbreaks. The deviance of the group sex in conjunction with the demographics of the affluent town drew media attention. The *Frontline* program was shocking—especially for those who had moved to Conyers so they would not have to worry about their children's lives being touched by the problems of the inner city.

Many viewers and researchers dismissed the Conyers syphilis epidemic as an aberration. Feminists were especially critical of PBS for "sensationalizing" the story. But as Dr. Robert Blum, director of pediatrics and adolescent health at the University of Minnesota, asserted, "What is so disturbing about the events in Conyers was not that we are witnessing a rare event in the United States, but rather an event that is quite common."[2] Blum noted grimly that it took a syphilis outbreak before anyone noticed that alienated suburban children were out of control.

According to the Centers for Disease Control in Atlanta, the sexual activities usually took place in a "party environment" in the homes of the teenage girls during the late afternoon and early evening— between 3 and 7 P.M.—before parents arrived home from work. While most of the girls were between 13 and 15 years old at the time, some were as young as 12. The CDC wrote that "the sexual activity was usually communal: girls would most often have sequential and simultaneous sex partners."[3] Researchers studying the syphilis epidemic reported that "the sexual activity ranged from oral sex, to vaginal sex, to anal sex and to group sex." Initially, the girls said, they would try to provide some privacy for those who were engaging in sex, but eventually the behavior went on with others watching. This often evolved into some of the girls having sex with other girls, primarily for the enjoyment of the boys looking on. Eventually, the group activity included scenarios like the one in which one female teen simultaneously had oral sex with one male, vaginal sex with another, and anal sex with a third.[4] Most of the girls involved in these activities and the eventual syphilis outbreak identified multiple sexual partners. One girl reportedly had intercourse with more than twenty-five boys during a single evening's "party"; others acknowledged a total of more than a hundred partners each.

Multiple partners for teens is not rare. According to Hymowitz, national survey data indicate that more than 55 percent of sexually active adolescent girls admit having had multiple partners, and 13 percent report at least six partners.[5] In her own qualitative study, sociologist Lillian Rubin described teenage girls she had interviewed who described sexual activity with "forty, maybe fifty different guys."[6] Looking at trends in teenage sexuality, the Centers for Disease Control found that although the teenage pregnancy rate declined in the 1990s, the rate of sexual activity among females increased. In the mid-1950s, fewer than one-fourth of females under nineteen were sexually active. In 1982, 47 percent of female teenagers polled reported having had sexual intercourse, and by 1990, that figure had increased to 55 percent. In 1995, 61 percent of black female teenagers reported having had sexual intercourse.

Increasing numbers of girls—some of them as young as ten or eleven years old—were engaging in oral sex but not defining this behavior as "having sex." In a nonscientific online sex survey for *Twist* magazine, 25 percent of the more than ten thousand girls who responded to the survey acknowledged having had oral sex, some describing it as "something to do for fun." The results of this survey were validated by a Guttmacher Institute report indicating that health care providers have found dramatic increases in oral herpes and gonorrhea of the pharynx in teenagers. Dr. Robert Blum also found that these behaviors "transcend race and income and family structure and are much more widespread than we might have thought."[7] In other words, what used to be considered seriously deviant behavior for a child of ten or twelve years is now being redefined as normative.

In this light, the **PBS** documentary on Conyers, Georgia, was riveting not so much because of the deviance of the adolescent sexual behavior, which was eye-opening enough, but because of its larger implications for our view of life in the suburbs. The real story was one of lost children without limits or structure in their lives—a textbook example of the anomie that even a first-year sociology student would recognize as a determinant of deviant behavior.

Yet some of the professionals and academic "experts" interviewed for the Conyers documentary applauded **PBS** for "finally acknowledging that young women have sexual desires and fantasies similar to young men."[8] In fact, one of the respondents used the presentation not to attack the nihilistic promiscuity it revealed, but to take a swing at abstinence-based sex education programs. (The program in Conyers' schools is "abstinence-based" but provides additional information about sexuality.)

For Deborah Tolman, a senior research scientist and director of the Adolescent Sexuality Project at the Wellesley College Center for Research on Women, the real deviance was not preteen sex with multiple partners, but abstinence. She blamed the "poor" sex education program in the Conyers schools as having contributed to the syphilis epidemic because it "denied sexuality" to teens. According to Tolman, abstinence education was guilty because "students who have had abstinence education who subsequently become sexually active are much less likely to take precautions."[9] Tolman argues that a more comprehensive approach to sex education is more likely to lead to responsible and protected or "safe sex" with more use of contraception and condoms. The behavior in the Conyers homes might still have occurred, in other words, but we would never have known about it because there would have been no syphilis.

THE CHARGE THAT ABSTINENCE-BASED programs contribute to deviant behavior is common, if not necessarily commonsensical. Critics of such programs have contended that many of them "rely on instilling fear and shame in adolescents in order to discourage premarital sexual behavior." The authors of an article entitled "Scared Chaste: Fear Based Educational Curricula," for instance, assert that abstinence programs exaggerate the physical and psychological risks of early sexual activity, encourage intolerant attitudes about homosexuality, fail to provide teenagers with adequate information about contraceptives, and promote gender stereotyping.[10]

Defining abstinence as deviance is the other side of the coin that defines promiscuous sexuality as "healthy." Such a redefinition has actually been occurring in slow motion in America for more than three decades. Spearheaded by influential organizations like Planned Parenthood, the Sexuality Information and Education Council of the United States, and the National Organization for Women, a movement began in the 1960s with the goals of destigmatizing female sexuality and fighting the repression that prevented women from becoming "fully sexual." This feminist-led movement has campaigned for "equal access to sexuality" for women and teenage girls. The underlying message is that women are sexual beings from the day they are born, and need to learn to enjoy sex as much as men. From this perspective, sexuality is a "right" as well as a natural urge. In *Raising Sexually Healthy Children*, Lynn Leight writes that "We need to stop using the word should or should not with regard to teenage sexuality because this sets them up to feel guilty," and that society's obsession with virginity has made women lose touch with their "natural and true sexuality."

Despite efforts to stigmatize abstinence programs themselves as deviant, however, it is undeniable that these programs have had some success in reducing teenage pregnancy rates. In San Marcos, California, a 20 percent rate of teenage pregnancy declined to 1.5 percent within four years after the schools implemented an abstinence-only sex education program. A five-year study of the twenty-six schools using the "Sex-Respect" abstinence-based curriculum showed the pregnancy rate among teenage girls who had participated in the program to be 44 percent lower than that among girls who had not participated.[11] Despite such data, advocates of comprehensive sex education continue to charge that in addition to promoting "unsafe sex" and even causing deaths from AIDS, abstinence programs promote gender stereotypes by putting the burden of responsibility upon females to set the tone for chastity in relationships.

According to Deborah Tolman, the PBS program on the Atlanta suburb was gender-biased because it implicitly "denied female sexuality" by interviewing the girls only about their negative experiences, and it supported the view that "it is normal for adolescent boys (but not girls) to engage in wild sexual activity." She continues, "When the boys talk about sex in the program, it is to comment on the behavior of the girls, about whom they are socialized to observe, judge, talk about and treat disrespectfully if it is considered deserved. These boys report male sexual fantasies coming true over and over again in those empty houses."[12]

Tolman suggests that instead of abstinence, "we should teach girls that they are entitled to their own sexual desire or sexual pleasure, and, that 'good' and 'nice' girls are depriving themselves of a full life." Rather than teach girls to be the objects of others' sexual longings, we should advise them that "becoming a sexual person is a normal part of growing up."[13] Had the Conyers teens been given comprehensive sex education, as Tolman recommends, they would have used condoms, thus preventing the syphilis epidemic. There would have been no PBS program and we would never have known about the teen sex in the suburb.

Tolman's 1996 article entitled "How Being a Good Girl Can Be Bad for Girls" is a classic redefinition of deviance, in which what has been regarded as "good" is recast as "deviant" and what was seen as "bad" becomes "normal."[14] In a more recent article, "Femininity As a Barrier to Positive Sexual Health for Girls," Tolman argues that feminine and masculine ideals are problematic, creating rigid stereotypes that inhibit girls from truly enjoying their own sexual experiences and cause both boys and girls to "commodify" girls' sexuality. Tolman advises females to become "more like males" in their pursuit of sexual pleasure.

But in fact, as the Conyers episode showed, those girls who have become "more like males" in their choices for multiple partners and little intimacy suffer the greatest emotional harm. When the girls involved in the syphilis epidemic were asked if they were "getting to be more like boys," most said yes. One of them commented: "Some girls are starting to act like, 'I just wanted to have sex with him. Now it's over.'" Another said that "girls are just starting to feel the same way about using guys, because guys have done that so many times to them they are just doing the same." Yet another said: "Yeah, it's kind of like the girls are coming back and treating the guys like they treated us. Like, playing them, and going out with three different guys at a time instead of the guy going out with three different girls at a time." It would appear that these teens have already discarded gender stereotypes—without the liberating results that Tolman might have predicted.

Most viewers would not have been concerned about the "commodification of sex," the derogation of female teen eroticism, or other issues raised by some academics. They would have seen the Conyers teens as simply out of control. In fact, when the teenagers were interviewed for the documentary, most of the girls, far from feeling "sexually empowered," felt melancholy about their experiences. One fifteen-year-old girl said bluntly: "Sex sucks actually.... I think only guys are gonna benefit from it.... You're just like, get off me, what are you doing?" Another said glumly, "The first time you have sex, you think it's cause it means something. But, then you realize it doesn't. You just don't really care anymore. So that's pretty much how it is now."[15]

The words of the Conyers teens are echoed by many other sexually precocious teenagers. A 1996 national poll found that 81 percent of sexually active female teenagers age 15 to 19 wished they had waited. They expressed regret that they "felt pressured" to have sex before they were "ready."[16] Drained of emotion and authentic feelings, these "sexually adventurous" teens can be seen (as many see themselves) as victims of seriously misguided social policy on sex education and advocacy. They learned that the pleasure experienced from sex is not uncomplicated. And, while teenagers generally may not have been taught of the power and mystery of intercourse in their techno-sex education courses, the children of Conyers learned something of this from their afternoons of sexual nihilism.

In an interview, one of the girls sadly referred to herself as "evil." Others described their lives as having been "out of control."[17] The concept of good and evil was a frequent theme in the interviews posted on the PBS website after the show, as the girls constantly referred to their behavior not as liberated and "adventurous," but simply as "bad."

When asked whether their parents were aware of their activities, most responded that parents had no idea. One teenager said,

> Most of the time they didn't even know that I was doing drugs or that you know that I'd had sex. They didn't find any of that out until later. And when they figured it out, that's when they tried to jump in, but I really wouldn't let them. So I mean, it's completely not my parents' fault at all. I just would not let them you know interfere with what I was doing because that's what I like to do.

When asked if Conyers parents were "strict," the answer from those teenagers interviewed was nearly unanimous: their parents were "easy." One fifteen-year-old girl responded, "No, they're not strict. They're—we're pretty much like best friends or something. I mean I can pretty much tell them how I feel, what I wanna do and they'll let me do it." A second girl agreed: "She was more of a friend than a parent. She tried to be. She just tried different ways to get me to do right. And that was one of the ways she tried was to talk to me like a friend would."[18]

Although these teenagers talked about their parents being their friends, they still acknowledged little communication or even contact with them. When asked if they were close to their parents, most respondents said no. One explained,

> We don't—we never ate together. Maybe once every three months or something. I mean, we don't sit down and eat. Everybody just gets their plate and goes in the living room and eats…. We're kind of—it's just like another piece of the day. You just go fix your plate, eat, watch TV, finish watching whatever you're watching.[19]

Clearly these young people got little in the way of moral guidance from their parents to supplement the nonjudgmental, value-free sex education they had received in school since their elementary days.

ALTHOUGH THERE IS SUPPOSEDLY an abstinence base to the sex education now offered in public schools, in many classrooms this message is subverted. In some independent private schools, the sex education is unapologetically graphic. One sex educator at an elite school in southern California demonstrates various intercourse positions for her middle school students. One year, this same instructor provided information about the caloric content of sperm to weight-watching eighth-grade girls who presumably were engaging in oral sex. Countless suburban and urban schoolchildren learn not only that sexual feelings and behaviors are "normal," but that it is perfectly acceptable to enjoy these pleasurable feelings no matter what their age, provided they feel they are "ready."

To assist in determining whether they are indeed ready, Planned Parenthood has created a unique website to help teens "decide for themselves." *Teenwire.com*, advertised in such girls' magazines as *Seventeen, CosmoGirl, LatinGirl, Teenstyle* and *TeenVoices*, and in the more male-oriented video game magazine *GamePro*, invites teens to visit the website for information on "relationships." *Teenwire* assures teens, "This is your private place on the internet where you can get information and news about your sexuality, sexual health, and relationships. While you're here, be sure to register (choose an anonymous screen name) so that you can tell other teens what you think about all the stuff you see here."

Once at the website, a teenager is offered a quick survey to determine whether he or she is "ready for sex." Respondents can answer this question in minutes without interacting with another person. The website advises: "Frankly a web page can't decide for you if you're ready or not—but, neither can your best friend, boyfriend, girlfriend, parent, brother, sister, teacher, minister, counselor, rabbi—well you get the idea. The only person who can know when the time's right is you!" Teens are invited to "Take our quick poll, find out if you're ready to have sex, read other stories teens have written, or go get the answers to your most pressing questions about sex in *Yikes.*" *Yikes* is an Internet link connected to *Teenwire* that offers preteens graphic instructions on how to perfect sexual techniques like oral sex. Like *Teenwire, Yikes* encourages young people to "think through" the decision.[20]

It would be hard to find a young person visiting *Teenwire* who, after "thinking it through," was not anxious to declare himself or herself "ready." Most teens think they are "ready" for anything. Traditionally it has been precisely the job of the parents, or a counselor, teacher, priest or rabbi to help teenagers realize that they are "not ready." But in many sex education classrooms, students not only learn to reject such authority figures, but also to suspect that they themselves may be "weird" if they abstain from sex. Without the mediating moral messages that parents might have provided in the past, and without any guidelines on what might constitute "normal" and "deviant" sexual behavior, teenagers simply emulate what they see in popular culture. For example, the PBS documentary reported that a favorite activity for the Conyers middle school students was to watch the Playboy Channel together and then imitate what they saw on the X-rated programming.

The questions we ask of teenagers to some degree determine the behavior in which they engage. In *The Assault on Parenthood*, Dana Mack points to a survey that was administered (without parental permission) to middle and high school students in Falmouth, Massachusetts, which assumed sexual activity by all students. Of 39 questions addressing the sexual behavior of children as young as twelve years old, 24 implied that all respondents were sexually active. For example, the question "When did you first have sexual intercourse?" listed various grade levels as possible responses, but gave no opportunity to answer "never."[21] Any sexually abstinent teenager who took the survey was bound to feel isolated from his or her peers. Mack points out that the survey was filled with questions designed to force children to describe their part in behaviors that at one time would have been defined as deviant for youngsters of their age. One question asked, "What is the sex of the person(s) with whom you have had sexual contact?" Not only did the available answers again assume sexual activity, but assumed a broad range of sexual behaviors.[22]

"Remember there are no right or wrong answers—just your answers," says the textbook *Learning about Sex*. "You have noticed how the kinds of food you like and dislike are different from some of those other people like and dislike…. It is much the same with the sexual appetites of human beings."[23] In sex education courses, issues are posed in terms of what "most teenagers" or "many people" feel, believe or do. The attitude conveyed is ostensibly nonjudgmental, yet implicitly hostile toward chastity. Apart from the values and behaviors of peers, there is no other guidance available to many students whose parents are their "friends."

Hard-line feminist perspectives have also acquired authority for students and teachers in the field of sex education. According to feminist writers such as Carol Gilligan, Naomi Wolfe and Mary Pipher, prepubescent girls are fully at ease with their bodies and themselves. But "society" cannot embrace their sexuality, so upon entering adolescence they lose the "voice" of their own desire and become "denatured." To keep this from happening, girls need to realize their sexuality at adolescence by listening to what Gilligan calls their "sexual voices."[24]

This viewpoint, which contributes to the redefinition of adolescent sexuality, holds that sex, left to itself, would be "natural" and "healthy." It is only because society is repressive that sexuality becomes distorted. But Kay Hymowitz argues that this feminist/revisionist view of sexuality, part of an ideological program, ignores the fact that children's sexual desires are neither temperate nor rational. Freud posited that somewhere around six or seven years of age, children enter a relatively calm, asexual period called "latency," which lasts until the storms of puberty. Latency is essential for children in modern societies, for it is during this time that they are able to focus their energy on cognitive achievement. Freud warned that while some less-developed cultures give free rein to sexual curiosity throughout childhood, even very early childhood, these cultures have paid a great price in diminished achievement and moral development.

Freud is today considered passé, particularly his ideas about sex. In contrast, the ideas of moral development popularized by feminist philosopher Carol Gilligan have become the "dominant theory." For Gilligan, children should be left to their own devices while finding their moral way. While it may seem obvious to the average person that adults civilize children by teaching them the rules of morality and insisting that they restrain their antisocial impulses, Gilligan maintains that adults are actually part of the problem, not the solution.

Children are pure and easily corrupted by adult interference and mor-alizing; without the static of adult messages, they would find the clear channel of their desires. To "prove" her theory, Gilligan observed female students at a private school in Ohio, and from these observa-tions concluded that preadolescent girls are "more moral" than either their older peers or their parents and teachers. It is at the point that adults interfere, attempting to "civilize" them, that these girls begin to have problems. As they mature, their "innately moral self" is drowned out by the "foreign voice-overs of adults."[25]

Such theories of moral development permeate much sex educa-tion programming today. Aptly titled "Choices," for instance, Planned Parenthood's peer education program replaces the adult teachers or counselors with other teens. The Choices philosophy asserts, "We are sexual beings from birth; however during adolescence, these feelings intensify and grow. These can be wonderful, loving feelings of being attracted to someone else. Individual growth may result from an inti-mate relationship with another person." However, Choices also cautions that there can be negative consequences, including sexually transmitted diseases and unintended pregnancy, for sexually active teenagers. Peer counselors are empowered to help teens make the right choices and avoid harmful outcomes. Peer counseling also avoids the intrusion of "adult voices."

In San Diego's Planned Parenthood peer education program (TRACE: Teens Responding to AIDS with Care and Education), peer educators drawn from La Jolla Country Day School, an exclusive pri-vate school, mentor female students from San Diego High School, an inner-city school.[26] While these students may be chronological "peers," the demographics of the two high schools could not be further apart. Tuition at La Jolla Country Day School is more than $12,000 per year. Its student body stands in marked contrast to the ethnically diverse and much less affluent students at San Diego High School. While 100 percent of the students at La Jolla Country Day School take the SAT and go on to college after graduation, only 40 percent of San Diego High School's students take the exam and a far lower percentage attend college. Still, the La Jolla teens visit the San Diego High School campus every week to teach the inner-city teens about responsibility in making decisions pertaining to "family planning."

The decision to tap an exclusive school like La Jolla Country Day for the delivery of sex education services to the urban youth of San Diego was a calculated one. Correctly anticipating that the privileged peers would arrive at the inner-city school with a message of "responsible sex" and a never-ending supply of designer condoms in their Prada handbags, Planned Parenthood continues its historic commitment to educating the masses about birth control and "safe sex." The San Diego TRACE message is a powerful one: you too can be attractive and enjoy a sexually active lifestyle without consequences—just look at me.

SADLY, THE NEWLY BROADENED sexual repertoire and adventurousness acquired by teenagers has not always had the desired outcome. There are signs that by the time these sexually precocious adolescents reach college, much of the pleasure and excitement of meeting potential partners has vanished. Indeed, today's college students no longer date, or even make commitments to see one another.

A survey of one thousand college women recently reported in the *Chronicle of Higher Education* found that "the date, alas, is all but dead."[27] Only half of the female college seniors surveyed had been asked out on more than five dates throughout their entire college career, and one-third were asked out on no more than two dates. According to the study, the choices for women consisted of "hooking up," hanging out, or flying into full-fledged commitment, with dating a very distant fourth. The article concluded: "If Ali MacGraw and Ryan O'Neal, who played the protagonists in the film *Love Story*, met on a college campus today, they would have 'hooked up' at a fraternity party and gone their separate ways." And while adult feminists may continue to celebrate the "broadened sexual repertoire" of "sexually adventurous adolescents," fewer than 40 percent of the female college students in the survey indicated that they were happy with the social scene on campus. They had been left to make up the rules for themselves—without adult guidance by parents and college administrators, who have withdrawn from this traditional role.

Until recently, it was commonly accepted that society had an important stake in how its young people interacted with each other, found potential mates, and married. Dating was important because it "provided rituals of growing up, for making clear the meaning of one's own human sexual nature, and for entering into the ceremonial and customary world of ritual and sanctification."[28] Yet even more importantly, as Leon Kass wrote recently in the *Public Interest*, "Courtship disciplined sexual desire and romantic attraction, provided opportunities for mutual learning about one another's character, and fostered salutary illusions that inspired admiration and devotion. By locating wooer and wooed in their familial settings, courtship taught the inter-generational meaning of erotic activity."[29]

The decline of courtship, viewed as an aspect of the sexualization of society, seems to reflect broader cultural trends. As we have redefined our culture from one that celebrates "couples" to one that celebrates "sexually adventurous" individuals, some problems have occurred in the transition. This is especially true on college campuses, where attraction and mate selection are gradually being reconfigured. As we will see in the next chapter, confusion and lapses in communication increasingly are resulting in devastating allegations of "date rape," which serve to polarize the sexes and further threaten the possibility for positive male-female relationships.

EIGHT

RAPE,

REAL AND IMAGINED

Shortly after midnight on a spring evening in 1996, three hundred angry Bates College students gathered outside the home of President Donald W. Harward to demand that he finally confront a growing menace on their campus in Lewiston, Maine. Fearing that the crowd was getting out of control—one witness compared it to a "lynch mob"—local and state police were summoned.[1] The agitated (mostly female) students were demanding that something be done at once to eradicate an evil stalking the campus: the vice of date rape. Chanting the names of the "evildoers" on campus, the protesters claimed that if the college had acted sooner, it could have stopped the "raping" of innocent students. They demanded that the president confront the crime and banish the offenders from campus.

Fearful for his life, one of the alleged "date rapists" fled Bates on the night of the protest and immediately withdrew from the college. The hostile mob demanded that other offenders be similarly cast out. In response, college administrators took quick action—expelling one freshman after finding him guilty of raping a female student and twice sexually assaulting another, and suspending a twenty-three-year-old senior who had been accused of raping his ex-girlfriend, forbidding him from graduating with his class.

The *Chronicle of Higher Education* reported that none of the women who had filed complaints about date rape that semester had reported the incidents to the police. This did not stop the administrators and student representatives who comprised the college judiciary board from convicting the students. During the judicial proceedings, the accused students were not permitted to have lawyers at the hearings, nor were they allowed to call witnesses to testify on their behalf. Such star chamber procedures caused lawyers for the accused to claim that Bates College "acted in haste to appease the protesters, and has tarred innocent students as rapists in the process." The lawyer for the expelled freshman described the action against his client as "the culmination of more than a month of confusion, prejudice and finally hysteria on the part of the administration at Bates College."[2]

It is important to try to understand how it happened that men not only at Bates, but at Harvard, Columbia, Yale, Dartmouth, Villanova, Antioch, Notre Dame and other elite campuses were held guilty of this new form of deviance. And, even more important, to understand how smart, and once-strong and independent women on these same campuses are now redefining themselves as helpless victims, powerless to prevent someone they know from taking advantage of them.

In considering the moral panic surrounding date rape, we must acknowledge, as we did in the previous chapter, that there remain deep divisions over important issues in our cultural dialogue about sex. Contentious debate continues, even within the feminist movement itself, over questions of male-female sexual activity and the threat posed by males. Norms are in flux. And this ambiguity affords an opportunity to see the politics of deviance at work.

EVEN DURING THE MOST contentious moments of the culture wars over sex, there was a time, not so long ago, when we could rely upon at least one area of agreement: the deviance of rape. There was consensus that rape is an outrage that cannot be tolerated in civilized society—a serious violation of the selfhood and dignity of an individual, and uniquely horrible in the trauma it inflicts and the long-term consequences it has for the victim. Because of these strong perceptions of deviance, the sanctions for the rapist have historically been severe. At one time, the penalty for rape was death. Even today, in some states, conviction for "aggravated rape" or "capital rape" qualifies for capital punishment.[3]

Yet for the past decade, a powerful element within the feminist advocacy community has waged a moral crusade to expand greatly the boundaries of violence against women, and by doing so has called basic definitions into question. Like all redefinitions of deviance, the process began slowly with a gradual expansion of the use and eventually the meaning of the word "rape." Some feminists began using the word in referring to acts that are not even related to sexual activity, but to power. Feminist legal scholar and anti-pornography activist Catharine MacKinnon, for instance has long contended that depictions of sex through pornography are equivalent to rape. In *Only Words*, she claims that "pornography is literally a form of assault by expression. Protecting pornography means protecting sexual abuse as speech." For MacKinnon, a woman can also be raped by criticism. When a reviewer wrote a negative evaluation of her book, she accused him of rape. In an interview for *Time*, MacKinnon asserted that the reviewer "wanted me as a violated woman with her legs spread—he needed me there before he could address my work."[4]

Most of us dismiss talk of "rape by paragraph"—or the even stranger assertion by MacKinnon's comrade-in-arms Andrea Dworkin that even consensual heterosexual sex is "rape"—as mere hyperbole. Of course "rape" had to some degree always been used as a metaphor, but it has come to have decidedly nonmetaphorical consequences on some of our college campuses. The first time I recall the metaphor applied in a context where it had implications for institutional outcomes was more than a decade ago during an especially contentious faculty senate meeting on an East Coast college campus. An angry feminist colleague complained that we were "raping the curriculum" by our reluctance to mandate suggestions she had made for course requirements for our students. This perceptive colleague knew that the (mostly male) faculty senators would pay attention when they were accused of rape, even if only metaphorically. And they did, particularly when she claimed to have been "violated" by a faculty committee. The tenor of the meeting changed immediately, and each of her suggestions for courses in gender was approved as a general education curriculum requirement for undergraduate students.

On many campuses today, the line between the metaphorical and the literal has disappeared as allegations of rape can now be made following any unpleasant, awkward or regrettable sexual encounter between students. The "rapist" is any male who participates in these encounters. And being found guilty of a metaphorical offense carries real consequences, as male students are increasingly being charged with rape when a date goes badly.

Instead of the few dozen satanic day care workers of the 1980s, the "folk devil" of this contemporary moral panic is nearly any male college student who engages in sexual relations with a female student who is ambivalent at the time, or, more often, after the fact. And while girls may be taught to celebrate sex and sexual adventurousness in sex education classes at the outset of their schooling, when they arrive on campus as freshmen they are immediately warned that they too might be the "one in four" females who will be raped that semester.[5] As a result, the same females who as girls seemed to have been leading a conga line of sexual suitors in suburbs like Conyers, Georgia, suddenly as young women became afraid of every man on campus.

This is not to imply that sexual behavior is actually discouraged by colleges and universities. Quite the contrary. Like the middle and high school sex education curricula, most colleges also promote the idea of "celebrating sexuality"—as long as it is as carefully scripted as a legal contract. Instructions on sexual activity and sex codes abound on college campuses. In some cases, students actually receive what are called "sex survival kits." Including an assortment of condoms, the kit distributed at Stanford University also contains a "how to" booklet entitled the *Safe Sex Explorer's Action Packed Starter Kit Handbook*, with advice such as this: "Mutual masturbation is great—but watch out for cuts on hands or raw genitals. Use condoms for fucking; and, remember, with several partners, always clean up and change rubbers before going from one person to another."[6]

This liberated sex advice is paralleled by a contradictory feminist agenda that defines all men as potential rapists and all women as potential victims. On many campuses, rape is now defined within the orientation materials and lectures as "any sexual intercourse without mutual desire." In fact, most first-year students are cautioned during orientation that "anyone who is psychologically or physically pressured into sexual contact on any occasion is as much a victim as the person who is attacked on the streets."[7] National data indicate that more than 75 percent of these sexual encounters are not initially defined as rape by the woman.[8] But this is before the relationship ends badly, or before a meeting with an enlightened friend, or a dorm advisor, "crisis intervention" counselor, or student affairs administrator provides an interpretation in which what was originally an embarrassing or regrettable sexual encounter is relabeled as rape. Feminist advocates have successfully convinced a growing number of young female college students that before they have sex with a man, they must give consent as explicit as a Miranda warning. And a growing number of young women have been persuaded that when such stipula-

tions don't formally occur—as they rarely do in moments of passion—
then they too have been the victims of rape.

One date-rape case that drew national attention involved students at Brandeis University. David Schaer was a junior when a female
student accused him of raping her. The two had met while working on
the student newspaper and had started dating the previous summer.
The couple engaged in sexual relations once during that time, but
eventually the relationship ended. Schaer claimed that the sex was
consensual, and the alleged victim acknowledged in a deposition that
when she telephoned him and asked him to come to her room to "fool
around," she meant it as an invitation to have sex.

The *Chronicle of Higher Education* reported that the young man
found the woman quite aware of what was going on when he arrived
at her on-campus apartment. She also provided him with a condom.
Midway through the intercourse, however, she said she would like to
stop and switch to oral sex. Schaer claimed that he asked if he could
"just finish."

His accuser had a slightly different interpretation of events. In
published reports, she said that although she did indeed invite Mr.
Schaer over for sex, she was intoxicated, and was in and out of sleep
and awoke to find Schaer having sex with her. She claimed that she
told him to stop and asked him to leave. She acknowledges that after a
short conversation, he left the room.

More than a month after this encounter, Schaer learned that the
woman had filed a complaint against him and that he would face a
hearing before a campus judicial panel. As part of his prosecution, a
Brandeis police officer who spoke with the accuser one month after
the encounter was allowed to testify that the woman "looked like a
rape victim." Another witness was allowed to describe Schaer as a
"self-motivated egotistical bastard." In total, there were thirteen witnesses in the case—yet the school maintained only a twelve-line record
of the entire proceedings. Still, a judicial panel at Brandeis found
David Schaer guilty not only of "unwanted sexual activity," but also of
creating a "hostile environment" for the woman who had lodged the
complaint against him.[9]

Schaer attempted to challenge the way Brandeis handled the
date-rape allegation against him. However, he lost his suit in 2000
when, in a 3-to-2 decision, the highest court in Massachusetts ruled
that Brandeis University's judicial system did not need to provide students with the same constitutional protections that criminal courts
provide the accused. Ten other Massachusetts private colleges, includ-

ing Boston University, filed a brief in support of the Brandeis decision.[10] All of these campuses maintain that they do not have to
provide "due process" in student judicial proceedings surrounding
date rape.

Feminists insist that there is no distinction between the aggression associated with violent stranger rape and the quite different
context of most date rapes. But there are differences, and as the
Schaer case suggests, the most disturbing is that in most cases, the
violent stranger rapist would have more legal rights and due process
than the campus "date rapist." On most college campuses, an accused
person has no right to confront his or her accuser, confront or examine witnesses, or have an attorney present during university
proceedings. Instead, the "crime" is defined, judged and punished by
campus student affairs judicial boards. Such boards deliberate in
secret, provide no explanation of why or how they reached their decisions, and assign punishments without regard to any uniform
sentencing code.[11]

The year before the Schaer appeal was decided, as 250 students
protested outside, the faculty of Harvard University voted to expel a
student for his role in a date rape. The protesters were not defending
the student, but demonstrating against some professors who had
argued for a lesser punishment that would have acknowledged that his
wrongdoing was not the same as more violent forms of rape. The
voices of these recalcitrant faculty members were quickly silenced.

The alleged date-rapist, a Harvard sophomore, was lying in bed
with his accuser in April 1998, following a night of drinking. After
some sexual touching, but no intercourse, the woman fell asleep. As
she drifted in and out of sleep, the male student attempted to have sex
with her. In a hearing before Harvard's judicial board, the male student admitted responsibility for the activity. The board recommended
dismissal—giving the feminist advocates the victory they demanded
without considering the role that "tacit consent" on the part of the
victim had played.

A case at another college involved a young woman who brought
marijuana to a young man's dormitory. According to published
reports, she smoked marijuana with him and then went to his bed-
room. To the annoyance of students in the adjacent room, the couple
engaged in noisy sexual activity for several hours. Sometime during
the night, the female student later claimed, she awoke to find her partner touching her face and attempting to have intercourse with her
again. She told him to stop—and she agreed that he had stopped at

once. The next day, friends with whom she discussed what had happened told her that she had been raped, and referred her to the university office that dealt with crimes against women. Once the sexual encounter had been designated as "rape," the university charged the young man, found him guilty and expelled him. Campus activists pressured the local district attorney to bring a criminal charge of rape against him. It took a real jury about half an hour to acquit the young man.[12]

This new sexual hysteria has been fueled by advocates who have created a date-rape industry complete with "spokespersons" for the "survivors." A popular lecturer on the date-rape circuit is Katie Koestner, a self-described date-rape "survivor" who claims to have visited more than eight hundred campuses to warn female students of what lies in wait for them. Weaving advocacy data with graphic descriptions of her own traumatic experience of being date-raped during her first year at William and Mary College, Koestner typically calls on college students to fight for "a day without rape"—claiming that in the United States, 1.3 women are raped every minute.[13] In her lectures, Koestner tearfully testifies that her "life was forever changed" during the fall of her freshman year when, after going out with a student she calls "Peter," she invited him back to her dorm room with "intentions of dancing." Peter apparently had other ideas. By Koestner's account, "Tickling and teasing transpired into a wrestling match that night that left her on the floor pinned under Peter, with him holding her hands above her head by her wrists and kissing her even though she said 'no.'" Koestner admits spending the night with Peter in her room after this incident. "I can't tell you why I didn't throw him out of my room," she recalls, "Maybe it was because I thought he would just sleep it off and then go home in the morning. But when he awoke, he saw me huddled in the corner, and I hadn't slept all night."[14]

When she arrived on Harvard's campus to help women in their "Take Back the Night Week," Koestner began to meet some resistance when she called upon the men in the audience, as she frequently does, to stand up and declare their support for women in their fight against rape. Although many of the males in the audience obliged, some of the Harvard female students were offended that Koestner's focus on men took power out of their own hands. One of them was quoted in the *Harvard Crimson* as saying, "I thought her view of men as the only agents of change undermined her point, and just wasn't true." Another female student also objected to the focus on men: "I was deeply offended, I wondered if all the women in the audience should give up the fight."[15]

This response points to the real problem with the expanded definition of rape: it actually ends up removing power from women— creating, instead, female children unable to stand up for themselves and in need of protection by the kind of men who attend date-rape lectures, or by the emerging sex codes created by campus feminists and college administrators.

Activist Camile Paglia has written persuasively of the moral panic surrounding date rape.[16] In an interview for *Playboy*, she asserted, "Date rape has swelled into a catastrophic cosmic event like an asteroid threatening the earth in a fifties science fiction film."[17] Commenting on the furor created by Brown University women when they posted names of alleged rapists in the toilet stalls, Paglia says the media completely missed the real story: "Why were squalid toilets now the forum for self-expression by supposed future leaders? These sewer spaces, converted to pagan vomitoria, offer women students their sole campus rendezvous with their own physiology."[18] Paglia believes that "the fantastic fetishism of rape by mainstream and anti-porn feminists has, in the end, trivialized rape, impugned women's credibility, and reduced the sympathy we should feel for legitimate victims of violent sexual assault."[19] She summarizes the issue crisply: "When feminist discourse is unable to discriminate the drunken fraternity brother from the homicidal maniac, women are in trouble."[20]

Paglia knows, as most strong and independent women do, that when a real rape occurs, the woman should report it to the real police, not campus committees. Complaining that the real courts "take too long" or are "too cold and impersonal" is a pretext. But Paglia's message of personal responsibility has been rejected by a growing number of young women, as campuses persist in canonizing the "rape survivors" who, instead of delivering a message of strength and independence for women, remind them of their fragility and vulnerability.[21]

As long as rape victims are venerated on college campuses, it should not surprise anyone that allegations of rape continue to increase—and that the cases begin to involve the confabulation that characterized the panic over child abuse in day care. The most recent rape fabrication was quietly revealed at Iowa State University when Katharine Robb, a second-year student, finally disclosed that the story she had tearfully told her sorority sister—of being forced into a car at gunpoint by four black men and raped in a wooded area—was untrue.[22] Thinking it was an actual rape, the sorority's president reported the story to the police without Robb's knowledge. By then, Robb admits, she was "too caught up" in the lie to confess to anyone.

During the early days of the rape allegation, Robb received all the rewards that accompany such victimhood, as campus feminists rallied to her side, held demonstrations to warn other students, and demanded that prosecutors find the perpetrators. Robb briefly became a campus heroine, widely praised for her "courage" in coming forward to face the horrible crime. By the time she admitted to lying about the rape, the story had spun into a criminal case that wasted investigators' time and thousands of dollars in taxpayer money, while spreading increased alarm among other female students. At the conclusion of the trial, as Robb's feminist supporters disappeared, a judge sentenced her to eighteen months of probation, psychiatric treatment and a hundred hours of community service.

WHILE PRESUMED RAPE VICTIMS are the new celebrities on campus, those who have questioned the research methodologies used to further the redefinition of rape have become the new enemy. This includes scholars as well as students themselves. When Neil Gilbert, a professor at the University of California at Berkeley's School of Social Welfare, first read the campus feminists' often-quoted "one in four" statistic for the incidence of rape, he became skeptical and set out to analyze the study on which the figure was based. Like most sociologists, Gilbert knew that this figure differed dramatically from national data collected by the Department of Justice, which reveal an annual rape rate of lower than 12 percent—less than half the figure cited by women's advocacy groups.

In his research, Gilbert reassessed the survey data compiled by Dr. Mary Koss of Kent State University as a basis of her contention that 15 percent of respondents had been raped and an additional 12 percent had been victims of "attempted rape," yielding a 27 percent rate for rape, as Koss defined it. Her findings were published with great fanfare in *Ms.* magazine and then generalized nationally.

Gilbert concluded that the Koss study was seriously flawed. In addition to an inadequate sample, Gilbert noted several questions in the survey that were vague or likely to create uncertainty in the respondent's mind. For example, Koss defined as a victim of rape any respondent who answered "yes" to the following question: "Have you had sexual intercourse when you didn't want to because a man gave you alcohol or drugs?" Similarly, anyone who answered "yes" to the question "Did anyone ever try to have sexual intercourse with you when you did not want to?" was counted as a victim of attempted rape.

Pointing out that these questions were far too ambiguous, Gilbert asked, "What does having sex 'because' a man gives you drugs or alcohol signify? A positive response does not indicate whether duress, intoxication, force, or the threat of force were present, whether the woman's judgment or control were substantially impaired, or, whether the man purposefully got the woman drunk in order to prevent her resistance to sexual advance."[23] Likewise, there are many men who "try" to have sex with a woman who doesn't want it. How much effort in that direction constitutes attempted rape?

In addition to ambiguity in the questions and poor sampling strategies, Gilbert also pointed out that the majority of women Koss classified as rape victims did not believe themselves to have been raped. (Koss herself admits that more than 75 percent of the students she defined as victims of rape did not think they had been raped.) And 42 percent of the students in the Koss study had sex again with the men who allegedly raped them the first time. Yet despite these women's reluctance to define their experience as "rape" and their continuing voluntary relationships with their "rapists," the Koss figure of "one in four" remains sacrosanct.

When Gilbert published his critical analysis of the Koss study, feminist activists reacted vigorously, making him the target of demonstrations, boycotts and denunciations. A date-rape clearinghouse in San Francisco devoted itself to sending out masses of literature attacking Gilbert. This organization advertised its outrage against him at feminist conferences with green and orange fliers bearing the headline "Stop It Bitch." At one anti-Gilbert demonstration on the Berkeley campus, students chanted, "Cut it out, or cut it off," and carried signs that read, "Kill Neil Gilbert!"[24]

Those who remind women of their own strength and personal responsibility also often find themselves targeted as part of the problem. When "Dr. Ruth" Westheimer gave a talk at Stanford University, she was vilified for suggesting that it might not be "fair" for a woman to get undressed and engage in sexual preliminaries with a man and then decide later to say "no." She was attacked for what most people off campus would see as common sense: "If there is foreplay and there is passion—for somebody who does not want to engage in sexual activity, then to play like this with fire is just not fair and right." Campus feminists accused Dr. Ruth of teaching the acceptability of date rape. Her plea for personal responsibility was rejected as another instance of "blaming the victim."[25]

The reactions to Paglia, Gilbert, Westheimer and others who have questioned the date rape issue clearly show that the power to define deviance in this case now rests within an advocacy community that has spun off from the feminist movement. This is especially true on college campuses, where local chapters of national women's organizations and gay and lesbian organizations function to protect their faculty "assets," pressure university administrators to expand resources in their areas of interest, and redefine as crimes those behaviors they find offensive.

GIVEN THE HOSTILITY AGAINST males in colleges today, it should not come as a surprise that men are becoming more scarce on campus. Nationally, fewer than 45 percent of today's undergraduates are men. The ratios are even worse at some private colleges, where females outnumber males by as much as 3 to 1. The Department of Education reports that in 1996 there were 8.4 million women enrolled in college but only 6.7 million men. By 2007, the numbers are expected to be 9.2 million women and 6.9 million men.

While the feminism of the last four decades has contributed significantly to gender equity, a new brand of feminism dismisses evidence of accelerating female attainment and continues to stamp males as oppressors. Notwithstanding the depressing data about male college attendance, programs such as "Vision 2000," proposed by female faculty and administrators and endorsed by the presidents of six New England land-grant universities, continue to cast women as the endangered group. Vision 2000 made recommendations covering salaries, course content, research, teaching styles and campus life to address what these authors believe to be the continued oppression of women. Drawing on the language of oppression and rape, Vision 2000 claims that

> women face sexual violence and sexual harassment in the classroom and in the workplace, and are too often silenced by a system that protects the perpetrators of these crimes. Women of color, lesbians and women with disabilities are further marginalized. At the same time, since men are over-represented in the curriculum and in lead-

ership roles, a system of privilege and gender inequity is perpetuated.[26]

Under the Vision 2000 guidelines, all faculty members at each of the six land-grant universities would be evaluated on how well they integrate themes of gender into their coursework. Departments that can demonstrate "measurable progress" in gender equity would be rewarded, while others would be punished by loss of funding and faculty promotions. To guide this feminist overhaul, the designers of the initiative demanded that an autonomous Women's Studies Center oversee the process. Women's studies faculty were proposed to be the arbiters of university policy with rights of supervision over administrators, faculty, curriculum and programs.[27]

While programs such as Vision 2000 meet some resistance, the fact remains that many male students arrive on college campuses to find a female-friendly environment that is most unfriendly to them. *Men's Health* magazine recently named the ten most "male-unfriendly" campuses for men and warned that "men should be wary of institutions with large women's studies departments." The article characterized Brown as "smothered in half-baked feminism" and depicted schools like Antioch, Bates, Columbia, Dartmouth, Georgetown, Oberlin, UMass and UC Santa Cruz as "creating a climate in which men feel silenced and besieged." It is not surprising that the greatest numbers of date-rape allegations have occurred not at the Big Ten football schools or the large state universities throughout the nation, but instead on elite campuses like those named above. When the power to redefine deviance is concentrated in strong women's studies centers, men will always be suspect and imaginary crimes such as date rape will always be indistinguishable from the real thing.

It is difficult to predict where the politics of date rape will lead us. While the panic has diminished on some campuses, many others still hold on to their annual "Take Back the Night" rituals. Still, a recent case that has made its way to the U.S. Supreme Court may prompt college administrators to be a bit more careful about the shadow judiciary they have created on their campuses. In January 2002, the Supreme Court announced that it would decide a case pitting Gonzaga University against a graduate who says he can't get a teaching job because college officials told representatives of the state's teacher-certification office that he had been accused of raping another student.[28]

The former student, Ru Paster, denied that he had ever assaulted

the woman, and like nearly all cases of "date rape," he was never convicted of a crime. College employees had reported that the student said
she had been raped, but she did not file charges against Mr. Paster and
she denied in a videotaped deposition that he had sexually assaulted
her. Nonetheless, Roberta League, Gonzaga's certification specialist,
revealed the allegations to officials at the Washington State teacher-
certification office. Gonzaga also refused to submit a statement of
good character required for Paster to be certified.

Paster sued the university for negligence, defamation and inva-
sion of privacy—and a state court jury awarded him $1.5 million.
While the state court of appeals overturned that decision, the Washington State Supreme Court reinstated the $1.5 million award, ruling
that Gonzaga had violated Paster's privacy and civil rights by reporting
the information in his educational records. Gonzaga has brought the
case to the Supreme Court, claiming that students have no right to sue
colleges following a violation of the privacy law. While not directly
dealing with the kangaroo courts that now flourish on many college
campuses, this case may indeed have an impact on the information
that colleges may disclose about their students—especially when the
information involves unsubstantiated, panic-driven allegations of date
rape.

NINE

A DEATH

OF ONE'S OWN

S uicide has traditionally been viewed as a deviant act because it contributes to a climate in which individual life is devalued. If the person committing suicide does not think life is worth living, why should others in the community? For this reason, the norms surrounding suicide have been powerful. Most societies have recognized that suicide is not simply an act of violence against the self, but a violent force in the lives of others as well—so much so that even the most isolated or troubled individual has been legally forbidden to commit this act. In England, suicide was once regarded as so damaging to society that the penalty for attempting it was a cruel death![1]

While we have moved beyond such a paradoxical response, the belief that suicide is deviant has until recently remained strong. But there are indications that this is beginning to change. On September 10, 2000, Bill Moyers introduced a four-part PBS series on "end of life concerns," entitled *On Our Own Terms: Moyers on Dying*, by cautioning views that we need to make "hard choices" about our lives and our deaths—and that we must "take charge" of these decisions. On the third program in the series, entitled "A Death of One's Own," suicide is embodied not by a kooky (and spooky) Jack Kevorkian, but by a benevolent, Birkenstock-wearing Oregon physician who softly speaks the language of choice as she discusses her state's "right to die" law and allays our fears of death. The Moyers team reassures viewers that we too can avoid the loss of control that death might bring if only we will make the "hard choices" about the end of our lives.

The program presents heartbreaking vignettes of people struggling with terminal illnesses, chief among them a once-strong veterinarian now debilitated with the degenerative Lou Gehrig's disease (ALS). Viewers learn that the man is planning to take his own life in order to avoid the slow death by suffocation that he faces. But he lives in Louisiana, a state without an assisted suicide option. In labored speech, the struggling man laments: "If I lived in Oregon, I could live longer, knowing that my doctor would help me die. But, since I live in Louisiana, I will have to kill myself sooner, when I can do it myself, rather than later, when my doctor would have been allowed to help me." The message is clear: It just isn't fair that some of us can have "a death of our own," while others are forced to die according to society's rules. Indeed, most of those interviewed for Moyers' program seem to agree that it is cruel to refuse to help this kindly veterinarian die after he has "spent a lifetime of kindness to animals by putting them out of their suffering when it was needed."[2]

The producers' decision to highlight an ALS sufferer was most likely a calculated one. The first televised act of euthanasia in the country was that of Thomas Youk, an ALS victim who was euthanized by "Dr. Death," Jack Kevorkian. In broadcasting his death on *60 Minutes*, Mike Wallace described Youk as the "poster boy for euthanasia," implying that because of the particular horror of the disease, surely no one would deny the relief of suicide to an ALS victim. *60 Minutes* viewers were told that ALS victims "choke to death," and while Kevorkian was later charged and convicted of killing the patient, the program unambiguously conveyed the view that a "merciful death" is truly an act of mercy.

At the same time that Thomas Youk was meeting his end at the hands of Kevorkian, many other ALS sufferers—including, for example, sociologist Morris Schwartz—were dying in a natural and dignified way from the disease. Schwartz, whose advance through the terminal stages of ALS was as well recorded as Youk's, provides a compelling contrast to the dreary death televised on *60 Minutes*. Indeed, in the best-selling *Tuesdays with Morrie* by Mitch Albom, readers are introduced to a debilitated but still vibrant man who died surrounded by friends and family. We learn that Schwartz died quietly, as most ALS patients do, "when the muscles of respiration slowly fail and the patient is gradually narcotized from the accumulation of carbon dioxide."[3] Such information was not available to the viewers of the lurid spectacle on *60 Minutes.* Nor did this program or Moyers' PBS special advise desperate patients and their families that proper medical care through hospice or other providers can spare people like the anxious ALS sufferer from the terrifying death he fears. Dame Cicely Saunders, the creator of the modern hospice movement, personally treated hundreds of ALS patients and always claimed that with proper care, they can be kept comfortable until they reach a peaceful death.[4]

The campaign to elevate suicide to an issue of "choice" was begun during the 1960s, like many of the other advocacy movements described in earlier chapters of this book. As social critics like Roger Kimball have pointed out, the work of Herbert Marcuse and the Frankfurt School of Marxist intellectuals popularized during that decade produced a vision of emancipating us from all anxiety—including anxiety over what Marcuse called the "inconvenient reality of death." Marcuse argued that "the meaning of death must be changed" and made "rational." He said, "Men can die without anxiety if they know that what they love is protected from misery and oppression. After a fulfilled life, they may take it upon themselves to die—at a moment of their own choosing."[5]

As in other aspects of the politics of deviance, the redefinition of suicide began with an effective campaign to market the "right to die" as a matter of rational choice. But death is a difficult sell—even with the most creative television infomercials—and suicide, however "rational," remains contested ground. Our ambivalence about it is evident in the fact that while voters throughout the country are being presented with an ever-increasing number of assisted suicide bills like the one passed in Oregon, the surgeon general was issuing a report with a warning about the "dangerous increase in suicide deaths" and implementing a fifteen-point plan to reduce suicide, "one of our most pressing public health concerns."[6]

We live in a time when there is "good" suicide and "bad" suicide. People are now called upon to compartmentalize these kinds of suicide, differentiating between those who kill themselves for the "right" reasons and those who do so for the wrong reasons. People with a terminal illness, like the ALS sufferer on "A Death of One's Own," are viewed as justified in committing suicide, while disturbed teenagers who shoot or hang themselves are not. Yet as this chapter will argue, the line between the two is far less definitive than it may seem.

BEST-SELLING BOOKS LIKE Derek Humphry's *Final Exit,* Betty Rollins'

Last Wish and Anna Quindlen's *One True Thing*, which define taking one's own life through suicide as the rational and courageous choice, contribute to what must now be seen as a culture of suicide. Today there are estimated to be more than a hundred thousand suicide sites on the Internet. Many are highly graphic, appealing to the voyeur even more than the sufferer, with copies of suicide notes, death certificates and color photographs designed to encourage self-destruction.[7]

Wesley Smith, in *Culture of Death*, argues that the responsibility for the growing support for suicide lies, in large part, with a culture that has been persuaded to view it as just another option that should be available to those who desire dominion over every aspect of their lives. However, Smith also suggests that this emerging suicide culture is given credibility by the new field of bioethics, whose radical notion of autonomy has helped make suicide respectable. He points out that many university and medical bioethics classes and professional articles and symposia claim that there are two kinds of suicide: those that should be prevented, and the "rational suicides" that should be respected, perhaps even facilitated.[8] This duality, Smith asserts, is now widely promoted not only within mainstream bioethics, but also among allied psychiatrists, psychologists and social workers—people who used to serve as the last line of defense in protecting suicidal people from their self-destructive desires:

> Under the theory of rational suicide, mental health professionals have a duty to stop suicides only if they are impulsive or frivolous. If the suicidal person is deemed to have a rational basis for self-destruction, the professional's primary duty is to help sort out the pros and cons of self-destruction nonjudgmentally and to assist the patient in the use of proper decision making techniques.[9]

From this perspective, the proper role of the mental health provider is not to strenuously argue the suicidal individual out of ending it, but to prepare the way.

Even those like the surgeon general who profess to be concerned about the growing number of "bad" suicides, especially among the very young and the very old, appear to ignore the role of culture and social structure in normalizing these suicides. Because self-destruction seems so obviously an individual act—the act most saturated with self that a human being is capable of—most of those who study suicide today believe that its causes are lodged in the depths of the individual's personality. Nearly all of the current published work on suicide and suicide prevention analyzes the phenomenon from a psychological or psychiatric perspective.

On the other hand, Herbert Hendin's *Suicide in America* claims that the dramatic increase in youth suicide is due "almost solely to the wider availability of guns."[10] To prevent suicide, he recommends a renewed commitment to gun control.[11] But he neglects to mention that gun deaths overall in the United States have been declining each year for the past decade, at the same time that the suicide rate continues to rise.[12] Ignoring the cultural fallout from the increasing propaganda on behalf of "good" suicide, Hendin's approach would impose structural impediments to make the suicide's task more difficult. He argues for such things as a guarded fence on the Golden Gate Bridge, a favorite jumping-off spot. But only 2 percent of all suicides in the U.S. each year are accomplished by jumping from a high place, while nearly 20 percent result from hanging, strangulation or suffocation. Wouldn't it therefore make more sense to restrict the sales of rope and plastic bags?

In fact, plastic bags have become the new weapon of choice for those who desire to kill themselves. They are most often used as a backup to ensure death for those who first take an overdose of pills and want to make sure they die. One suicide advocacy group even sells plastic bags with "flannelette lining" and velcro fasteners at the neck for "added comfort."[13] The availability of such macabre products and the proliferation of how-to websites are indicators of the cultural shift that has occurred in this country.

FOR A SOCIOLOGIST, THE CAUSES of suicide have nothing to do with the paraphernalia of death, but reside in the social structure and in the norms and beliefs of the culture. The suicidal impulse, moreover, is rooted less in the mind of the suicide victim than in group values. The decision to commit suicide is (as Emile Durkheim put it) "endowed with coercive power, independent of individual will."[14]

It was Durkheim, more than a hundred years ago, who first provided sociology with its raison d'être when he argued that social phenomena such as suicide rates can be adequately explained only through an analysis of social conditions, including the breakdown of norms that operate throughout a society. Durkheim's approach is described by contemporary social scientists as "radically sociological," because he was the first to insist that the theorist remain at the societal level of analysis rather than seek psychological or biological causes.[15]

In his classic book *Suicide*, Durkheim argued that while values, attitudes and beliefs about suicide may appear to be individually constructed, it is a collective force that moves individuals toward self-destruction. The individual pulls the trigger of the gun that ends his life, or chooses to jump from the Golden Gate Bridge, yet a number of social and cultural factors determine the likelihood of his climbing onto the guard rail, or putting the gun to his head in the first place.[16] While the individual is ultimately responsible for the act itself, sociology has until recently focused on the social forces that underlie it.

Durkheim argued that if suicide were purely an individual act, then the relative number of people who killed themselves each year should be the same in every social environment. But he discovered that suicides followed more variable (and predictable) patterns.[17] The first social scientist to construct elaborate statistical models in analyzing data, he demonstrated that the annual suicide rate is both relatively stable in a given society and perceptibly different from one society to another. He concluded that suicide can never be viewed as a purely individual event, a random act of will. On the contrary, the moral constitution of a society and its degree of integration or regulation establish its "natural aptitude" for suicide. The resulting rates of suicide are predictable—and amenable to change through social and culture shifts.

When Durkheim examined suicide death records in his pioneering research, he also found differences by religion, marital status, economic status, and degree of social integration. For instance, he found that Protestants had higher suicide rates than Catholics, and that Jews had the lowest rates of all. He found that males were significantly more likely to commit suicide than females, that elderly people had higher rates than the young, and that the rate was higher among single, widowed and divorced people than among the married. And he discovered that suicide rates climbed in times of economic crisis and fell during times of political crisis. Durkheim reasoned that these differences reflected forces that went far beyond individual personalities and troubles.[18]

He ruled out individualistic psychopathological causes by looking for relationships between mental illness and suicide, and found that suicide rates for each society he was studying showed no correlation with the rate of individual pathology. It must be acknowledged that there are differences in the way psychopathology is defined and measured across societies. Yet Durkheim maintained that while a psychopathic state may predispose individuals to commit suicide, it does not sufficiently explain the variability of suicide rates from one society to another.[19]

To understand these variable rates, Durkheim considered purely cultural factors—shared ideas about suicide that might explain the differences. Yet there was no reason to believe that married people within a specific society or culture should disapprove of suicide in principle more than single people in the same culture. And what to make of the fact that while Catholicism views suicide more harshly than Judaism, Catholics had a slightly higher suicide rate than Jews?

Durkheim then turned from cultural factors to the social structure. In particular, he became interested in the degree of social cohesion among people in different social categories, and he found that when social bonds are weak, people are more likely to kill themselves. Protestants stress independence and individualism, while Catholics historically have stressed a more active involvement with other members of their communities. A history of oppression has encouraged even greater social cohesion among Jews. Men are less likely than women to be embedded in social relationships of care and responsibility, leaving them more prone to commit what Durkheim identified as "egoistic suicide." Because marriage integrates people into primary groups—the marital couple, the family of in-laws, close friends of the spouse—married people are less likely to kill themselves than the unmarried.[20]

Durkheim's data showed that individual acts of suicide are extensions of underlying societal currents. The term he employed in making this argument, "collective tendencies," did not simply mean averaged-out individual states. Collective tendencies become social forces that dominate the consciousness of individuals and affect all kinds of behavior, including the motivation to commit suicide. What Durkheim demonstrated in 1897 is still true today: the stability and predictability of the suicide rate for any particular society is caused by social factors and can have no other explanation. This is why dramatic change in the culture or social structure will have an equally dramatic impact on suicide rates.

Analyzing contemporary rates of suicide, we can see the same patterns that Durkheim found. There is still variability among countries and within countries, and there is predictability: those societies with strong social bonds have low suicide rates, while those that have experienced rapid social change or have little social integration through religion or shared beliefs have very high rates.

Sociologists have always known that what gives society its cohesion is a system of shared beliefs, values and ideas. These can be based on religion, nationalism, close community ties, or other factors; but they are always moral in character. They enable others to learn the norms, values and appropriate behaviors of the culture. The question of how such values collapse and are replaced during periods of social change was the focus of Durkheim's work. He saw that the breakdown of values results in anomie, a condition of social lawlessness and personal disorientation, and he proposed that deficiency or ambiguity in social norms leads to an increase in suicide.

With these propositions in mind, we should not be surprised that contemporary rates of suicide are highest in those countries undergoing the greatest social change, such as the former Soviet Union. While the United States has a troubling annual rate, 11.3 per 100,000 persons, it is moderate compared with nations affected by the dramatic political upheaval that followed the fall of communism. While males in the United States commit suicide at an annual rate of 18.7 per 100,000, Lithuania leads the world with a male suicide rate of 73.7 per 100,000.* The Russian Federation rate for male suicides is second, at 66.4, with Belarus (63.4), Latvia (59.8), Estonia (59.4), the Ukraine (51.7) and Slovenia (49.3) close behind.[21]

On the other hand, while Albania might be expected to have a high suicide rate due to the political turmoil associated with its recent emergence from totalitarianism, that country has a relatively low rate (2.9) because it has maintained social integration through the strong influence of a religion that places high moral demands on individuals and provides meaning even in the face of dramatic change. Countries with strong social integration and shared religious or cultural values— even in the face of rapid social change—have extremely low suicide rates. The lowest rates for male suicide are in Jordan (0.02), Egypt (0.1), the Syrian Arab Republic (0.2), Peru (0.6), Jamaica (0.5), Iran (0.3) and Guatemala (0.9).[22]

Countries in economic transition like Ireland and Scotland are experiencing alarming increases in suicide rates. In the 24–45 age group, the suicide rate among Scottish men has more than tripled since the 1970s.[23] Ireland is experiencing an even greater increase in the rate of suicide among males—even as the Irish economy expands. Indeed, despite tremendous growth in the technology sector and a greatly improving overall economy throughout Ireland, the suicide

---

* Suicide rates are calculated by dividing the number of suicides in a population by the size of the population and multiplying the result by 100,000. In most countries, males have rates of suicide that are more than four times that of females.

rate in the Republic increased more than sixfold since 1970—from a low of 1.8 suicides per 100,000 in 1970, to 11.7 per 100,000 in 1998.

Suicide in Ireland and in Scotland is primarily a male phenomenon. Likewise, in the United States, white males account for more than 73 percent of all suicides, and white males and white females together account for more than 90 percent of all suicides nationwide.[24] White males have an annual suicide rate of 20.9, while white females have a rate of 4.5. Black males have a suicide rate of 11.4, and black females have the lowest rate of all, 2.0. Older Americans (over 65 years of age) have a high rate of suicide, at 17.3. The highest rate is among what demographers call the "oldest old," white males over 85 years old, whose rate is 65.3 for every 100,000—comparable to the rate for males within the former Soviet Union.[25]

Suicide rates within the United States follow many of the same patterns as those shown among different countries. The states with low levels of church attendance and affiliation, and comparatively high levels of divorce, migration and social flux, show consistently high suicide rates. For the past decade, as the western mountain states have experienced tremendous in-migration and social change, suicide rates have risen. The rate of 17.2 per 100,000 people in the states of New Mexico, Arizona, Colorado, Utah, Nevada, Idaho, Wyoming and Montana is nearly double the 9.6 rate in New England. Nevada, which was named in a recent geographical mobility survey as the number one destination for those who "move for work," has also experienced the highest suicide rate in the country each year for the past decade (twice the national average).[26] Nevada also ranks poorly on nearly any index of social well-being: the highest adult smoking rate, the highest death rate from smoking, the highest percentage of teenagers who are high school dropouts, the highest teenage pregnancy rate and so on.[27]

Skeptics might conclude that losses by gambling tourists are driving the rate of suicide in Nevada, but the reality is that 95 percent of those who kill themselves in the state are Nevada residents, not outsiders who come there just to play.[28] According to Bob Fulkerson, state director of the Progressive Alliance of Nevada, an umbrella lobbying consortium of forty-five organizations including labor and civil rights groups, the state's "Wild West culture" and a high degree of geographical mobility contribute to the high suicide rate. "We have 10,000 people moving here each month and roughly 5,000 moving out, so lack of community and lack of connection to one another is a huge factor. This is the Wild West. The feeling is that if you can't pull yourself up by your bootstraps, then it's your own damn fault." Cultural norms of self-efficacy and autonomy, combined with the high turnover in population, have resulted in anomic conditions in Nevada.

In contrast, Washington, D.C., has enjoyed the lowest suicide rates in the nation for more than a decade. This may at first be puzzling because during that same decade, the nation's capital has also experienced an epidemic of teenage pregnancy and unmarried parenthood, high dropout rates, and among the highest homicide rates in the country. All of these variables are normally predictive of the anomie that leads to a high rate of suicide. Yet a large population of African-Americans, who historically have had an extremely low suicide rate, can be viewed as a partial explanation for the low rate in D.C., 6.6 per 100,000.

Durkheim would have predicted that the history of shared oppression suffered by African-Americans has largely inoculated the community against suicide. However, in a departure from Durkheim, some sociologists maintain that homicide and suicide represent aggressive responses linked by the common cause of frustration. Suicide thus represents inward aggression and homicide represents outward aggression.[29] From this theoretical perspective, those who view the source of their frustration as arising from sources external to themselves are more likely to commit homicide, while those who internalize their rage commit suicide. It is difficult to say which of these theories can explain the historically low rate of suicide for African-Americans. However, from the classically Durkheimian social-structural perspective, their tight social integration within their neighborhoods has provided the strong bonds that virtually will not allow suicide.

IT IS AGAINST THIS BACKDROP that the contemporary debate over the deviance of suicide takes place. Anti-suicide laws do much more than simply affirm the sanctity of life; they also establish and support social boundaries. While we might be "seduced by death," in Herbert Hendin's phrase, most societies have recognized that suicide must not be encouraged through downgrading the deviance of the act.[30] The will to live is a basic prerequisite not only for individuals, but also for groups and societies.

Durkheim argued that one reason that suicide has historically been so severely punished is that the entire social order is threatened by it. Judging suicide as deviant is thought to affirm the collective beliefs of the society, reinforce social order, and inhibit future suicides.

Stigmatizing suicide is how the community reaffirms its values and fosters solidarity.

In earlier times, evil spirits capable of possessing an individual were thought to be the cause of suicide. Such notions gradually evolved into explanations based on individual psychology, and then into our current medicalized model. And as we have seen throughout this book, once deviant behavior is medicalized, the stigma is soon removed from it.

Indeed, as in the medicalization of drug and alcohol abuse, contemporary perspectives of "irrational" suicide draw on a biological and biochemical perspective. Genetic factors are increasingly viewed as key to understanding the significantly higher rate of suicidal behavior in certain families—although it might also be possible to look at the ways in which a family member's suicide gives tacit permission to others in the family to do the same. But the medical model is in the ascendant.

Brain serotonin levels as a predictor of suicide has been the subject of intense research over the past several years. (Those with low levels of serotonin are viewed as most "at risk.")[31] Proponents of this biochemical perspective maintain that if only we would "listen to Prozac" or any of the similar antidepressants known as selective serotonin reuptake inhibitors (SSRIs), we would certainly reduce our rate of suicide. But as Herbert Hendin points out in *Suicide in America,* despite the popularity of this newer class of antidepressants, it is still true that many who kill themselves do so only after their depression has lifted somewhat in response to medication. These victims who were "successfully treated" with antidepressants must serve as a reminder that factors other than depression are involved in suicide, and that "severity of depression is a poor predictor of suicide risk."[32]

In fact, even Kay Redfield Jamison, one of the strongest proponents of the biochemical explanation for deviant behavior, admits that suicide takes too much effort when one is "curled up in a ball." She acknowledges that "suicide takes a little more clarity, a little more energy and sometimes, a little more cunning." Suicide is more complex than we may realize, she notes, and the smarter, better-informed patient is often the one who is more likely to be successful in ending his life.

Hendin's *Suicide in America* and Jamison's *Night Falls Fast* are symptomatic of the shifting definitions of suicide in that neither pays attention to the sociological dimension of suicide. However, the sociological data are becoming much more difficult to dismiss now that a pro-suicide culture has emerged. It is clear that the movement to make suicide acceptable has succeeded by influencing the subtle and sometimes not so subtle changes in societal values and norms that might block such deviance.

The Hemlock Society has taken the lead in marketing suicide for more than twenty years. Society founder Derek Humphry has traveled throughout the country with his message of "rational" suicide, primarily targeting senior citizens. In February 1997 the *Los Angeles Times* reported on Humphry's presentation to more than two hundred residents of Leisure World, Orange County's senior community, of the "options" for suicide open to them. Humphry reminded those in attendance that the Hemlock Society's first member, back in 1980, "when the group was considered a crazy suicide club," was Shirley Carroll O'Connor, a Leisure World resident, and that Leisure World's Hemlock Society now had more than a hundred members. According to the *Times* reporter, however, "the Leisure World crowd was less interested in the group's history than in learning the nuts and bolts of death with dignity from the activist famous for helping his first wife kill herself by drinking a poisoned cup of coffee."[33]

Today, an ever-increasing number of advocacy groups with names like "Compassionate Friends" or "Compassion in Dying" provide volunteers to help those who seek assistance in suicide. Several of these groups offer handbooks and recipes for a quick and painless death. The Hemlock Society's "Caring Friends Program" provides volunteer mentors to work with dying members who want "someone to provide support, comfort and information as they die."[34] Applying the marketplace metaphor, one would have to say that anxious consumers, worried about a painful or protracted death for themselves and their loved ones, provide a receptive audience for the marketing of the "rational choice" of suicide.

Assisted suicide advocates have successfully advanced their cause with compelling stories of suffering patients whose last hours were eased by a courageous family member who assisted with the suicide. In *Last Wish*, journalist Betty Rollins chronicles her role in helping her mother take her own life. Book reviewers throughout the country praised the book as a document of "personal compassion and public importance." One review commented, "The book was not really about death. It is instead, a loving tribute to a mother and daughter's spirited progress through life."

Rollins describes her assistance in the planning and implementation of the act as initially "upsetting." But after a short time, she says,

"I got up and blew my nose and came back and sat down. Then we resumed our plotting." The plotting involved stockpiling and later administering a deadly dose of pills, described in detail as "Compazine followed by 20 tiny 100 mg tabs of Nembutal, chased by Dalmane, washed down with soda water."

There are dozens of similar stories of assisted suicide in books and magazines. In fact, a 1995 article in the *New Yorker* by Andrew Solomon entitled (like the PBS series) "A Death of One's Own" drew national attention to assisted suicide as a "rational" choice. The chilling article describes the suicide of Mr. Solomon's mother in the late stages of ovarian cancer. Solomon recounts how the entire family, including his father and brother, were present at the time his mother took her fatal overdose of Seconal. Solomon claims to have supported his mother's decision for "rational" suicide, and writes that his entire family, including his mother, had supported assisted suicide and euthanasia in principle. In fact, Solomon recalls that several years before her cancer diagnosis, his mother had expressed to her family her desire eventually to die this way.

Yet Solomon's ambivalence comes through clearly.[35] The "comfort of control" that his mother exerted gave her solace, he says, but "the fact is that a suicide is a suicide—over determined, sad and somewhat toxic to everyone it touches."[36] He writes that he rarely talks with his father or his brother anymore. The family appears to have fallen apart in the aftermath of the suicide. And in his best-selling book called *The Noonday Demon: An Atlas of Depression*, written ten years after his mother's suicide, Solomon details what seems to have been a futile effort to treat his own depression through a regimen of sometimes more than a dozen pills a day, including, at one time or another, Zoloft, Paxil, Navane, Effexor, Wellbutrin, Serzone, BuSpar, Zyprexa, Dexedrine, Xanax, Valium, Ambien and Viagra. Having participated in his mother's death, Solomon admits that he too has viewed suicide as an option to escape his psychic pain. In fact, he writes that he tried to contract HIV by having unprotected sex with male strangers—not to die of AIDS, but to have a reason to kill himself. In the ambiance created by the suicide of one family member, others receive tacit permission to do the same. "Euthanasia breeds euthanasia" is how Solomon describes the "toxic environment" of assisted suicide—just as a Christian might claim that "sin breeds sin."[37]

In fact, the barrage of pro-suicide messages in the media has led even Herbert Hendin to finally acknowledge, in *Seduced by Death*, that we are witnessing a "selling of suicide." Hendin cites the ways in which the media invisibly redefines suicide: from an issue with broad social consequences to simply a matter of individual choice. He refers to recent books advocating assisted suicide as "marketing tools" and identifies the "marketing technique" of using short case reports, limited to one or two paragraphs focusing on the medical symptoms and unbearable suffering that the potential assisted suicide patient has endured. And he acknowledges that these accounts usually leave out the social context in which euthanasia is being considered, obscuring the complex and often subtle pressures on patients' allegedly autonomous decisions to seek death.

Words like "empowerment" and "dignity" are associated only with the choice of dying, not with the choice to struggle on. The patient who may have asked to die in the hope of receiving emotional reassurance that those around her want her to live, may find that she has set in motion a process whose momentum she cannot control.[38] Hendin acknowledges that with a life-or-death "purchase" like suicide, people should be given more information about what they are buying and how payment will be exacted. As he admits, "Death ought to be hard to sell."[39]

The truth is that suicide is becoming easier to sell. In Oregon, suicide advocates successfully convinced voters, frightened by horror stories of suffering and prolonged death, that the best way to ensure a death with dignity was to support assisted suicide. In the marketing campaign, advocates of Oregon's "death with dignity" measure assured voters that those in unbearable pain would at last have a way to end their suffering. However, since the implementation of the law, those Oregonians who have availed themselves of its provisions have not always been in intractable, terminal pain, as the referendum envisioned. A study in the *New England Journal of Medicine* reported that not a single one of those who chose suicide in Oregon was driven by the pain of end-stage disease. Instead, the most common reason that people chose to take advantage of the new law was "concern about the loss of autonomy or control of bodily functions."[40] Rather than a limited procedure performed out of extreme medical urgency, in other words, assisted suicide in Oregon has become primarily a replacement for caregiving.[41]

Richard McDonald, a California physician and president of the World Federation of Right to Die Societies, acknowledges that "pain is rarely the reason given for ending life." Instead, it is primarily a sense that disease has taken away control and dignity. Yet McDonald does not view such a development with alarm. On the contrary, he and other advocates of suicide maintain that the purpose of assisted suicide is to provide a "choice." (In redefining the meaning of suicide, the assisted death movement has piggybacked on the rhetoric of autonomy developed by the abortion lobby.) Whether or not one is in intractable pain is irrelevant to the suicide advocacy community. McDonald and others travel through the country training volunteers to work with those who are desperate for expertise in successfully ending life. "What we want is to support dying people in what they want," says McDonald. "We don't make judgments or try to convince anyone what is appropriate for them. If they decide the time has come for death, we want to ensure that their death is peaceful, speedy and sure. Nothing is worse than a bungled attempt."[42]

The advocacy groups in Oregon want to make assisted suicide even easier to accomplish than it already is. The organization Compassion in Dying, for instance, believes that Oregon's requirement of a fifteen-day waiting period is "overly restrictive."[43] Also, Oregon's guideline requiring that the drugs used by the one choosing assisted suicide be self-administered is now also under attack by euthanasia advocates. When Oregon resident Patrick Matheny's brother-in-law claimed to have been forced to help in his suicide because Matheny's ALS prevented him from swallowing the prescribed pills, the state deputy attorney general, David Schuman, suggested that in order to avoid discrimination against disabled people, Oregon might have to make "reasonable accommodation." To prevent "discrimination," in other words, Oregon will have to offer direct assistance to those who want to commit suicide but cannot self-administer their lethal drugs.[44]

Many of the safeguards that Oregon voters were promised have already been ignored. The requirement that a doctor familiar with the patient's case must prescribe the lethal drugs has been bypassed. In Oregon, family members "shop" for doctors willing to accommodate them—or find such doctors through suicide advocacy organizations. As a result, many of those who choose to end their lives in Oregon do so with doctors they barely know. The first woman to commit assisted suicide in Oregon had an eighteen-day relationship with the doctor who helped her die. Her own doctor had refused, as did a second, who diagnosed her with depression. One of the many right-to-die advocacy groups in Oregon finally found her a physician willing to overlook her depression and help her end her life. Likewise, an eighty-five-year-old dementia patient committed assisted suicide after her daughter shopped for doctors willing to provide lethal drugs to a woman who had been diagnosed by previous psychiatrists as not "possessing the capacity required to weigh options for assisted suicide."[45]

In such a culture of suicide, we should not be surprised that a growing acceptance of suicide has trickled down even to the very young. Oregon's state health division reported an all-time record number of suicides since 1994—the year voters passed the assisted suicide initiative. The increase, boosted by a 26 percent increase in suicides among 15-to-24-year-olds, has given Oregon a suicide rate more than 35 percent higher than the national average.[46]

Opponents of Oregon's assisted suicide law said that it was a step down a "slippery slope." They claimed that the state's future could be seen in the Netherlands, which is already near the bottom of the slope. Until recently, Dutch penal codes made both assisted suicide and euthanasia illegal. However, doctors who directly euthanized patients or helped patients kill themselves were not prosecuted as long as they followed certain guidelines, including reporting every euthanasia or assisted suicide to the local prosecutors. All of this became moot in 2001 when assisted suicide was officially legalized, despite government studies showing that in many cases, euthanized patients were not even terminally ill. For example, a Dutch pro-euthanasia documentary presented in this country on PBS told the story of a young woman in remission from anorexia. But she was so worried about returning to "food abuse" that she asked her doctor to kill her. He did so without legal consequence.[47]

Those who have dementia and are mentally incompetent are particularly vulnerable in the evolving suicide/euthanasia culture. According to the Remmelink Report, a 1991 government study on assisted suicide and euthanasia in Holland, Dutch doctors in a single year (1990) euthanized more than two thousand patients who had not asked to die.[48] Only 14 percent of those whose lives were ended by doctors were fully competent. In 45 percent of the euthanasia cases involving hospitalized patients who were killed without their permission, the patients' families had no knowledge that their loved ones' lives were deliberately terminated by doctors. The Dutch findings are contrary to the right-to-die rhetoric of advocacy groups, which holds that euthanasia and assisted suicide are simply "choice issues." The data demonstrate that where a culture of euthanasia and assisted suicide is allowed to grow, patients sometimes have little choice at all.

FOR DR. PAUL McHUGH, the movement toward assisted suicide and euthanasia is "a special kind of nihilism—a kind of atomism." He writes:

> In the Kevorkian worldview, the patient is a solitary figure, related to nothing or no one beyond himself, with neither a past to honor nor a future to influence.... The euthanasia movement dismisses the role of the physician as a provider of reason or one who helps a patient differentiate good from bad, right from wrong, responsible decisions from impulses; the movement privileges instead, the momentary inclinations of the patient who is most often *in extremis*.[49]

In many ways, the suicide advocacy community has benefited from the incarceration of Jack Kevorkian. He had become a stigmatized figure—an unattractive, rather scary representative of the movement. But this is not the case with the new generation of sympathetic choice advocates like Oregon's latest angel of death portrayed on PBS. This beneficent physician softly advises her patients that "the choice is theirs" as she prepares the lethal cocktail for them to drink.

The growing assisted suicide movement has a powerful appeal. Even sociological arguments for the common good have failed in the face of Oregon's antiseptic benevolence. Ethicist Daniel Callahan, director of the Hastings Center, maintains that assisted suicide can never be classified simply as a private matter of choice, because it is a social decision. Like Durkheim, Callahan claims that the way we die is important not only to us, but to society at large. The individual will flourish only to the degree that society as a whole flourishes. Yet the common good is a concept that in this field at least has been trumped by individual rights.

In addition to the quest for autonomy, there is another factor driving the debate over assisted suicide: the financial incentive. This dimension of the issue is a major concern of observers like Wesley Smith, who has written widely about the transformation of the American medical system from one based on the sanctity of life into a starkly utilitarian, corporate model in which the medically defenseless (and expensive) are seen as having not just a "right" but also a "duty" to die. Smith focuses on the revealing words used by those who promote death: "Organizations that once called themselves euthanasia societies have now renamed themselves using soothing words such as 'compassion' and 'dignity' along with the language of rights, such as 'choice.'" Thus the Euthanasia Society of America was transformed into the Society for the Right to Die, and then into Choice in Dying. Assisted suicide has been renamed "aid in dying."[50]

This new language redefines suicide from a deviant act that

harms individuals and society, to an act of courage and empowerment. And whoever wins control over the language will likely control how we regard suicide in the future.

TEN

THE LANGUAGE

OF DEVIANCE

I n major cultural transitions, words often change their meanings as new norms evolve and old cultural constraints loosen. As the preceding chapters show, those involved in the politics of deviance often foster subtle changes in the language as part of a larger campaign to alter perceptions. An effective media campaign—one, for instance, that pushes for standards of behavior based on individual desires rather than moral categories—begins the redefinition with a linguistic assault. The man who preys on boys becomes someone seeking only "intergenerational intimacy," and the promiscuous teenager is redefined as simply "sexually adventurous." In an age of imagery and sound bites, the reality of a given behavior can be less important than the emotions with which that behavior is packaged.

From the rights-based, pro-choice rhetoric of those promoting assisted suicide, to the medical jargon of those promoting the disease model of addiction, advocates for redefinitions of deviance know that the side that wins the linguistic high ground generally wins the debate. In the not-so-distant past, words like "crazy" and "deeply disturbed" were connected with suicide. Today, they have been replaced with words like "dignity" and "autonomy," while those who oppose assisted suicide legislation are themselves stigmatized as "zealots" who want to strip the vulnerable of their last rights in the pursuit of cold moral abstractions.

The process of redefining deviance is a subtle one, and the changes in language we have discussed are so incremental and innocuous that the new meanings appear almost invisibly. Social philosopher Alasdair MacIntyre implores us all to examine this process more closely when he writes, "Ours is a culture dominated by experts, experts who profess to assist the rest of us, but who often instead make us their victims." MacIntyre says that we must be able to identify the particular set of precepts that will help us achieve that which contributes to the common good.[1] Most of us know what will contribute to the common good. Most of us know that there are unwritten, morally based "laws" that tell us what kind of behavior is deviant. They have not necessarily been codified within the legal system, but are nonetheless binding.[2]

In an age of technology and expertise, we have been convinced that we should listen to the "experts" rather than common sense in determining the norms, values and attitudes of our families, our churches and other trusted institutions. Cultural relativists urge us to adapt to the changes of our times, which they define as "progress" rather than mere change whose inevitability is not assured.

As the previous chapters have shown, the postmodernists' rejection of concepts of good and evil appeared to have won the day. Yet the politics of deviance do not exist in a vacuum; they are networked into larger social movements and affected by history. The events of September 11, 2001, profoundly affected the context in which these politics play out. The slaughter of American innocents called into question the relativism that has controlled our moral conversations and our scholarship for the past three decades. Confronted with an act of mass murder and the implacable hatred of our enemies, we found that those seemingly outworn moral categories of good and evil were suddenly relevant again.

Many realized that our failure to support structures of authority and to recognize and censure the deviance that has confronted us played some role in our vulnerability to the attack. Our unwillingness to make judgments about the behavior of others—no matter how reprehensible—coupled with the requirement to honor claims of multiculturalism and diversity—however divisive and morally questionable—had weakened our resistance and lowered our defenses. We knew about the treatment of women in Afghanistan, for instance, who under Taliban rule were prohibited from working, attending school or leaving their homes without their husbands or a male relative escort. We knew that these women could be beaten on the street by male strangers for some supposed infraction of a medieval behavioral code. Yet we said this was simply "their way," which, by postmodern principles, could be no worse than "our way." The cruelest and most repressive practices of Islamic fundamentalists were viewed as matters of culture and tradition, not for us in the West to judge.

For postmodernists inside and outside of academia, the values of Western culture—of personal freedom and democracy, and freedom of inquiry—had long ago been dismissed as "reactionary" and even "xenophobic." Social scientists had continued to romanticize the alleged victims of American aggression. For many of these self-defined oppositionists, in fact, September 11 was "payback" for what they see as a history of genocide committed by the United States. MIT linguist Noam Chomsky, a cult figure for those who hold this view, continues to claim that the terrorist attack must be viewed as no worse than the Clinton administration's 1998 bombing of Sudan, and that the death toll of Americans was minimal in comparison with the toll exacted by a generation of American "imperialism."[3] A professor in New Mexico lauded the terrorist attack by flippantly remarking to his students, "Anyone who can bomb the Pentagon has my vote." And, while he later recanted his statement by lamely averring that it was a joke, there are many who did not blurt out the fact that they shared kindred sentiments. In a cover story in *The Nation,* the "postcolonial" scholar Edward W. Said medicalized (and therefore minimalized) the terrorism of September 11 by calling it an act by a "small group of deranged militants in a pathologically motivated suicide attack." Said was especially harsh in his criticism of what he called the xenophobic response to the attacks by people who wanted to "rant on about the West's superiority."[4]

The continued attempts to psychologize and "understand" deviance—even in the face of evil such as that which appeared in America on September 11—show the distance some will go to avoid applying moral categories of judgment. Sociologists Peter Conrad and Joseph Schneider cautioned us more than three decades ago that the medicalization of deviance would eventually "shroud conditions, events and people and prevent them from being confronted as evil."[5] Said's suggestion that the terrorists who tried to blow up America were deranged but not evil demonstrates how prophetic they were. Although medicalizing deviance does not automatically render evil consequences good, the assumption that behavior is the product of a "sick" mind or body gives it a status similar to that of "accidents." Removing intent or motive hinders us from comprehending the human element in the decisions we make, the actions we take and the social structures we create.

The reluctance of sociologists to acknowledge that there are moral judgments to be made when discussing a subject like deviance shows how far this discipline has strayed from its origins. From the earliest days of sociology, scholars were concerned about the question of social order and the common good. Emerging in the midst of major social, economic and political transformation sweeping across ninetheenth-century Europe as a result of the Industrial Revolution, the discipline of sociology sought to explain how societies maintain stability in the face of dramatic social change. From this time onward, until the upheavals of the 1960s, sociologists continued to assert that social stability is founded on moral order—a common worldview that binds people to their families, to their communities, and to the larger economic and political institutions. Integral to this moral order is a shared concept of deviance, and a willingness to identify the boundaries of appropriate behavior.[6]

Today, few sociologists hold these convictions. Yet ironically, the world from which sociology emerged more than a century ago was, in many ways, similar to our own contemporary world of rapid, often overwhelming, social change. Just as the Industrial Revolution brought deplorable living conditions to the industrialized cities, including poverty, sickness and dramatic changes within the family, so today's technological society presents profound challenges to social order and the common good. Globalization has created societies based less on shared culture than on narrow calculations of individual self-interest.[7] A commitment to a common moral order is much more difficult within a culture of such strong individualism.

The policymakers of the past paid attention when social scientists like Daniel Bell, Edward Banfield, James Coleman, James Q. Wilson and Daniel Patrick Moynihan spoke out on issues of morality and deviance. But today, compelling pleas for a rational response to deviant behavior are often drowned out by the more emotional appeals—and political cunning—generated by advocacy groups. In 1965, Moynihan tried to warn us of the impending problems in the inner cities when he predicted that chaos would result from single-parent households. Using the language of Durkheim, Moynihan warned that society's mechanisms for social control were breaking down. He was correct—yet for the past thirty years, instead of attacking the problem of fatherless children in the inner cities, social scientists have been more likely to attack Senator Moynihan and any other sociologist who dared to "blame the victims" of poverty.

For the first sociologists, definitions of deviance marked the outer edges of group life, thus supplying the framework within which the people of the group develop an orderly sense of their own cultural identity and social order. This process allows for some deviation—sociologists have long known that testing the boundaries of established norms can be positive. Indeed, some of the most progressive social change we have experienced in this country has been the result of subtle changes in definitions of deviance—in the direction of common sense and the common good. In the 1950s and 1960s, identifying racism and bigotry as deviance led to positive social change in which discrimination was appropriately stigmatized in our culture and censured in our legal system.

However, this dynamic process of boundary maintenance can also create the kind of social change that is not positive, the kind that Senator Moynihan cautioned us about. His concern was that our refusal to acknowledge as deviant and negatively sanction the increase in out-of-wedlock births would have a detrimental effect upon the black community. He was correct about that. What he did not foresee was that those like himself who challenged the dysfunction in the inner cities would themselves be viewed as deviant for judging the behavior of others.

In large part, the success of the civil rights movement was due to the moral authority that religious leaders brought to it. Under the leadership of Martin Luther King Jr., the movement became ecumenical, with representatives from diverse faith traditions, all of them contributing resources and volunteers to assist in the progress toward equal rights. Stamping discrimination and racism as deviant was greatly facilitated by an appeal from the religious sources of moral authority.

Today the most influential definers of deviance are not moral figures but political advocates whose efforts often involve defending those previously regarded as deviant and attacking those previously regarded as normal. These advocacy groups have sought and acquired a certain authority. Campus feminists, for instance, who have successfully convinced college administrators of their particular interpretation of date rape, have gained a significant increase in the resources devoted to women's issues. Women's centers, women's studies programs, rape awareness seminars and, on some campuses, a total reshaping of the campus and curriculum to further women's interests were some of the benefits that followed the successful redefinitions of sexual assault and victimization of women.

Meanwhile, once-respected organizations, like the Salvation

Army or the Boy Scouts, that have been slow to change their views on homosexuality and have attempted to preserve a moral commitment to their own historic mission find themselves defined as sites of deviance. The Boy Scouts organization in particular is on the verge of acquiring a stigmatized identity because of its unwillingness to allow openly gay men to be troop leaders. The organization has tried to defend itself with an appeal to traditional values, protesting that homosexuality is counter to its morally based mission and a threat to its organizational integrity. Yet, as we have seen throughout this book, such pleas tend to fail in the face of organized resistance by advocates and a growing social reluctance to judge the behavior of others.

More than a half-century ago, T. S. Eliot wrote about the sense of alienation that occurs when social regulators begin to splinter and the controlling moral authority of a society is no longer effective. In his play *The Cocktail Party,* a troubled young protagonist visits a psychiatrist and confides that she feels a "sense of sin" because of her relationship with a married man. She is distressed not so much by the illicit relationship, but rather by the strange feeling of "sinfulness." Eliot writes, "Having a sense of sin seems abnormal" to her—she had never noticed before that such behavior might be seen in those terms. She believed that she had become "ill."[8]

When Eliot speaks of his protagonist's feeling unease or uncertainty about her behavior, he is really speaking of the sense of normlessness that has traditionally been a focus of sociology. In many ways, Eliot's play is about anomie—the state that sociologists identify as resulting when one is caught between the loosening moral norms regulating behavior and one's own moral misgivings. Eliot's play echoes the scholarship of Durkheim. Both men saw that the identification and stigmatization of deviant behavior is functional for society because it can produce certainty for individuals and solidarity for the group. And both recognized that dramatic social change through rapid redefinition of deviance can be dysfunctional for society. Strong cultural values and clear concepts of good and evil integrate members into the group and provide meaning. When traditional cultural attachments are disrupted, or when behavior is no longer regulated by these common norms and values, individuals are left without a moral compass.[9]

As we have seen, Durkheim knew that social facts like crime statistics and suicide rates can be adequately explained only by analyzing the unique social conditions that evolve when norms break down.[10] The resulting anomic state leads to deviant behavior as the individual's attachment to social bonds is weakened. According to this view, people internalize social norms because of their attachments to others. People care what others think of them and attempt to conform to expectations because they accept what others expect.[11] However, when these same people are unsure about the norms, or when the norms are changing rapidly, there is a growing unwillingness to make moral judgments about all behavior. The door is open to moral panics, which flourish in such a climate of anomie.

When a society's moral boundaries are sharp, clear and secure, and the central norms and values are strongly held, moral panics rarely take hold. When the moral boundaries are fuzzy and shifting, poorly defined by ineffective authority and constant testing, as we see so often now on college campuses, moral panics are far more likely to grow—in an attempt to clarify the moral boundaries.[12]

Reporting on a national study of attitudes and values a few years ago, sociologist Alan Wolfe found that the people he interviewed—whatever their different beliefs—were unified by their increasing reluctance to judge the behavior of others. In interviews with more than two hundred middle-class respondents, Wolfe found that the refusal to judge others was mentioned so often that he identified it as the "Eleventh Commandment for the middle class: Thou Shalt Not Judge."[13] This value-free ideology was predicted thirty years ago by psychologist Philip Rieff, who warned in his now-classic book *The Triumph of the Therapeutic* that "psychological man" was beginning to replace "Christian man" as the dominant character type in our society.[14] Unlike traditional Christianity, which made moral demands on believers, the secular world of "psychological man" rejected both the idea of sin and the need for salvation.

The only time the word "sin" was mentioned during 2001 in my hometown newspaper, the *San Diego Union-Tribune*, for instance, was in a headline describing the "capitalist price-gouging" surrounding the California energy crisis.[15] In contrast, when Kathleen Soliah (a.k.a. Sara Jane Olson), a former member of the radical Symbionese Liberation Army, was captured after twenty-three years of evading arrest for conspiracy to commit murder, leaders of the Methodist Church she had been attending quickly rallied to her defense without ever speaking of her need to demonstrate remorse or repentance, and scrambled to provide over $1 million for her defense, proclaiming their "unconditional love." After interviewing these church representatives, journalist Katherine Kersten reported in the *Wall Street Journal* that they believed any crimes Olson may have committed were now "canceled out" by the many good works she had done.[16]

Perhaps it is exactly this aversion to making moral demands that has kept "psychological man" going to church all these years. Rieff predicted this too when he wrote that churches would retain members because "psychological man seeks to enlist all institutions in his service. Independent from any god, psychological man is drawn to any faith that lends itself to therapeutic use." Psychological man can embrace a faith, in other words, only so long as it imposes no real moral imperatives, and consoles but does not judge.[17]

SOCIOLOGISTS LIKE ALAN WOLFE find that "tolerance" is America's principle value, one so consensual that its virtue seems unarguable. Yet it is only during the past few decades that we have become so hesitant to judge the behavior of others. For most of this country's history, we had no difficulty placing moral demands on ourselves and others. In fact, this was viewed as "functional," a survival benefit for society.

Vestiges of this functionalist perspective—and of our continued need to identify moral boundaries—perhaps explain the popularity of "Judge" television shows like *Judge Judy* and *The People's Court,* where people are told what is right and wrong. Yet these representations are feeble and secularized attempts to use public shaming or sanctioning in what has become deviance-as-entertainment. Likewise, the high ratings of *Court TV* and reality shows like *COPS,* and the broad appeal of widely publicized presentations of sex scandals involving government officials or high-profile murder trials on the 24-hour news stations all provide examples of the public desire to see deviance negatively sanctioned. In some ways, these programs recall the practice of publicly displaying criminals in the stocks during colonial times. Parading high-profile offenders in shackles and prison garb before the television cameras each night is a reminder of how important defining deviance is to our survival. Thus does television—which has otherwise done so much to deconstruct traditional standards of deviance—also contribute to defining what is normative.

New laws also serve a similar purpose of affirming solidarity and reinforcing social norms. Megan's Law, for example, requires that sex offenders be publicly identified to residents of the neighborhoods where they seek to live after their release from prison. Clearly this law protects the safety of those residents and their children, but the early sociologists would have argued that its more important function is to affirm the standards of presumably normal sexual behavior by identifying and sanctioning behavior that is abnormal and destructive. It sends the message that if an individual participates in this unacceptable sexual behavior, he or she will suffer the consequences of being stigmatized as "deviant."

But in the long run, laws are inadequate to do what must be culture's job. There was a time, not so long ago, when moral concerns strongly affected private judgments and public policy. Throughout the nineteenth century, the English people spoke the language of morality because they truly believed in the reality and the importance of virtue as a factor in public as well as private life. Historian Gertrude Himmelfarb has suggested that while Victorian liberals and conservatives may have disagreed about specific social policies, they usually agreed on the moral principles that served as the foundation for those policies. This was especially true when they provided welfare—or "relief," as they called it—to the poor. In designing programs to benefit the poor, the Victorians agreed that any charity had to be viewed as contributing to the "character" or moral well-being of the recipient.

To support the value of work, the Victorians believed that pauperism for the "able-bodied" should be stigmatized. But there was no stigma for the "deserving poor." Poor children, or those adults who were poor because of illness or advanced age, received greater charity and benevolence than those who were poor because they chose not to work. In the marketing of morals, Victorians elevated the working man in their art, showing work as honorable and good, and a worthy subject for high culture. The Victorian family home was also sanctified in the artwork of the time as a place of cherubic children and Madonna-like mothers. Of course, Karl Marx defined it all as an example of "false consciousness," just as some later sociologists would see a capitalist plot underlying such "propaganda." Still, the Victorians knew that morals worked better than laws in creating community and solidarity, and they marketed this morality in many of the same ways that the current advocacy groups have marketed dysfunction.

The re-moralizing of society worked for the Victorians. Himmelfarb provides data indicating that over the course of the nineteenth century, all the key indicators of deviance or social pathology in Britain improved markedly. The illegitimacy rate, 7 percent in 1845, plunged below 4 percent by the century's end, dropping even more dramatically in the poorest sections of London. Between 1857 and 1901, the crime rate declined by 50 percent, so that even while the population grew from 19 million to 33 million, the absolute number of serious crimes actually fell. Prostitutes and alcoholics, quite common on the streets at the middle of the nineteenth century, had become scarce by 1900.

Himmelfarb writes that all of these improvements in the quality of moral life in Britain occurred against a background of urbanization and industrialization that theoretically should have produced social disintegration, not improvement. Yet despite the presence of what sociologists would have defined as structural causes of poverty, a much stronger cultural force was in operation that created dramatic social improvement. The lesson to be learned from the success of the Victorian era is that social policy must never be divorced from moral principles. Contemporary efforts to devise social policies that are "value-free" and do not stigmatize those who refuse to work, for instance, or actually reward those who abuse drugs, end up "demoralizing" us all.

Despite or perhaps because of what seems to be the chaos of popular culture, people still search for meaning and order in their lives and the lives of their families, and many of them seek such meaning in religion. It is not off our subject to point out that just as nonjudgmental, mainline Christian churches continue to lose members, there has been a significant growth in the fundamentalist, Pentecostal and evangelical churches, whose greatest strength is in offering believers real guidance in how to live their lives.

In fact, data from the Gallup polling organization's most recent *Surveying the Religious Landscape* reveal a dramatic decline in the churches that make the fewest moral demands on believers— Methodist and Presbyterian.[18] Some of the deepest divisions are within the Episcopalian Church, much of it concerning the ordination of gay men and lesbian women as priests.[19] Gallup documents a growing trend in denomination switching as people's beliefs and situations change. About one adult in four (23 percent) has moved from the religion in which he or she was raised. The smaller, yet fastest-growing Protestant denominations, including the Pentecostal Assembly of God, have often been the beneficiaries of these switches in allegiance. The religious denominations that provide moral guidance and make demands are flourishing. Gallup found that almost seven in ten adults (68 percent) believe that religious leaders must exert a much greater influence in reinvigorating American morality[20]

However, when religious leaders attempt to assert public morality too dramatically, they also run the risk of being rebuked. Even Pope John Paul II, arguably the most powerful religious authority in the world, is now criticized when he attempts to affirm Catholic teaching on sexual morality. When the Pope pronounced the 2001 Gay Pride festival in Rome "offensive to Christians" and declared that homosexual acts are "contrary to natural law," the government of Holland attempted to prosecute him for "hate speech." While Holland's bid to prosecute failed, the Pontiff's words were strongly denounced by the international supporters of the gay community and by much of the international media.

In an effort to avoid alienating members with diverse lifestyles and values, some religious leaders have become hesitant to speak of morals at all. But in their place, a powerful advocacy community stands ready, willing and able to define deviance. The only sufficient response to the compelling marketing techniques of these advocacy groups is a renewed willingness to make moral judgments.

In the aftermath of September 11, President George W. Bush repeatedly called the terrorist acts "evil" and those who perpetrated them "evildoers." This language drew only a minor protest from those who on September 10 would have had a field day if the President had used similar terminology. Reassessing the politics and culture after terrorists declared war on America, social critic David Brooks writes,

> Life in times of war and recession reminds us of certain hard truths that were easy to ignore during the decades of peace and prosperity. Evil exists. Difficulties, even tragedies are inevitable. Human beings are flawed creatures capable of monstrosity. Not all cultures are compatible. To preserve order, good people must exercise power over destructive people.

Brooks reminds us that in order to cope with the implications of the new reality, we must "construct hard principles" of moral consensus. "When you are faced with the problem of repelling evil, you absolutely must be able to reach a conclusion on serious moral issues."[21]

Perhaps this re-moralization of our public discourse—despite the agitation and murmuring it has caused in certain academic circles—will be the only good to come out of our national tragedy. Perhaps we will begin to recognize that a society that continues to redefine deviance as disease, or refuses to acknowledge and negatively sanction the deviant acts our common sense tells us are destructive, is a society that has lost the capacity to confront evil that has a capacity to dehumanize us all.

ACKNOWLEDGMENTS

Of the many who helped with this book, I am most indebted to my mentor and longtime friend, Professor J. M. Lewis of Kent State University. Since the days of the Kent State tragedy in 1970, "Dr. J" has devoted his life to his students, and I continue to be a grateful beneficiary. I am also grateful to my friend Fr. Peter Bosque, who read most of the manuscript and offered helpful criticisms and moral support. His willingness to check facts, look for primary sources and locate obscure laws defining deviance went well beyond the call of friendship.

At the University of San Diego, a very special thank-you to my students for their enthusiasm and continued willingness to think rationally and to use common sense and their moral convictions to see through the politics of deviance. Their observations and insights about emerging definitions of deviance are reflected throughout these pages. I am grateful also to Monsignor Dan Dillabough, Vice President of Mission and Ministry, for his careful reading and criticism of the chapter on suicide. Thank you to colleagues Jan Fain and Alberto Restrepo, who helped with the research and provided ongoing feedback. While they often disagreed with the conclusions throughout the book, I have always been grateful for the support and friendship they have provided.

And finally, thank you to Peter Collier, publisher of Encounter Books, for his generosity of time and effort throughout the entire writing process, and to copy editor Carol Staswick for her attention to detail. Their patient reading and re-reading of the manuscript was greatly appreciated.

NOTES

Introduction

1 Emile Durkheim, *Rules of Sociological Method* (New York: The Free Press, 1964; first pub. 1895).

2 Lewis A. Coser, *Masters of Sociological Thought* (New York: Harcourt Brace Jovanovich, 1977).

3 Colin Sumner, *The Sociology of Deviance: An Obituary* (New York: Continuum Press, 1994), p. ix.

4 C. Wright Mills, *The Power Elite* (New York: Oxford University Press, 1956).

5 Sumner, *The Sociology of Deviance*, p. 203.

6 Erving Goffman, *Stigma: Notes on the Management of Spoiled Identity* (Englewood Cliffs, New Jersey: Prentice Hall, 1963).

7 Myron Magnet, *The Dream and the Nightmare: The Sixties' Legacy to the Underclass* (San Francisco: Encounter Books, 2000; first pub. 1993).

8 Howard S. Becker, *The Outsiders* (New York: Free Press of Glencoe, 1963), p. 9.

9 Michel Foucault, *Madness and Civilization: A History of Insanity in the Age of Reason* (London: Tavistock, 1967).

10 Sumner, *The Sociology of Deviance*, p. 297.

11 Alexander Liazos, "The Poverty of the Sociology of Deviance: Nuts, Sluts and Perverts," *Social Problems,* vol. 20, no.1 (summer 1972), pp. 103–20.

12 Cited by Sumner, *The Sociology of Deviance*, p. 261.

13 Herbert Gans, quoted from the back cover of William Ryan, *Blaming the Victim* (New York: Pantheon, 1971).

14 Sumner. *The Sociology of Deviance*, p. 309.

15 Daniel Patrick Moynihan, *Miles to Go* (Cambridge, Massachusetts: Harvard University Press, 1996), p. 144.

16 Ibid., p. 156.

17 Cited by Andrew Karmen, " 'Defining Deviancy Down': How Senator Moynihan's Misleading Phrase about Criminal Justice Is

Rapidly Being Incorporated into Popular Culture," *Journal of Criminal Justice and Popular Culture*, vol. 2, no. 5 (1994), pp. 99–112.

18   Ibid., p. 100.

19   Pete DuPont IV, "Defining the Presidency Down," www.intellectualcapital.com, 8 October 1998.

20   Jeff Barker, "Duncan Vetoes Bill Targeting Secondhand Smoke: Law Would Have Banned Lighting Up at Home If Fumes Imperil Neighbor," *Baltimore Sun*, 28 November 2001, p. B2.

21   Philip Jenkins, *Pedophiles and Priests* (New York: Oxford University Press, 1996), p. 4.

Chapter 1: Medicalizing the Deviance of Drug Abuse

1   Peter Conrad and Joseph Schneider, "Medicine As an Institution of Social Control: Consequences for Society," in *Deviance and Medicalization: From Badness to Sickness* (Philadelphia: Temple University Press, 1993), pp. 241–60.

2   Ibid., p. 588.

3   "Strawberry's Wife to Head Florida Drug Addiction Council," *Atlanta Journal-Constitution*, 11 April 2001, p. B7.

4   Matthew Gilbert, "Is Robert Downey Jr. a Lost Cause?" *Boston Globe*, reprinted in *San Diego Union-Tribune*, 1 May 2001, p. E2.

5   Mary Murphy, televised interview, *Rivera Live*.

6   Sean Mitchell, "Protesting Another Misguided War," *Los Angeles Times*, 7 January 2001. Bennett responded to the accusations in an opinion piece in which he pointed out, among other things, that Bingham's drug abuse long predated his own tenure as "drug czar." "The Real Lessons from Traffic," *Pittsburgh Post-Gazette*, 25 March 2001, p. E4. Bennett's deputy, Herbert Kleber, concurred with this. "Traffic Screenwriter's Sentiment Is Misguided," *Los Angeles Times*, 29 January 2001, p. F3.

7   Cited by Neil Kendricks, "Mainlining Traffic," *San Diego Union-Tribune*, 1 January 2001, p. E1.

8   *Moyers on Addiction: Close to Home*, 4-part PBS documentary aired March 1998; see www.pbs.org.

9   "The Hijacked Brain," part 2 of *Moyers on Addiction: Close to Home*, www.pbs.org.

10   Sharon Begley, "How It All Starts inside Your Brain," *Newsweek*, 12 February 2001, p. 42.

11   David F. Musto, *The American Disease* (New York: Oxford University Press, 1999), p. 5.

12   Ibid., p. 273.

13 D. Stanley Eitzen and Macine Bacca Zinn, *Social Problems*, 8th ed. (Boston: Allyn & Bacon, 2000), p. 522.

14 Ibid.

15 Chris Harry, "It Was Our Wake-Up Call: Fifteen Years Ago, Bias's Death Shook a Nation," *Washington Post*, 24 June 2001, p. D1.

16 "The Wrong Way to Drug-Law Reform," *St. Petersburg Times*, 8 February 2000, p. A8.

17 Eitzen and Zinn, *Social Problems*, p. 526.

18 Musto, *The American Disease*, p. 279.

19 Health and Human Services News, *Fact Sheet*, U.S. Department of Health and Human Services, HHS Press Office, Thursday, 14 December 2000.

20 Harry, "It Was Our Wake-Up Call."

21 Alex Roth, "Two in Court Scandal Cut Prison Time via Program for Addicts," *San Diego Union-Tribune*, 18 December 2001, p. B1.

22 Sally Satel, *PC, M.D.: How Political Correctness Is Corrupting Medicine* (New York: Basic Books, 2000), p. 132.

23 Ibid.

24 Ibid., p. 133.

25 Ibid., p. 135.

26 Bill Moyers, "An Interview with Bill White," *Moyers on Addiction: Close to Home*, www.pbs.org/wnet/closetohome/policy/html/white.html.

27 Satel, *PC M.D.*, p. 137.

28 Cited by Sally Satel, "Opiates for the Masses," *Wall Street Journal*, 8 June 1998.

29 Ibid.

30 Ibid.

31 Ulysses Torassa, "Changing Method of Treatment for Drug Addiction: San Francisco Models Harm Reduction Theory," *San Francisco Chronicle*, 15 January 2001, p. A21.

32 Ibid.

33 Cited in "Drive-Thru High," Editorial, *Wall Street Journal*, 6 May 2001.

34 Larry Kessler, "Addiction Is Not a Moral Lapse," Letters to the Editor, *Boston Globe*, 20 February 2001, p. A14.

35 Jeff McDonald. "The Detox Paradox," *San Diego Union-Tribune*, 3 June 2000, p. A20.

36 Thomas Szasz, *Our Right to Drugs* (Syracuse, New York: Syracuse University Press, 1992), p. 136.

37 Claudia Kolb, "Can This Pill Stop You from Hitting the Bottle?"

Newsweek, 12 February 2001, p. 48.

38   Geoffrey Cowley, "New Ways to Stay Clean," *Newsweek,* 12 February 2001, p. 47.

39   Mary Duenwald, "Rapid Detox a Controversial Addiction Cure," *San Diego Union-Tribune,* 12 December 2001.

40   Ibid.

41   Troy Duster, *The Legislation of Morality* (New York: The Free Press, 1970).

42   Peter Conrad and Joseph Schneider, "Medicine As an Institution of Social Control: Consequences for Society," in *Deviance and Medicalization: From Badness to Sickness* (Philadelphia: Temple University Press, 1993), p. 244.

43   Website for Melanie Griffith, www.melanieonline.com.

44   Talcott Parsons, "Definitions of Illness and Health in Light of American Values and Social Structure," in *Patients, Physicians and Illness,* ed. E. G. Jaco (1972), cited by Peter Conrad and Joseph Schneider, "Medicine As an Institution of Social Control: Consequences for Society," in *Theories of Deviance* (Itasca, Illinois: Peacock Press, 1999), p. 574.

45   Conrad and Schneider, "Medicine As an Institution of Social Control," in *Deviance and Medicalization.*

46   Conrad and Schneider, "Medicine as an Institution of Social Control," in *Theories of Deviance,* p. 574.

47   Peter Conrad, "The Discovery of Hyperkinesis: Notes on the Medicalization of Deviant Behavior," *Social Problems,* vol. 23 (1975), pp. 12–21.

48   Conrad and Schneider, "Medicine As an Institution of Social Control," in *Deviance and Medicalization.*

49   Jeffrey Schaler, *Addiction Is a Choice* (Chicago: Open Court Press, 2000), p. 38.

50   A. Bandura, "Self Efficacy: Towards a Unifying Theory of Behavioral Change," *Psychological Review,* 1977, pp. 191–215.

51   Cited by Schaler, *Addiction Is a Choice,* p. 44.

52   Barry McCaffrey, director of the Office of National Drug Policy, luncheon speech, "Our Balanced Approach to Drug Policy," 4 October 2000, online at www.pbs.org.

53   Hanna Rosin, "George W. Bush: The Record in Texas: Putting Faith in a Social Service Role: Church-Based Providers Freed from Many Rules," *Washington Post,* 5 May 2000, p. A1.

54   James Q. Wilson, *The Moral Sense* (New York: The Free Press, 1997), p. 96.

55 Ibid., p. 93.

56 Stanton Peele, *Diseasing of America* (San Francisco: Jossey Bass, 1995), p. 269.

57 Ibid., p. 261.

Chapter 2: Removing the Stigma from Mental Illness

1 Gerald N. Grob, *The Mad Among Us: A History of the Care of America's Mentally Ill* (Cambridge, Mass.: Harvard University Press, 1994).

2 Heather MacDonald, "Homeless Advocates in Outer Space," *City Journal*, vol. 7, no. 4 (Autumn 1997).

3 Erving Goffman, *Stigma: Notes on the Management of Spoiled Identity* (Englewood Cliffs, New Jersey: Prentice Hall, 1963).

4 Thomas Szasz, *The Manufacture of Madness* (St. Albans: Paladin, 1972), p. xxv.

5 Thomas Szasz, *The Myth of Mental Illness: Foundations of a Theory of Personal Conduct* (New York: Harper & Row, 1974), p. 262.

6 Stanton Peele, *Diseasing of America* (San Francisco: Jossey Bass, 1995), p. 13.

7 R. D. Laing, *The Politics of Experience* (London: Penguin Books, 1990), p. 24.

8 John Clay, *R. D. Laing: A Divided Self*, pp. 170–71, cited on "The Unofficial R. D. Laing Website," www.decaelo.com/relaing.-unidexfr.htm.

9 R. D. Laing, *The Divided Self* (London: Penguin Books, 1990), p. 12.

10 James Verniere, "Movies: Multiplex Personalities: Films Grapple with Mental Illness by Reviling, Revealing, Celebrating," *Boston Herald*, 16 January 2000, p. 47.

11 Mary Pemberton, "Mentally Ill Alaskan Can Carry Gun," *San Diego Union-Tribune*, 11 January 2000, p. A13.

12 Henry Weinstein, "Furrow Gets 5 Life Terms for Racist Rampage," *Los Angeles Times*, 27 March 2001.

13 Robert Epstein, "Tipper Gore and Rosalynn Carter on America's Mental Health Crisis," *Psychology Today*, vol. 21 (1999), pp. 31–34.

14 Cited by E. Fuller Torrey, "Sanity on Mental Illness," *City Journal*, vol. 10, no. 3 (Summer 2000), pp. 10–11.

15 Ibid., p. 10.

16 Andrew Maykuth, "A Nether World They Call Home: They Seek Security by Retreating Underground," *New York Times*, 26 February 199s, p. A1.

17 Fred Siegel, *The Future Once Happened Here* (New York: The Free

Press, 1997), p. 175.

18   Ibid., p. 172.

19   Myron Magnet, *The Dream and the Nightmare: The Sixties' Legacy to the Underclass* (San Francisco: Encounter Books, 2000; first pub. 1993).

20   Patrick Hoge, "Squalor in the Streets: Public Health Toll," *San Francisco Chronicle*, 4 November 2001, p. A18.

21   Ibid.

22   Ibid.

23   Siegel, *The Future Once Happened Here*, p. 185.

24   Ibid.

25   James Barron, "Pushed to Tracks, Woman Is Killed by F Train," *New York Times*, 5 January 1995, p. A1.

26   Barbara Ross, "Put Subway Pusher in Hospital, Lawyer Urges," *New York Daily News*, 12 April 1996, p. 32.

27   Cited by Jonathan Gregg, "Will the Real Andrew Goldstein Take the Stand," www.time.com.

28   Laurie Flynn, "The Kendra Webdale–Andrew Goldstein Tragedy: One More Failure in America's Mental Healthcare System," National Alliance for the Mentally Ill, www.ami.org/pressroom.

29   "TV View of Schizophrenia Perpetuates Stereotypes," *St. Louis Post-Dispatch*, 3 April 2000, p. E4.

30   Shawn Hubler, "Looking Mental Illness in the Eye," *Los Angeles Times*, 6 April 2000, p. B1.

31   Edward Mulvey and Jess Fardella, "Are the Mentally Ill Really Violent?" *Psychology Today*, December 2000, p. 39.

32   Julio Arboledo-Florez, Heather Holley and Annette Crisanti, "Mental Illness and Violence: Proof or Stereotype?" Health Promotion and Programs Branch, Health Canada, National Clearinghouse on Family Violence, 1996.

33   Laurie Goodstein and William Glaberson, "The Well Marked Roads to Homicidal Rage," *New York Times*, 10 April 2000, p. A1.

34   Ibid.

35   Anne Marie O'Connor, "High School Frets about Taint of Troubled Alumnus," *Los Angeles Times*, 27 February 2001, p. B5.

36   Joe Mozingo and Jennifer Ragland, "Other Students Saw Signs of Trouble: Before Driver Plowed into a Crowd, Killing Four, He Acted Weirder and Crazier and Was Starved for Attention, Classmates Say," *Los Angeles Times*, 26 February 2001, p. B1.

37   Joe Mozingo, "Freshman Is Charged with Murder in 4 Deaths near UC Santa Barbara," *Los Angeles Times*, 27 February 2001,

NOTES   171

38   Mozingo and Ragland, "Other Students Saw Signs of Trouble."

39   David Edwards and Mary Allen, "Stigma: Perpetuating Misper-
ceptions," http//home.earthlink.net, 2001.

40   Shelby Oppel and Jo Becker, "Bill Combats Mental Illness
Stigma," *St. Petersburg Times*, 4 April 2000, p. B6.

Chapter 3: Expanding the Market for Mental Illness

1   Steven Wharry, *eCMAJ Today*, website of the Canadian Medical
Association, 3 October 2000, www.cma.ca/cmaj.htm.

2   Elise Tanouye, "Mental Illness: A Rising Workplace Cost," *Wall
Street Journal*, 13 June 2001, p. B1.

3   Karen Davis, "Fired Worker Allowed to Sue under Disabilities
Act," *San Diego Union-Tribune*, 24 March 2001, p. A3.

4   Joel Best and Frank Furedi, "The Evolution of Road Rage in
Britain and the United States," in *How Claims Spread*, ed. Joel
Best (Hawthorne, New York: Aldine de Gruyter, 2001), p. 108.

5   Terry Rodgers, "Local Man Accused in Surf Rage Attack Case,"
San Diego Union-Tribune, 15 March 2001, p. B6.

6   Peter Conrad, "The Discovery of Hyperkinesis," in *Deviant Behavior*, ed. Delos Kelly (New York: St. Martin's Press, 1993), p. 46.

7   John Ratey and Catherine Johnson, *Shadow Syndromes* (New
York: Pantheon Books, 1997).

8   John Ratey and Catherine Johnson, "Out of the Shadows," *Psychology Today*, May/June 1997, p. 46.

9   Ibid., p. 47.

10 Jonathan Leo, "Attention Deficit Disorder: Good Science or Good
Marketing?" *Skeptic*, vol. 8 (2000), p. 63.

11 National Institutes of Health, "Diagnosis and Treatment of Attention Deficit Hyperactivity Disorder," Consensus Development
Conference, 1998, cited by Leo, "Attention Deficit Disorder."

12 Jennifer Coleman, "Emotional Check-ups for Tots," *San Diego
Union-Tribune*, 3 June 2000.

13 Kelly Patricia O'Meara, "Doping Kids," *Insight on the News*,
28 June 1999, p. 10.

14 Lawrence Diller, "Kids on Drugs," 9 March 2000, www.salon.-
com/health/feature.

15 Cited by O'Meara, "Doping Kids."

16 Cited by Leo, "Attention Deficit Disorder."

17 O'Meara, "Doping Kids."

18 Richard Schmitt, "Maker of Ritalin, Psychiatric Group Sued,"

Wall Street Journal, 14 September 2000, p. B19.

19   Alex Roth, "Judge Tosses Suit against Ritalin Maker, Psychiatric Association," *San Diego Union-Tribune,* 16 March 2001, p. B6.

20   "Give Your Dog an 'A' in Behavior," marketing materials promoting Clomicalm, produced by Novartis Pharmaceuticals, 2001.

21   Daniel Rockmore, "Exploiting a Beautiful Mind," *Chronicle of Higher Education,* 25 January 2002, p. B18.

22   Kay Redfield Jamison, *Touched by Fire* (New York: The Free Press, 1993), p. 6.

23   Ibid., p. 8.

24   Ibid., p. 82.

25   Kay Redfield Jamison, *An Unquiet Mind* (New York: Vintage Books, 1996), p. 129.

26   Elaine Showalter, *Hystories: Hysterical Epidemics and Modern Media* (New York: Columbia University Press, 1997), p. 22.

27   Ibid.

28   Interview with Paul R. McHugh for "Hot Type," *Chronicle of Higher Education,* 4 June 1999, p. A24.

29   Dan Flynn, "Temple University Sued for Hauling Christian Student to Psychiatric Ward," *Campus Report,* The Newspaper of Academic Accuracy, February 2001, p. 1.

30   Herbert London, "A New Mental Disability: Political Incorrectness," *Insight on the News,* 28 February 2000, p. 44.

31   Thomas Scheff, *Being Mentally Ill,* 3rd ed. (Hawthorne, New York: Aldine de Gruyter, 1999).

32   David Satcher, "Mental Health: A Report of the Surgeon General," 16 December 1999, available online at www.surgeongeneral.com.

33   Jamie Dettmer, "Mentally Sick or Crazy Like a Fox?" *Insight on the News,* 25 October 1999, p. 8.

34   Patrick Langan, Ph.D., *Spouse Murder Defendants in Large Urban Counties,* U.S. Department of Justice, Office of Justice Programs, Bureau of Justice Statistics, 1995, p. 2.

35   Bill Callahan, "Probation Ordered in Killing of Husband," *San Diego Union-Tribune,* 8 March 1996, p. B1.

36   Cited by Stanton Peele, *Diseasing of America* (San Francisco: Jossey Bass, 1995), p. 219.

37   Ibid., p. 220.

38   Ibid., p. 212.

39   Showalter, *Hystories,* p. 16.

40   Joan Acocela, "The Politics of Hysteria," *New Yorker,* 8 April 1998, pp. 64–79.

41 Tara Parker-Pope, "Drug Companies Push Use of Antidepressants to Treat Severe PMS," *Wall Street Journal*, 23 February 2001, p. B1.
42 Ibid.
43 Paul R. McHugh, "How Psychiatry Lost Its Way," *Commentary*, December 1999.

Chapter 4: Moral Panics and the Social Construction of Deviance
1 Cited by Jeffrey Victor, "Moral Panics and the Social Construction of Deviant Behavior," *Sociological Perspectives*, vol. 41, no. 3 (1988), p. 541.
2 Erich Goode and Nachman Ben-Yehuda, *Moral Panics: The Social Construction of Deviance* (Malden, Massachusetts: Blackwell Books, 1999), p. 29.
3 Victor, "Moral Panic and the Social Construction of Deviant Behavior," p. 541.
4 Dorothy Rabinowitz, "A Darkness in Massachusetts III" *Wall Street Journal*, 12 May 1995.
5 Ron Geraci and Greg Gutfeld, "Scared out of Our Wits," *Men's Health*, December 1996, p. 54.
6 Philip Jenkins, *Moral Panic: Changing Concepts of the Child Molester in Modern America* (New Haven: Yale University Press, 1998), pp. 119–20.
7 Ibid., p. 126.
8 Ibid., p. 128.
9 Ibid., p. 129.
10 Ibid., p. 135.
11 Joan Acocella, "The Politics of Hysteria," *New Yorker*, 8 April 1998, p. 68.
12 Ibid.
13 Dorothy Rabinowitz, "Afterward," *Wall Street Journal*, 29 December 2000.
14 Rabinowitz, "A Darkness in Massachusetts III."
15 Rabinowtz, "Afterward."
16 Dorothy Rabinowitz, "A Darkness in Massachusetts," *Wall Street Journal*, 30 January 1995.
17 Lisa Miller and David France, "Sins of the Father," *Newsweek*, March 4, 2002.
18 Cited by Philip Jenkins, *Pedophiles and Priests: Anatomy of a Contemporary Crisis* (New York: Oxford University Press, 1996), p 4.
19 Interview with Tom Economus, "John Paul II: The Millennial Pope," *Frontline: The Church and Sexuality*, available online at

www.pbs.org, 1999.

20 Miller and France, "Sins of the Father."

21 Tom Economus, "Catholic Pedophile Priests: The Effect on United States Society," www.thelinkup.com, 15 January 2001.

22 A. Ross, "Blame It on the Devil," *Redbook*, June 1994, pp. 86–89.

23 Jenkins, *Pedophiles and Priests*, p. 170.

24 Ibid., p. 8.

25 Ibid., p. 10.

26 Ibid., p. 11.

27 Frank Reeves, "Catholic Groups Assail Remarks on Vouchers: Democrat Charges Church Would Use Public Funds to Settle Pedophilia Suits," *Pittsburgh Post-Gazette*, 10 June 1999, p. B1.

28 Jenkins, *Pedophiles and Priests*, p. 170.

29 Frank Furedi, "A Plague of Moral Panics," *Living Marxism*, vol. 63 (January 1994). Cited by Lesley Sands, 1999, www.aber.ac.uk/education/undergrad/ed30620/lcs602.

30 George Weigel, "The Neoconservative Difference," in *Being Right: Conservative Catholics in America*, ed. Mary Jo Weaver and R. Scott Appleby (Bloomington, Indiana: University of Indiana Press, 1995), p. 148.

31 Ibid., p. 140.

32 Jenkins, *Pedophiles and Priests*, p. 16.

33 Ibid., p. 78.

34 Ibid., p. 100.

35 Lisa Sowle Cahill, "A Crisis of Clergy, Not of Faith," *New York Times*, 6 March 2002, p. A21.

36 Jenkins, *Pedophiles and Priests*, p. 17.

37 Ibid., p. 122.

38 Scott Heller and Alison Schneider, "Boston College Feminist Fights Order to Allow Men in Her Class," *Chronicle of Higher Education*, 5 March 1999, p. A50. See also Beth McMurtrie, "How Catholic Should Catholic Colleges Be?" *Chronicle of Higher Education*, 17 September 1999, p. A16. See also Robin Wilson, "Judge Denies Bid to Stop Retirement by Boston College Professor," *Chronicle of Higher Education*, 4 June 1999, p. A16.

39 Cited by Jenkins, *Pedophiles and Priests*, p. 119.

40 Ibid., p. 120.

41 Cited by *The Linkup* website. Based on data published in *National Catholic Reporter*, 15 January 1999.

42 Joseph Cardinal Bernardin, *The Gift of Peace: Personal Reflections* (New York: Bantam Doubleday Dell, 1998).

43 Ibid., p. 37.

44 Jenkins, *Pedophiles and Priests*, p. 54.

45 Charles R. Morris, *American Catholic* (New York: Vintage Books, 1997).

46 News Around the World, "Pope Deplores Pedophilia, But Won't Lift Priests' Celibacy," *Seattle Times*, 27 June 1999, p. A15.

47 Paul Wilkes, "Priests Who Prey," *New York Times*, 26 September 1992, p. A21.

48 Jenkins, *Pedophiles and Priests*, p. 55.

49 Ibid., p. 56.

50 Ibid., p. 58.

51 Ibid., p. 15.

52 Ibid., p. 106.

53 Eugene Kennedy, "Saving Fr. Ryan: Understanding the Good Priest," *National Catholic Reporter*, 31 March 2000.

54 Ibid.

55 Andrew Sullilvan, "They Still Don't Get It," *Time*, 27 February 2002.

56 Stacy Finz, "Teenagers Banned as Rectory Workers: Archdiocese Attempts to Avoid Abuse Lawsuits," *San Francisco Chronicle*, 5 August 2000.

57 Laurie Goodstein, "No Longer Eager to Say, My Son, the Priest: Religious Careers Lose Luster for Catholic Parents," *New York Times*, 19 November 2000.

58 Michael S. Rose, "Who's Afraid of the 'New Breed' of Priests?" *New Oxford Review*, December 2001, p. 34.

59 Kenneth Woodward, "Bing Crosby Had It Right," *Newsweek*, 4 March 2002.

Chapter 5: Postmodern Pedophilia

1 Charles R. Tittle and Raymond Paternoster, *Social Deviance and Crime* (Los Angeles: Roxbury, 2000), p. 13.

2 Theo Sandfort, Ph.D., Edward Brongersma, J.D., and Alex van Naerssen, Ph.D., *Male Intergenerational Intimacy* (New York: Haworth, 1991).

3 Ken Plummer, Ph.D., "Understanding Childhood Sexualities," in *Male Intergenerational Intimacy*, ed. Sandfort et al.

4 Ibid., p. 245.

5 Ibid., p. 246.

6 Gerald P. Jones, Ph.D., "The Study of Intergenerational Intimacy in North America: Beyond Politics and Pedophilia," in *Male Inter-*

generational Intimacy, p. 276.

7   Ibid., p. 278.

8   Ibid., p. 279.

9   Ibid., p. 289.

10   David Thorstad, "Man/Boy Love and the American Gay Move-ment," in *Male Intergenerational Intimacy*, p. 269.

11   Ibid., p. 254.

12   Judy Rakowsky, "Curley Parents Sue Man-Boy Love Group," *Boston Globe*, 17 May 2000, p. B1.

13   Carolyn Tuft, "Boy-Love Day Raises Concerns about Pedophilia," *St. Louis Post-Dispatch*, 20 December 1999, p. A8.

14   Arne Frederiksen, "Pedophilia, Science and Self-Deception: A Criticism of Sex Abuse Research," website of the Danish Pedophile Association, www.danpedo.to/english/.

15   Ibid.

16   Bruce Rind, Phillip Tromovitch and Robert Bauserman, "A Meta-Analytic Examination of Assumed Properties of Child Sexual Abuse Using College Samples," *Psychological Bulletin*, American Psychological Association, July 1998.

17   Laura Schlessinger, "Article on Pedophilia Is Just Junk Science," *New Orleans Times-Picayune*, 18 April 1999, p. E6.

18   Carol Tavris, "Commentary: Perspective on Psychology: Uproar over Sexual Abuse Study Muddies the Waters," *Los Angeles Times*, 19 July 1999, p. B5.

19   Mary Eberstadt, "Pedophilia Chic Reconsidered," *Weekly Standard*, 8 January 2001, p. 19.

20   Ibid.

21   "Georgetown University Newspaper Fires Student Who Cried Censorship," *Chronicle of Higher Education*, 7 April 2000, p. A49.

22   Cited in Eberstadt, "Pedophilia Chic Reconsidered," p. 25.

Chapter 6: Stigma and Sexual Orientation

1   Raul Ramirez, "The Night That Gave Birth to a Movement," *San Francisco Examiner*, 4 June 1989, p. B6.

2   Ibid.

3   Joe Hughes, "San Diego Police Department Is Praised for Hiring of Gays and Lesbians," *San Diego Union-Tribune*, 14 November 2001, p. B2.

4   Ronald Alsop, "As Same-Sex Households Grow More Main-stream, Businesses Take Note," *Wall Street Journal*, 8 August 2001, p. B1.

5   Marshall Kirk and Hunter Madsen, *After the Ball* (New York:

Plume, 1989), p. 172.

6   Bruce Bawer, *A Place at the Table* (New York: Touchstone Books, 1993), p. 31.

7   Cited by Kirk and Madsen, *After the Ball*, p. 47.

8   Gabriel Rotello, *Sexual Ecology: AIDS and the Destiny of Gay Man* (New York: Dutton, 1998).

9   Kirk and Madsen, *After the Ball*, p. xxvii.

10 Ibid., p. 154.

11 Ibid., p. 149.

12 Ibid., p. 216.

13 Ibid., p. 188.

14 Ibid.

15 Peter Monaghan, "Lesbian Studies Pioneer Traces What Lesbians Have Done for America," *Chronicle of Higher Education*, 11 June 1999, p. A14.

16 Course description of "Finding Common Ground: Using Adolescent and Children's Literature to Explore Issues Related to Gay, Lesbian, Bisexual and Straight Identities," Spring 2001.

17 Camile Paglia, "It Wasn't Romeo and Julian," *Wall Street Journal*, 2 February 1999.

18 Cited by Kirk and Madsen, *After the Ball*, p. 223.

19 Ibid., p. 222.

20 Ibid.

21 Paglia, "It Wasn't Romeo and Julian."

22 Kirk and Madsen, *After the Ball*, p. 151.

23 Ibid., p. 221.

24 Wendy Shalit in *Commentary*, August 1995; cited in Alan Kors and Harvey Silverglate, *The Shadow University* (New York: The Free Press, 1998), p. 226.

25 Cited in Kors and Silverglate, *The Shadow University*, p. 217.

26 Thomas Sowell, *Inside American Education* (New York: The Free Press, 1993), p. 182.

27 Ronald Gramieri, "The Politics of Punishment," *Harvard Salient*, November 1987, p. 4; cited in Sowell, *Inside American Education*.

28 Kirk and Madsen, *After the Ball*, p. 153.

29 Ibid., p. 154.

30 Ibid., p. 233.

31 Ibid., p. 241.

32 Ibid., p. 245.

33 General Social Survey, 1996, www.ssdc.ucsd.edu/gss. Survey respondents were asked: "Do you think sexual relations between

two adults of the same sex are always wrong, almost always wrong, wrong sometimes, or not wrong at all?" Only 29 percent of all respondents answered "not wrong at all."

34 Alan Wolfe, *One Nation, After All* (New York: Penguin, 1998), p. 77.

35 Cheryl Clark, "AIDS Researchers Report an Increase in Unsafe Sex," *San Diego Union-Tribune,* 19 February 2001, p. A1.

36 Bob Egelko, "AIDS Activists Charged with Stalking: Two Taken into Custody, Held on $500,000 Bail after Hearing," *San Francisco Chronicle,* 29 November 2001, p. A23.

37 Maureen Orth, *Vulgar Favors: Andrew Cunanan, Gianni Versace and the Largest Failed Manhunt in United States History* (New York: Delacorte Press, 1999), p. 323.

38 Maureen Orth, "On the Trail of the Gay Serial Killer," *Vanity Fair,* September 1997.

39 Glaad Alert, "Two Magazines Look at Spree Killer's Sexual Orientation," 16 May 1997, www.glaad.org.

40 Andrew Sullivan, *Virtually Normal* (New York: Vintage, 1996), p. 21.

41 Ibid., p. 92.

42 Ibid., p. 177.

43 Ibid., pp. 183–84.

44 Jonathan Rauch, "Leave Gay Marriage to the States," *Wall Street Journal,* 27 July 2001.

45 Judith Stacey and Timothy Biblarz, "Does the Sexual Orientation of Parents Matter?" *American Sociological Review,* 25 April 2001, p. 164.

46 Fiona Tasker and Susan Golombok, *Growing Up in a Lesbian Family* (New York: Guilford, 1997); cited in Stacey and Biblarz, "Does the Sexual Orientation of Parents Matter?" p. 171.

47 Stacey and Biblarz, "Does the Sexual Orientation of Parents Matter?" pp. 170–71.

Chapter 7: Celebrating the Sexually Adventurous Adolescent

1 Kay Hymowitz, *Ready or Not* (New York: The Free Press, 1999), p. 164.

2 Transcript of interview with Dr. Robert Blum, M.D., Ph.D., *The Lost Children of Rockland County,* www.pbs.org, April 2000.

3 Richard Rothenberg, C. Sterk, K. Toomey, J. Potterat, D. Johnson, M. Schrader and S. Hatch, "Using Social Network and Ethnographic Tools to Evaluate Syphilis Transmission," *Sexually*

Transmitted Diseases, vol. 25, no. 3 (1988), pp. 154–60.

4   Transcript of interview with Claire Stark, *The Lost Children of Rockland County.*

5   Cited in Hymowitz, *Ready or Not,* p. 174.

6   Ibid., p. 164.

7   Karen S. Peterson, "For Many Teens, Oral Sex Doesn't Count," *USA Today,* Health section, 15 November 2000.

8   Interview with Deborah Tolman, Ed.D., *The Lost Children of Rockdale County.*

9   Ibid.

10 Cited in Dana Mack, *The Assault on Parenthood* (San Francisco: Encounter Books, 2000), p. 189.

11 Ibid.

12 Transcript of interview with Deborah Tolman, *The Lost Children of Rockdale County.*

13 Ibid.

14 Deborah Tolman, "How Being a Good Girl Can Be Bad for Girls," in *Good Girls/Bad Girls: Women, Sex, Violence and Power in the 1990s,* ed. N. Bauer Maglin and D. Perry (New Brunswick, New Jersey: Rutgers University Press, 1996).

15 Transcript of interview with Brandi, *The Lost Children of Rockland County.*

16 Cited in Hymowitz, *Ready or Not,* p. 174.

17 Transcript of interview with Brandi, *The Lost Children of Rockland County.*

18 Transcript of interview with Conyers teens, *The Lost Children of Rockland County.*

19 Ibid.

20 *Teenwire,* sponsored by Planned Parenthood, October 2000, www.teenwire.com.

21 Mack, *The Assault on Parenthood,* p. 185.

22 Ibid.

23 Cited by Thomas Sowell, *Inside American Education* (New York: The Free Press, 1993), p. 54.

24 Cited in Hymowitz, *Ready or Not,* p. 168.

25 Ibid., p. 4.

26 Personal communication with Planned Parenthood representative Erica Johnson, the community educator overseeing the La Jolla Country Day School program TRACES, 1 May 2000.

27 Dana Mulhauser, "Dating among College Students Is All but

Dead," *Chronicle of Higher Education*, 10 August 2001.

28   Leon R. Kass, "The End of Courtship," 2001, www.thepublicinter-est.com.

29   Ibid.

Chapter 8: Rape, Real and Imagined

1   Ben Gose, "Men Accused of Sex Crimes at Bates Say They Are Victims of Hysteria," *Chronicle of Higher Education*, 29 May 1998, p. A37.

2   Ibid.

3   Tracy Snell, "Capital Punishment 1999," U.S. Department of Justice, Office of Justice Programs, December 2000.

4   Richard Lacayo, "Assault by Paragraph," *Time*, 17 January 1994, p. 62.

5   The 25 percent figure for campus date rape was first posited in research by Mary Koss. See Mary Koss, Thomas Dinero and Cynthia Seibel, "Stranger and Acquaintance Rape," *Psychology of Women Quarterly*, vol. 12 (1988). For a thorough analysis and critique of this figure, see Neil Gilbert, "Examining the Fact: Advocacy Research Overstates the Incidence of Date and Acquaintance Rape," in *Current Controversies in Family Violence*, ed. Richard Gelles and Donileen Loseke (Newbury Park, California: Sage Publications, 1993), pp. 120–32.

6   Thomas Sowell, *Inside American Education* (New York: The Free Press, 1993), p. 180.

7   Cited by Christina Hoff Sommers, *Who Stole Feminism? How Women Have Betrayed Women* (New York: Touchstone Books, 1995).

8   Koss, Dinero and Seibel, "Stranger and Acquaintance Rape."

9   Ben Gose, "Brandeis Wins Legal Dispute over Its Handling of a Date-Rape Charge," *Chronicle of Higher Education*, 6 October 2000, p. A52.

10 Cited in ibid.

11 Dawn Santoli, "New York University Rejects Columbia University-like Sexual Misconduct Policy," *University Wire*, 13 October 2000.

12 Alan Charles Kors and Harvey A. Silverglate, *The Shadow University: The Betrayal of Liberty on America's Campuses* (New York: Harper-Perennial, 1998), p. 290.

13 Kim Claussen, "Iowa Speaker Warns of Date Rape," *Iowa State Daily*, 11 February 2000.

14 Colleen McCarthy, "Speaker Tells University of Notre Dame, St. Mary's Students, about Date Rape," *The Observer*, 15 November

2000.

15 Nell Haddock, "Harvard Vigil Condemns Sexual Violence," *Harvard Crimson*, 14 April 2000.

16 Camile Paglia, "Rape and the Modern Sex War," in *Sex, Art, and American Culture* (New York: Vintage Books, 1992), p. 53.

17 Camile Paglia, "The Return of Cary Nation," *Playboy*, October 1992, p. 36.

18 Camile Paglia, *Vamps and Tramps* (New York: Vintage, 1994), p. 31.

19 Ibid., p. 25.

20 Ibid., p. 33.

21 Kathleen Belew, "A Woman's Right to Safety," *University of Washington Daily*, 9 January 2001.

22 Staci Hupp, "Ex Student Sentenced for Rape Lie," *Des Moines Register*, 8 January 2002.

23 Sommers, *Who Stole Feminism?*, p. 212.

24 Ibid.

25 Sowell, *Inside American Education*, p. 179.

26 University of Massachusetts Vision 2000, www.umass.edu/wost/articles/vision2K/forward.htm.

27 Daphne Patai, "Why Not a Feminist Overhaul of Higher Education?" *Chronicle of Higher Education*, 23 January 1998, p. A56.

28 Ben Gose, "U.S. Supreme Court Agrees to Hear Case on Whether Private Colleges May Be Sued for Violating Student-Privacy Law," *Chronicle of Higher Education*, 14 January 2002.

Chapter 9: A Death of One's Own

1 Alan Johnson, *Human Arrangements* (New York: Harcourt Brace Jovanovich, 1989), p. 248.

2 "A Death of One's Own," part 3 of *On Our Own Terms: Moyers on Dying*, www.pbs.org.

3 Paul R. McHugh, "Dying Made Easy," *Commentary*, February 1999.

4 Cited by Wesley J. Smith, *Culture of Death* (San Francisco: Encounter Books, 2001), p. 100.

5 Cited by Roger Kimball, *The Long March* (San Francisco: Encounter Books, 2000), p. 169.

6 The surgeon general's *Call to Action to Prevent Suicide*, 1999, www.surgeongeneral.gov.

7 Smith, *Culture of Death*, p. 95.

8 Ibid., p. 96.

9 Ibid., p. 97.

10 Herbert Hendin, *Suicide in America* (New York: Norton, 1995),

author comment on back cover.

11   Ibid., p. 184.

12   Bill Rankin and Gracie Bonds Staples, "United States Gun Deaths at Lowest Level in 30 Years, CDC Reports," *Atlanta Journal-Constitution*, 13 April 2001, p. A1.

13   Smith, *Culture of Death*, p. 95.

14   Emile Durkheim, *The Rules of Sociological Method* (New York: The Free Press, 1938), p. 2.

15   Stuart Traub and Craig Little, *Theories of Deviance* (Itasca, Illinois: Peacock Publishers, 1999), p. xiv.

16   Cited in George Bryjak and Michael Soroka, *Sociology: Changing Societies in a Diverse World* (Boston: Allyn & Bacon, 2001), p. 14.

17   Ibid.

18   Johnson, *Human Arrangements*, p. 29.

19   Robert Alan Jones, *Emile Durkheim: An Introduction to Four Major Works* (Beverly Hills: Sage Publications, 1986).

20   Margaret L. Anderson and Howard Taylor, *Sociology: Understanding a Diverse Society* (Belmont, California: Wadsworth, 2000), p. 205.

21   World Health Organization, Geneva, October 2000.

22   Ibid.

23   Lorna Martin, "Suicide Takes One in Three Men," *The Herald* (Glasgow), 6 October 2000, p. 8.

24   The surgeon general's *Call to Action to Prevent Suicide*.

25   Ibid.

26   American Asociation of Suicidology, *USA Suicide: State and Regional Data, 1990–1998*.

27   Todd Purdum, "Bleak Statistics Tarnish Nevada's Glitter," *New York Times*, 19 May 2001, p. 1.

28   Ibid.

29   Andrew Henry and James Short, *Suicide and Homicide* (New York: The Free Press, 1954).

30   Herbert Hendin, *Seduced by Death* (New York: Norton, 1998).

31   Leslie Knowlton, "Scientists Study Serotonin Markers for Suicide Prevention," *Psychiatric Times*, vol. 12, no. 9 (September 1995).

32   Ibid.

33   Renee Tawa, "Orange County Seniors Hear Tips on Final Exit," *Los Angeles Times*, Orange County Edition, 4 February 1997, p. A1.

34   Warren Wolfe, "Program Helps Those Choosing Death over Illness," *Minneapolis Star Tribune*, 28 October 2000, p. B5.

35   M. Scott Peck, *Denial of the Soul* (New York: Three Rivers Press,

1997), p. 191.

36 Andrew Solomon, "A Death of One's Own," *New Yorker,* 22 May 1995, pp. 54–69.

37 Andrew Solomon, *The Noonday Demon: An Atlas of Depression* (New York: Scribner, 2001).

38 Herbert Hendin, *Seduced by Death,* p. 60.

39 Ibid., p. 62.

40 Arthur Chin, Katrina Hedberg, Grant Higginson and David Fleming, "Legalized Physician-Assisted Suicide in Oregon—The First Year's Experience," *New England Journal of Medicine,* vol. 340, no. 7 (18 February 1999).

41 Smith, *Culture of Death,* p. 115.

42 Wolfe, "Program Helps Those Choosing Death over Illness."

43 Cited by Smith, *Culture of Death,* p. 112.

44 Ibid., p. 113.

45 Ibid.

46 Cited by Richard John Neuhaus, "A Continuing Survey of Religion and Public Life," *First Things,* vol. 65 (August/September 1996), pp. 64–80; available online at www.firstthings.com/ftissues/ft9608/public.html.

47 Smith, *Culture of Death,* p. 110.

48 Remmelink Report (The Hague: Edo Uitgeverij, 1991). Translated later by the Hemlock Society, "Euthanasia and Assisted Suicide by General Practitioners in the Netherlands," undated. The Hastings Center has also released several publications describing Dutch practices of euthanasia and assisted suicide, including Maurice A. M. deWachter, "Euthanasia in the Netherlands," *Hastings Center Report* 22 (March/April 1992), pp. 22–30. Also Daniel Callahan's *Troubled Dream of Life* (Simon & Schuster, 1993) presents an overview of the Remmelink Report, pp. 112–16.

49 Paul R. McHugh, "Dying Made Easy," *Commentary,* February 1999.

50 Smith, *Culture of Death,* p. 232.

Chapter 10: The Language of Deviance

1 Alasdair MacIntyre, "Theories of Natural Law in the Culture of Advanced Modernity," in *Common Truths: New Perspectives on Natural Law*, ed. Edward B. McLean (Wilmington, Delaware: ISI Books, 2000), p. 90.

2 Janet E. Smith, "Natural Law and Sexual Ethics," in *Common Truths: New Perspectives on Natural Law,* ed. McLean, p. 195.

3 Noam Chomsky, "Reply to Hitchens," *The Nation* website, 1 Octo-

ber 2001.

4   Edward W. Said, "The Clash of Ignorance," *The Nation*, 22 October 2001.

5   Peter Conrad and Joseph Schneider, "Medicine As an Institution of Social Control: Consequences for Society," in *Theories of Deviance*, ed. Stuart Traub and Craig Little (Itasca, Illinois: Peacock Publishers, 1999), p. 577.

6   George J. Bryjak and Michael Soroka, *Sociology: Changing Societies in a Diverse World* (Boston: Allyn & Bacon, 2001), p. 17.

7   Ibid.

8   T. S. Eliot, *The Cocktail Party* (Orlando, Florida: Harcourt Brace Jovanovich, 1950), p. 156.

9   Cited by Margaret Anderson and Howard Taylor, *Sociology* (Belmont, California: Wadsworth, 2000), pp. 504–6.

10 Stuart Traub and Craig Little, *Theories of Deviance*, p. xiii.

11 Travis Hirschi, *Causes of Delinquency* (Berkeley: University of California Press, 1969).

12 Erich Goode and Nachman Ben-Yehuda, *Moral Panics: The Social Construction of Deviance* (Malden, Massachusetts: Blackwell, 1999), p. 52.

13 Alan Wolfe, *One Nation After All: What Middle-Class Americans Really Think about God, Family, Racism, Welfare, Immigration, Homosexuality, Work, the Right, the Left and Each Other* (New York: Penguin Books, 1998).

14 Cited by Katherine Kersten, "To Hell with Sin," *Wall Street Journal*, 17 September 1999, p. W15.

15 Sandi Dolbee, "Pastors Call Power Prices Sinful," San Diego Union-Tribune, 5 August 2000, p. A21.

16 Kersten, "To Hell with Sin."

17 Ibid.

18 George Gallup Jr. and D. Michael Lindsay, *Surveying the Religious Landscape: Trends in U.S. Beliefs* (Harrisburg, Pennsylvania: Morehouse Publishing, 1999), p. 19.

19 Andrew Ferguson, "Intolerant Episcopalians," *Weekly Standard*, 16 July 2001, p. 28.

20 Gallup and Linsay, *Surveying the Religious Landscape*, p. 98.

21 David Brooks, "The Age of Conflict," *Weekly Standard*, 5 November 2001, p. 21.

INDEX

"metaphorical," 99n; in military, 100; as parents, 107–8; and pedophilia, 83–90; Stonewall uprising, 94, 95
hospice, 137
Hughes, Francine, 61–62
Humphrey, Carolyn, 47–48
Humphry, Derek, 137, 146
Hymowitz, Kay, 109–10, 111, 118
hyperkinesis (ADD), 27
hysteria, 62

ibogaine, 25
incest, 66
institutional deviance, 5–6
interactionism, 4

Jamison, Kay Redfield, 54–55, 145
Jaynes, Charles, 87
Jenkins, Philip, 11, 66, 71–78
John Paul II, Pope, 70, 162–63
Johnson, Catherine, 49–50
Jones, Gerald, 84–85
J. P. Morgan & Co., 95
Judge Judy (TV), 160

Kass, Leon, 120–21
Kelley, David, 13
Kennedy, Eugene, 79–80
Kennedy, Rory, 21
Kennedy, Ted, 39
Kersten, Katherine, 159
Kesey, Ken, 4, 34
Kevorkian, Jack, 135, 136, 151
KGO (radio), 78
Kimball, Roger, 137
King, Martin Luther, Jr., 157
Kinkel, Kip, 53
Kirk, Marshall, 97–103
Koestner, Katie, 128
Koppel, Ted, 21
Kos, Rudy, 69–70, 71
Koss, Mary, 130–31
Ku Klux Klan, 73

Laing, R. D., 33–34
La Jolla Country Day School, 119–20
Last Wish (Rollins), 138, 146
Law, Cardinal Bernard, 80
League, Roberta, 134
Leight, Lynn, 113
Leisure World, 146
Leonardo da Vinci, 98, 99
Lesbian and Gay Public Awareness Project, 103
lesbians, 90–91, 98–99
Leshner, Alan, 15–16
Letourneau, Mary Kay, 90
Levada, Archbishop William, 80–81
Lewinsky, Monica, 9, 58
Leyva, Tony, 72
Liazos, Alexander, 5
Linkup, 71, 76–77
Little Rascals Day Care Center, 67
Log Cabin Republicans, 92
Lost Children of Rockdale County (PBS), 110, 112, 113–16

MacIntyre, Alasdair, 154
Mack, Dana, 117
MacKinnon, Catharine, 124
Madness and Civilization (Foucault), 5, 33
Madsen, Hunter, 97–103
Magnet, Myron, 38
Male Intergenerational Intimacy, 83–86
manic-depression, 55
Marcavage, Michael, 57
Marcuse, Herbert, 137
marijuana, 16–17
Marx, Karl, 161
Marxism, 137
masochistic personality disorder, 61
Matheny, Patrick, 149
Mattachine Society, 94
McCaffrey, Barry, 28
McColl, Bill, 29